NIST Special

Systems Security Engineering

Considerations for a Multidisciplinary Approach in the Engineering of Trustworthy Secure Systems

RON ROSS
MICHAEL McEVILLEY
JANET CARRIER OREN

This publication contains systems security engineering considerations for **ISO/IEC/IEEE 15288:2015**, *Systems and software engineering — System life cycle processes*. It provides security-related implementation guidance for the standard and should be used in conjunction with and as a complement to the standard.

National Institute of Standards and Technology
U.S. Department of Commerce

NIST Special Publication 800-160

Systems Security Engineering

Considerations for a Multidisciplinary Approach in the Engineering of Trustworthy Secure Systems

RON ROSS
Computer Security Division
National Institute of Standards and Technology

MICHAEL McEVILLEY
The MITRE Corporation

JANET CARRIER OREN
Legg Mason

November 2016

U.S. Department of Commerce
Penny Pritzker, Secretary

National Institute of Standards and Technology
Willie May, Under Secretary of Commerce for Standards and Technology and Director

Authority

This publication has been developed by NIST to further its statutory responsibilities under the Federal Information Security Modernization Act (FISMA) of 2014, 44 U.S.C. § 3551 et seq., Public Law (P.L.) 113-283. NIST is responsible for developing information security standards and guidelines, including minimum requirements for federal information systems, but such standards and guidelines shall not apply to national security systems without the express approval of appropriate federal officials exercising policy authority over such systems. This guideline is consistent with the requirements of the Office of Management and Budget (OMB) Circular A-130.

Nothing in this publication should be taken to contradict the standards and guidelines made mandatory and binding on federal agencies by the Secretary of Commerce under statutory authority. Nor should these guidelines be interpreted as altering or superseding the existing authorities of the Secretary of Commerce, Director of the OMB, or any other federal official. This publication may be used by nongovernmental organizations on a voluntary basis and is not subject to copyright in the United States. Attribution would, however, be appreciated by NIST.

National Institute of Standards and Technology Special Publication 800-160
Natl. Inst. Stand. Technol. Spec. Publ. 800-160, **257 pages** (November 2016)
CODEN: NSPUE2

Certain commercial entities, equipment, or materials may be identified in this document in order to describe an experimental procedure or concept adequately. Such identification is not intended to imply recommendation or endorsement by NIST, nor is it intended to imply that the entities, materials, or equipment are necessarily the best available for the purpose.

There may be references in this publication to other publications currently under development by NIST in accordance with its assigned statutory responsibilities. The information in this publication, including concepts, practices, and methodologies, may be used by federal agencies even before the completion of such companion publications. Thus, until each publication is completed, current requirements, guidelines, and procedures, where they exist, remain operative. For planning and transition purposes, federal agencies may wish to closely follow the development of these new publications by NIST.

Organizations are encouraged to review draft publications during the designated public comment periods and provide feedback to NIST. Many NIST cybersecurity publications, other than the ones noted above, are available at http://csrc.nist.gov/publications.

Comments on this publication may be submitted to:

National Institute of Standards and Technology
Attn: Computer Security Division, Information Technology Laboratory
100 Bureau Drive (Mail Stop 8930) Gaithersburg, MD 20899-8930
Electronic Mail: sec-cert@nist.gov

All comments are subject to release under the Freedom of Information Act.

Reports on Computer Systems Technology

The Information Technology Laboratory (ITL) at the National Institute of Standards and Technology (NIST) promotes the U.S. economy and public welfare by providing technical leadership for the Nation's measurement and standards infrastructure. ITL develops tests, test methods, reference data, proof of concept implementations, and technical analyses to advance the development and productive use of information technology (IT). ITL's responsibilities include the development of management, administrative, technical, and physical standards and guidelines for the cost-effective security and privacy of other than national security-related information in federal information systems. The Special Publication 800-series reports on ITL's research, guidelines, and outreach efforts in information systems security and its collaborative activities with industry, government, and academic organizations.

Abstract

With the continuing frequency, intensity, and adverse consequences of cyber-attacks, disruptions, hazards, and other threats to federal, state, and local governments, the military, businesses, and the critical infrastructure, the need for trustworthy secure systems has never been more important to the long-term economic and national security interests of the United States. Engineering-based solutions are essential to managing the growing complexity, dynamicity, and interconnectedness of today's systems, as exemplified by cyber-physical systems and systems-of-systems, including the Internet of Things. This publication addresses the engineering-driven perspective and actions necessary to develop more defensible and survivable systems, inclusive of the machine, physical, and human components that compose the systems and the capabilities and services delivered by those systems. It starts with and builds upon a set of well-established International Standards for systems and software engineering published by the International Organization for Standardization (ISO), the International Electrotechnical Commission (IEC), and the Institute of Electrical and Electronics Engineers (IEEE) and infuses systems security engineering methods, practices, and techniques into those systems and software engineering activities. The objective is to address security issues from a stakeholder protection needs, concerns, and requirements perspective and to use established engineering processes to ensure that such needs, concerns, and requirements are addressed with appropriate fidelity and rigor, early and in a sustainable manner throughout the life cycle of the system.

Keywords

Assurance; developmental engineering; disposal; engineering trades; field engineering; implementation; information security; information security policy; inspection; integration; penetration testing; protection needs; requirements analysis; resiliency; review; risk assessment; risk management; risk treatment; security architecture; security authorization; security design; security requirements; specifications; stakeholder; system-of-systems; system component; system element; system life cycle; systems; systems engineering; systems security engineering; trustworthiness; validation; verification.

Acknowledgements

The authors gratefully acknowledge and appreciate the significant contributions from individuals and organizations in the public and private sectors, whose thoughtful and constructive comments improved the overall quality, thoroughness, and usefulness of this publication. In particular, we wish to thank Beth Abramowitz, Max Allway, Kristen Baldwin, Dawn Beyer, Deb Bodeau, Paul Clark, Keesha Crosby, Judith Dahmann, Kelley Dempsey, Holly Dunlap, Jennifer Fabius, Daniel Faigin, Jeanne Firey, Jim Foti, Robin Gandhi, Rich Graubart, Richard Hale, Daryl Hild, Kesha Hill, Peggy Himes, Danny Holtzman, Cynthia Irvine, Brett Johnson, Ken Kepchar, Stephen Khou, Elizabeth Lennon, Alvi Lim, Logan Mailloux, Dennis Mangsen, Doug Maughn, Rosalie McQuaid, Joseph Merkling, John Miller, Thuy Nguyen, Lisa Nordman, Dorian Pappas, Paul Popick, Roger Schell, Thom Schoeffling, Matt Scholl, Peter Sell, Gary Stoneburner, Glenda Turner, Mark Winstead, and William Young for their individual contributions to this publication.

We would also like to extend our sincere appreciation to the National Security Agency; Naval Postgraduate School; Department of Defense Office of Acquisition, Technology, and Logistics; United States Air Force; Department of Homeland Security Science and Technology Office, Cyber Security Division; Air Force Institute of Technology; International Council on Systems Engineering, and The MITRE Corporation, for their ongoing support for the systems security engineering project.

Finally, the authors also respectfully acknowledge the seminal work in computer security that dates back to the 1960s. The vision, insights, and dedicated efforts of those early pioneers in computer security serve as the philosophical and technical foundation for the security principles, concepts, and practices employed in this publication to address the critically important problem of engineering trustworthy secure systems.

Table of Contents

Prologue

"Among the forces that threaten the United States and its interests are those that blend the lethality and high-tech capabilities of modern weaponry with the power and opportunity of asymmetric tactics such as terrorism and cyber warfare. We are challenged not only by novel employment of conventional weaponry, but also by the hybrid nature of these threats. We have seen their effects on the American homeland. Moreover, we must remember that we face a determined and constantly adapting adversary."

Quadrennial Homeland Security Review Report
February 2010

Foreword

The United States has developed incredibly powerful and complex systems—systems that are inexorably linked to the economic and national security interests of the Nation. The complete dependence on those systems for mission and business success in both the public and private sectors, including the critical infrastructure, has left the Nation extremely vulnerable to hostile cyber-attacks and other serious threats, including natural disasters, structural/component failures, and errors of omission and commission. The susceptibility to such threats was described in the January 2013 Defense Science Board Task Force Report entitled *Resilient Military Systems and the Advanced Cyber Threat*. The reported concluded that—

"...the cyber threat is serious and that the United States cannot be confident that our critical Information Technology systems will work under attack from a sophisticated and well-resourced opponent utilizing cyber capabilities in combination with all of their military and intelligence capabilities (a full spectrum adversary) ..."

The Task Force stated that the susceptibility to the advanced cyber threat by the Department of Defense is also a concern for public and private networks, in general, and recommended that steps be taken immediately to build an effective response to measurably increase confidence in the systems we depend on (in the public and private sectors) and at the same time, decrease a would-be attacker's confidence in the effectiveness of their capabilities to compromise those systems. This conclusion was based on the following facts:

- The success adversaries have had in penetrating our networks;

- The relative ease that our Red Teams have in disrupting, or completely defeating, our forces in exercises using exploits available on the Internet; and

- The weak security posture of our networks and systems.

The Task Force also described several tiers of vulnerabilities within organizations including known vulnerabilities, unknown vulnerabilities, and adversary-created vulnerabilities. The important and sobering message conveyed by the Defense Science Board is that the top two tiers of vulnerabilities (i.e., the unknown vulnerabilities and adversary-created vulnerabilities) are, for the most part, totally invisible to most organizations. These vulnerabilities can be effectively addressed by sound systems security engineering techniques, methodologies, processes, and practices—in essence, providing the necessary trustworthiness to withstand and survive well-resourced, sophisticated cyber-attacks on the systems supporting critical missions and business operations.

To begin to address the challenges of the 21st century, we must:

- Understand the modern threat space (i.e., adversary capabilities and intentions revealed by the targeting actions of those adversaries);

- Identify stakeholder assets and protection needs and provide protection commensurate with the criticality of those assets and needs and the consequences of asset loss;

- Increase the understanding of the growing complexity of systems—to more effectively reason about, manage, and address the uncertainty associated with that complexity;

- Integrate security requirements, functions, and services into the mainstream management and technical processes within the life cycle processes of systems; and

- Build trustworthy secure systems capable of protecting stakeholder assets.

System Security as a Design Problem

"Providing satisfactory security controls in a computer system is in itself a system design problem. A combination of hardware, software, communications, physical, personnel and administrative-procedural safeguards is required for comprehensive security. In particular, software safeguards alone are not sufficient."

-- The Ware Report
  Defense Science Board Task Force on Computer Security, 1970.

This publication addresses the engineering-driven actions necessary to develop more defensible and survivable systems—including the components that compose and the services that depend on those systems. It starts with and builds upon a set of well-established International Standards for systems and software engineering published by the International Organization for Standardization (ISO), the International Electrotechnical Commission (IEC), and the Institute of Electrical and Electronics Engineers (IEEE), and infuses systems security engineering techniques, methods, and practices into those systems and software engineering activities. The ultimate objective is to address security issues from a stakeholder requirements and protection needs perspective and to use established engineering processes to ensure that such requirements and needs are addressed with the appropriate fidelity and rigor across the entire life cycle of the system.

Increasing the trustworthiness of systems is a significant undertaking that requires a substantial investment in the requirements, architecture, design, and development of systems, components, applications, and networks—and a fundamental cultural change to the current "business as usual" approach. Introducing a disciplined, structured, and standards-based set of systems security engineering activities and tasks provides an important starting point and forcing function to initiate needed change. The ultimate objective is to obtain trustworthy secure systems that are fully capable of supporting critical missions and business operations while protecting stakeholder assets, and to do so with a level of assurance that is consistent with the risk tolerance of those stakeholders.

-- Ron Ross
  National Institute of Standards and Technology

Disclaimer

This publication is intended to be used in conjunction with and as a supplement to **International Standard ISO/IEC/IEEE 15288**, *Systems and software engineering — System life cycle processes*. It is strongly recommended that organizations using this publication obtain the standard in order to fully understand the context of the security-related activities and tasks in each of the system life cycle processes. Content from the international standard that is referenced in this publication is reprinted with permission from the Institute of Electrical and Electronics Engineers and is noted as follows:

ISO/IEC/IEEE 15288-2015. Reprinted with permission from IEEE, Copyright IEEE 2015, All rights reserved.

How to Use This Publication

This publication is intended to be extremely flexible in its application in order to meet the diverse needs of organizations. It is *not* intended to provide a specific recipe for execution. Rather, it can be viewed as a catalog or handbook for achieving the identified security outcomes of a systems engineering perspective on system life cycle processes—leaving it to the experience and expertise of the engineering organization to determine what is correct for its purpose. Thus, organizations choosing to use this guidance for their systems security engineering efforts can select and employ some or all of the thirty **ISO/IEC/IEEE 15288** processes and some or all of the security-related activities and tasks defined for each process. Note that there are process dependencies, and the successful completion of some activities and tasks necessarily invokes other processes or leverages the results of other processes.

The system life cycle processes can be used for new systems, system upgrades, or systems that are being repurposed; can be employed at any stage of the system life cycle; and can take advantage of any system or software development methodology including, for example, *waterfall*, *spiral*, or *agile*. The processes can also be applied recursively, iteratively, concurrently, sequentially, or in parallel and to any system regardless of its size, complexity, purpose, scope, environment of operation, or special nature.

The full extent of the application of the content in this publication is informed by stakeholder capability, protection needs, and concerns with particular attention to considerations of cost, schedule, and performance. The tailorable nature of the engineering activities and tasks and the system life cycle processes will ensure that the specific systems resulting from the application of the security design principles and concepts have the level of *trustworthiness* deemed *sufficient* to protect stakeholders from suffering unacceptable loss of assets and the associated consequences. Such trustworthiness is made possible by the rigorous application of those design principles and concepts within a disciplined and structured set of processes that provides the necessary evidence and transparency to support risk-informed decision making and trades.

Context-Sensitive Security — Getting the Maximum Benefit from This Publication

This publication is **not** intended to formally define Systems Security Engineering (SSE); make a definitive or authoritative statement of what SSE is and what it is not; define or prescribe a specific process; or prescribe a mandatory set of activities for compliance purposes. This publication **is** intended to address the activities and tasks, the concepts and principles, and most importantly, what needs to be "considered" from a security perspective when executing within the context of Systems Engineering (hence the alignment to the international standard **ISO/IEC/IEEE 15288**). The title of the publication, *Systems Security Engineering – Considerations for a Multidisciplinary Approach in the Engineering of Trustworthy Secure Systems*, was chosen to appropriately convey how the content can be used to achieve the maximum benefit.

- The use of the term "considerations" is intended to emphasize that this document is not claiming to be "the" answer for the formal statement of SSE and all forms of its application. It does not define SSE, but rather offers considerations towards what can and should be done now and from which there can be continued evolution and maturation towards more effective and *context–sensitive* application of the considerations to address the breadth and depth of system security problems. In that regard, the document is not "a process" but a collection of related processes, where each process addresses an aspect of the system security problem space and offers a cohesive set of activities, tasks, and outcomes that combine to achieve the end goal of a trustworthy secure system. The application of any process must be properly calibrated to the objectives and constraints in the *context* to which the process is applied— and conducted with an appropriate level of rigor.

- The use of the term "in the engineering of" is intended to emphasize that the focus is on engineering (as opposed to building, integrating, or assembling). The core objective of the publication is to be engineering-based, not operations- or technology-based. Considerations are grounded in a systems engineering viewpoint of system life cycle processes. Organizations using the publication will certainly tailor the life cycle processes for effectiveness, feasibility, and practicality, but in doing so they have the responsibility to achieve the stated outcomes nonetheless. There can be legitimate variances with the activities and tasks and how they are or are not accomplished, or whether they do or do not have value in the particular context of their application. These variances occur when differing and sometimes conflicting views must be addressed and traded among to achieve the combined objectives of all stakeholders in a cost-effective manner.

Context-sensitive security means that stakeholders establish the value of their assets and the context to subsequently apply the SSE activities and tasks that provide a level of asset protection and trustworthiness that falls within their tolerance of loss and associated risk—through custom development and fabrication to the procurement of commercial products and services to achieve the required level of protection and trustworthiness. Context-sensitive application of the SSE activities and tasks in this publication is precisely what systems engineering expects. With sufficient understanding of SSE, the context-sensitive application happens as a natural by-product of systems engineering. It is essential that the processes be adaptable and tailorable to address the *complexity* and *dynamicity* of all factors that define the system and its environmental context. This includes the system-of-systems environment where such systems may not have a single owner, may not be under a single authority, or may not operate within a single set of priorities. The system-of-systems context potentially requires the execution of these processes along a different line of reasoning. The fundamentals and concepts of SSE are still applicable, but may have to be applied differently. This is one of the primary design objectives for the *Systems Security Engineering Framework* and the associated SSE activities and tasks provided in this publication.

NIST Systems Security Engineering Initiative

NIST Special Publication 800-160 is the flagship publication in a series of planned systems security engineering publications. The series of 800-160 publications will include several important systems security engineering topics, for example: *hardware security and assurance*; *software security and assurance*; and *system resiliency*. Each topic will be addressed in the context of the system life cycle processes contained in ISO/IEC/IEEE 15288 and the security-related activities and tasks that are described in SP 800-160.

NIST plans to update its foundational security and risk management guidance to describe how such guidance might be interpreted and applied at both the enterprise level and in association with systems engineering processes.

Errata

This table contains changes that have been incorporated into Special Publication 800-160. Errata updates can include corrections, clarifications, or other minor changes in the publication that are either *editorial* or *substantive* in nature.

DATE	TYPE	CHANGE	PAGE

CHAPTER ONE

INTRODUCTION

THE NEED FOR SYSTEMS ENGINEERING-BASED TRUSTWORTHY SECURE SYSTEMS

The need for trustworthy secure systems[1] stems from a wide variety of *stakeholder* needs that are driven by mission, business, and a spectrum of other objectives and concerns. The characteristics of these systems include an ever-evolving growth in the geographic size, number, and types of *components* and technologies[2] that compose the systems; the complexity and dynamicity in the interactions, behavior, and outcomes of systems and their system elements; and the increased dependence that results in *consequences* of major inconvenience to catastrophic loss due to disruptions, hazards, and threats within the global operating *environment*. The basic problem can be simply stated—today's systems have dimensions and an inherent complexity that require a disciplined and structured engineering approach in order to achieve any expectation that the inherent complexity can be effectively managed within the practical and feasible limits of human capability and certainty.

Managing the complexity of today's systems and being able to claim that those systems are trustworthy and secure means that first and foremost, there must be a level of confidence in the feasibility and correctness-in-concept, philosophy, and design, regarding the ability of a system to function securely as intended. That basis provides the foundation to address any of the additional security concerns that provide confidence for the expectation that the system functions only as intended across the spectrum of disruptions, hazards, and threats, and to realistically bound those expectations with respect to constraints, limitations, and uncertainty. The level of trustworthiness that can be achieved in today's complex systems is a function of our ability to think about *system security* across every aspect of every activity, and in our ability to execute with commensurate fidelity and rigor to produce results that provide the confidence in the basis for those claims of trustworthiness. Failure to address the complexity issue in this manner will continue to leave the Nation susceptible to the consequences of an increasingly pervasive set of disruptions, hazards, and threats with potential for causing serious, severe, or even catastrophic consequences.

Systems engineering provides the basic foundation for a disciplined approach to engineering trustworthy secure systems. Trustworthiness, in this context, means simply worthy of being trusted to fulfill whatever critical *requirements* may be needed for a particular component, subsystem, system, network, application, mission, enterprise, or other entity [Neumann04]. Trustworthiness requirements can include, for example, attributes of safety, security, reliability, dependability, performance, resilience, and survivability under a wide range of potential adversity in the form of disruptions, hazards, and threats. Effective measures of trustworthiness are meaningful only to the extent that the requirements are sufficiently complete and well-defined, and can be accurately assessed.

---

[1] A *system* is a combination of interacting elements organized to achieve one or more stated purposes. The interacting elements that compose a system include hardware, software, data, humans, processes, procedures, facilities, materials, and naturally occurring entities [ISO/IEC/IEEE 15288].

[2] The term *technology* is used in the broadest context in this publication to include computing, communications, and information technologies as well as any mechanical, hydraulic, pneumatic, or structural components in systems that contain or are enabled by such technologies. This view of technology provides an increased recognition of the digital, computational, and electronic machine-based foundation of modern complex systems and the growing importance of the trustworthiness of that foundation in providing the system's functional capability and explicit interaction with its physical machine and human system elements.

From a security perspective, a trustworthy system is a system that meets specific *security requirements* in addition to meeting other critical requirements. Systems security engineering, when properly integrated into systems engineering, provides the needed complementary engineering capability that extends the notion of trustworthiness to deliver trustworthy secure systems. Trustworthy secure systems are less susceptible, but not impervious to, the effects of modern adversity that includes attacks orchestrated by an intelligent adversary.

While it is impossible to know all potential forms of adversity or to stop all anticipated disruptions, hazards, and threats, the basic architecture and design of systems can make those systems inherently less vulnerable, provide an increased level of penetration resistance, and offer engineered-in tolerance and resilience that can be leveraged by system owners and *operators*— allowing missions and business functions to exercise resilience techniques even when the systems are operating in degraded or debilitated states. Moreover, the effects of disruptions, hazards, and threats to include sophisticated and well-orchestrated cyber-attacks can be reduced or controlled by the application of well-defined security design principles, concepts, and techniques upon which systems security engineering activities and tasks are based. And finally, having a greater level of trustworthiness in a system means it is possible to put procedures in place to help individuals (i.e., human system element) respond more effectively to attacks and other disruptions, in concert with or independent of, the machine/technology system elements.

This publication defines *security* as the freedom from those conditions that can cause loss of *assets*[3] with unacceptable consequences.[4] The specific scope of security must be clearly defined by stakeholders in terms of the assets to which security applies and the consequences against which security is assessed.[5] This publication defines *systems security engineering* as a specialty discipline of systems engineering.[6] It provides considerations for the security-oriented activities and tasks that produce security-oriented outcomes as part of every systems engineering process *activity* with focus given to the appropriate level of fidelity and rigor in analyses to achieve assurance and trustworthiness objectives.

Systems security engineering contributes to a broad-based and holistic security perspective and focus within the systems engineering effort. This ensures that stakeholder *protection needs* and *security concerns* associated with the system are properly identified and addressed in all systems engineering tasks throughout the system *life cycle*. This includes the protection of intellectual property in the form of data, information, methods, techniques, and technology that are used to create the system or that are incorporated into the system. Systems security engineering activities draw upon the combination of well-established systems engineering and security principles, concepts, and techniques to leverage, adapt, and supplement the relevant principles and practices of systems engineering. Such engineering activities are performed systematically and consistently to achieve a set of outcomes within every stage of the system life cycle, including concept, development, production, utilization, support, and retirement.

---

[3] The term *asset* refers to an item of value to stakeholders. An asset may be tangible (e.g., a physical item such as hardware, firmware, computing platform, network device, or other technology component) or intangible (e.g., data, information, software, trademark, copyright, patent, intellectual property, image, or reputation). The value of an asset is driven by the stakeholders in consideration of life cycle concerns that include, but are not limited to, those concerns of business or mission. Refer to Section 2.3 for discussion of the system security perspective on assets.

[4] Security is concerned with the protection of *assets*. Assets are entities that someone places value upon. Summarized from [ISO/IEC 15408-1], Section 7.1 *Assets and countermeasures*.

[5] Adapted from [NASA11].

[6] Summarized from [MIL-HDBK].

The effectiveness of any engineering discipline first requires a thorough understanding of the problem to be solved and consideration of all feasible solution options before taking action to solve the identified problem. To maximize the effectiveness of systems security engineering, security requirements for the protection against loss in the context of all relevant assets, driven by business, mission, and all other stakeholder asset loss concerns, must be defined and managed as a set of engineering requirements and cannot be addressed independently or after the fact. Rather, the *protection*[7] capability must be engineered in and tightly integrated into the system as part of the system life cycle process. Understanding stakeholder asset protection needs (including assets that they own and assets that they do not own but must protect) and expressing those needs through well-defined security requirements becomes an important *investment* in mission/business success in the modern age of global commerce, powerful computing systems, and network connectivity.

1.1 PURPOSE AND APPLICABILITY

The purpose of this publication is:

- To provide a basis to formalize a discipline for systems security engineering in terms of its principles, concepts, and activities;

- To foster a common mindset to deliver security for any system, regardless of its scope, size, complexity, or stage of the system life cycle;

- To provide considerations and to demonstrate how systems security engineering principles, concepts, and activities can be effectively applied to systems engineering activities;

- To advance the field of systems security engineering by promulgating it as a discipline that can be applied and studied; and

- To serve as a basis for the development of educational and training programs, including the development of individual certifications and other professional assessment criteria.

The systems security engineering discipline is applicable at each stage of the system life cycle and provides security considerations towards the engineering of systems in the following types:

- **New systems**

  The engineering effort includes such activities as concept exploration, analysis of alternatives, and preliminary or applied research to refine the concepts and/or feasibility of technologies employed in a new system. This effort is initiated during the concept and development stages of the system life cycle.

- **Modifications to Systems**

  - *Reactive modifications to fielded systems:* The engineering effort occurs in response to adversity in the form of disruptions, hazards, and threats such as cyber-attacks, incidents, errors, accidents, faults, component failures, and natural disasters that diminish or prevent the system from achieving its design intent. This effort can occur during the production, utilization, or support stages of the system life cycle and may be performed concurrently with or independent of day-to-day operations.

---

[7] The term *protection*, in the context of systems security engineering, has a very broad scope and is primarily oriented on the concept of assets and asset loss. Thus, the protection capability provided by a system goes beyond *prevention* and has the objective to control the events, conditions, and consequences that constitute asset loss. Refer to Section 2.3 for discussion of the system security perspective on assets and loss.

- ***Planned upgrades to fielded systems while continuing to sustain day-to-day operations:*** The planned system upgrades may enhance an existing system capability, provide a new capability, or constitute a technology refresh of an existing capability. This effort occurs during the production/utilization/support stages of the system life cycle.

- ***Planned upgrades to fielded systems that result in new systems:*** The engineering effort is carried out as if developing a new system with a system life cycle that is distinct from the life cycle of a fielded system. The upgrades are performed in a development environment that is independent of the fielded system.

- **Dedicated or Special-Purpose Systems**

  - ***Security-dedicated or security-purposed systems:*** The engineering effort delivers a system that satisfies a security-dedicated need or provides a security-oriented purpose, and does so as a stand-alone system that may monitor or interact with other systems. Such systems can include, for example, surveillance systems, monitoring systems, and security service provisioning systems.

  - ***High-confidence, dedicated-purpose systems:*** The engineering effort delivers a system that satisfies the need for real-time control of vehicles, industrial or utility processes, weapons, nuclear, or other special-purpose needs. Such systems may include multiple operational states or modes with varying forms of manual, semi-manual, automated, or autonomous modes. These systems have highly deterministic properties; strict timing constraints and functional interlocks; and severe if not catastrophic consequences of failure.

- **System-of-Systems**

  The engineering effort occurs across a set of constituent systems, each system with its own stakeholders, primary purpose, and planned evolution. The composition of the constituent systems into a *system-of-systems* [Maier98] produces a capability that would otherwise be difficult or impractical to achieve. This effort can occur across a continuum of system-of-systems types from a relatively informal, unplanned system-of-systems concept and evolution that emerges over time via voluntary participation, to degrees of more formal execution with the most formal being a system-of-systems concept that is directed, planned, structured, and achieved via a centrally managed engineering effort.

- **Evolution of Systems**

  The engineering effort involves migrating or adapting a system or system implementation from one operational environment or set of operating conditions to another operational environment or other set of operating conditions.[8]

- **Retirement of Systems**

  The engineering effort removes system functions or services and associated system elements from operation, to include removal of the entire system, and may also include the transition of system functions and services to some other system. The effort occurs during the retirement stage of the system life cycle and may be carried out while sustaining day-to-day operations.

---

[8] Increasingly, there is a need to reuse or leverage system implementation successes within operational environments that are different from which they were originally designed and developed. This type of reuse or reimplementation of systems within other operational environments is more efficient and represents potential advantages in maximizing interoperability between various system implementations. The engineering of agile systems offers unique challenges to the system security engineer based on the *similarities* and *differences* between the systems. The similarities offer the potential for reuse of development, assessment, and related approaches, whereas the differences increase the likelihood of invalidly applying assumptions from one operating environment to another with potentially adverse consequences.

The considerations set forth in this publication are applicable to all federal systems other than those systems designated as national security systems as defined in 44 U.S.C., Section 3542. These considerations have been broadly developed from a technical and technical management perspective to complement similar considerations for national security systems and may be used for such systems with the approval of federal officials exercising policy authority over such systems. State, local, and tribal governments as well as private sector entities are encouraged to consider using the material in this publication, as appropriate. The applicability statement above is not meant to *limit* the technical and technical management application of these considerations therein. That is, the security design principles, concepts, techniques, and best practices described in this publication can be broadly applied to any system to achieve system-oriented security and the trustworthiness objectives.

> **"This whole economic boom in cybersecurity seems largely to be a consequence of poor engineering."**
> -- Carl Landwehr, *Communications of the ACM*, February 2015

1.2 TARGET AUDIENCE

This publication is intended for security engineering and other engineering professionals who are responsible for the activities and tasks that are defined by the life cycle processes described in Chapter Three. The term *systems security engineer* is used specifically to include those security professionals who perform any or all of the activities and tasks in Chapter Three. It may apply to an individual or a team of individuals from the same organization or different organizations.[9] This publication can also be used by professionals who perform other system life cycle activities or activities related to the education and/or training of systems engineers and systems security engineers. These include, but are not limited to:

- Individuals with systems engineering, architecture, design, development, and integration responsibilities;

- Individuals with software engineering, architecture, design, development, integration, and software maintenance responsibilities;

- Individuals with security governance, risk management, and oversight responsibilities;

- Individuals with independent security verification, validation, testing, evaluation, auditing, assessment, inspection, and monitoring responsibilities;

- Individuals with system security administration, operations, maintenance, sustainment, logistics, and support responsibilities;

- Individuals with acquisition, budgeting, and project management responsibilities;

- Providers of technology products, systems, or services; and

- Academic institutions offering systems security engineering and related programs.

---

[9] Systems security engineering activities, tasks, concepts, and principles can be applied to a mechanism, component, system element, system, or system-of-systems. While a mechanism can be routinely addressed by a small team, the engineering of a system-of-systems may require an organizational structure with multiple coordinating and interacting teams, each reporting to a lead systems engineer. The processes are intended to be tailored accordingly to facilitate their effectiveness.

1.3 ORGANIZATION OF THIS SPECIAL PUBLICATION

The remainder of this special publication is organized as follows:

- **Chapter Two** describes the specialty discipline of systems security engineering; defines the foundational systems engineering constructs of system, system elements, system-of-interest, system environment, enabling systems, and other systems in the operational environment; describes the security perspective of a system including the concepts of protection needs, security relevance, security architecture, trustworthiness, and assurance; and introduces a notional systems security engineering framework.

- **Chapter Three** describes systems security engineering considerations, contributions, and extensions to the system life cycle processes defined in the international systems and software engineering standard ISO/IEC/IEEE 15288. Each of the system life cycle processes contains a set of security enhancements that augment or extend the process outcomes, activities, and tasks defined by standard. The enhanced system life cycle processes address system security as they are applied throughout the system life cycle.

- **Supporting appendices** provide additional information for the effective application of the systems security engineering activities and tasks in this publication. These include: references (Appendix A); definitions and terms (Appendix B); acronyms (Appendix C); a summary of the security engineering activities and tasks (Appendix D); roles, responsibilities, and skills associated with systems security engineering (Appendix E); design principles for security (Appendix F); and engineering and security fundamentals (Appendix G).

Systems Security Engineering — A Specialty Discipline

Security, like safety and other system quality properties, is an emergent property of a system. System security is the application of engineering and management principles, concepts, criteria, and techniques to optimize security within the constraints of operational effectiveness, time, and cost throughout all stages of the system life cycle. When performing appropriate analysis, the evaluation is performed holistically by tying into systems security engineering concepts and best practices and ensuring that system security has an integrated, system-level perspective.

Systems security engineering focuses on the protection of stakeholder and system assets so as to exercise control over asset loss and the associated consequences. Such protection is achieved by carrying out the specific activities and tasks in the system life cycle processes with the objective of eliminating or reducing vulnerabilities and minimizing or constraining the impact of exploiting or triggering those vulnerabilities. The ability to minimize or constrain impact includes continued delivery of partial or full secure system function at some level of acceptable performance. This approach helps to reduce the susceptibility of systems to a variety of simple, complex, and hybrid threats including physical and cyber-attacks; structural failures; natural disasters; and errors of omission and commission. This reduction is accomplished by fundamentally understanding stakeholder protection needs and subsequently employing sound security design principles and concepts throughout the system life cycle processes. These life cycle processes, if properly carried out (to include the identified systems security engineering activities and tasks), result in systems that are adequately secure relative to the asset loss consequences and associated risk based on measurable assurance and trustworthiness in the systems security performance and effectiveness.

To accomplish the security objectives described above, systems security engineering, as a specialty discipline of systems engineering, provides several distinct perspectives and focus areas which set it apart from other engineering disciplines. These include the engineering of security functions; addressing the security aspects associated with the engineering of non-security functions; and protecting the intellectual property and otherwise sensitive data, information, technologies, and methods utilized as part of the systems engineering effort.

CHAPTER TWO

THE FUNDAMENTALS

THE PRINCIPLES AND CONCEPTS ASSOCIATED WITH SYSTEMS SECURITY ENGINEERING

Systems engineering is a collection of system life cycle technical and nontechnical processes with associated activities and tasks. The technical processes apply engineering analysis and design principles to deliver a system with the capability to satisfy stakeholder requirements and critical quality properties.[10] The nontechnical processes provide engineering management of all aspects of the engineering project, agreements between parties involved in the engineering project, and project-enabling support to facilitate execution of the engineering project.

Systems engineering is *system-holistic* in nature, whereby the contributions across multiple engineering and specialty disciplines are evaluated and balanced to produce a coherent capability that is in fact, the *system*. Systems engineering applies *critical systems thinking* to solve problems and balances the often-conflicting design constraints of operational and technical performance, cost, schedule, and effectiveness to optimize the solution—and to do so with an acceptable level of risk. Systems engineering is *outcome-oriented* and leverages a flexible set of engineering processes to effectively manage complexity and that serve as the principal integrating mechanism for the technical, management, and support activities related to the engineering effort. Finally, systems engineering is *data-* and *analytics-driven* to ensure that all decisions and trades are informed by data produced by analyses conducted with appropriate level of fidelity and rigor.

Systems engineering efforts are a very complex undertaking that requires the close coordination between the *engineering team* and stakeholders throughout the various stages of the system life cycle.[11] While systems engineering is typically considered in terms of its developmental role as part of the acquisition of a capability, systems engineering efforts and responsibilities do not end once a system completes development and is transitioned to the environment of operation for day-to-day operational use. Stakeholders responsible for utilization, support, and retirement of the system provide data to the systems engineering team on an ongoing basis. This data captures their experiences, problems, and issues associated with the utilization and sustainment of the system. They also advise on enhancements and improvements made or that they wish to see incorporated into system revisions. In addition, field engineering (also known as sustainment engineering) efforts provide on-site, full life cycle engineering support for operations, maintenance, and sustainment organizations. Field engineering teams coexist with or are dispatched to operational sites and maintenance depots to provide continuous systems engineering support.

An important objective of systems engineering is to deliver systems that are deemed *trustworthy* in general. Specifically, for security, this objective translates to providing *adequate security* to address stakeholder's concerns related to the consequences associated with the loss of assets throughout the system life cycle with respect to all forms of adversity. Security is one of several emergent properties of a system and it shares the same foundational issues and challenges in its

---

[10] *Quality properties* are emergent properties of systems that include, for example: safety, security, maintainability, resilience, reliability, availability, agility, and survivability. The International Council on Systems Engineering (INCOSE) identifies specialty engineering disciplines within systems engineering that are necessary to deliver a complete system, some of which address one or more system emergent properties.

[11] Nomenclature for stages of the system life cycle varies, but includes, for example: concept analysis; solution analysis; technology maturation; system design and development; engineering and manufacturing development; production and deployment; training, operations and support; and retirement and disposal.

realization as does every other emergent property of the system.[12] Achieving security objectives therefore **requires** system security activities and considerations to be tightly integrated into the technical and nontechnical processes of an engineering effort—that is, *institutionalizing* and *operationalizing* systems security engineering as a proactive contributor and informing aspect to the engineering effort. This means full integration of systems security engineering into systems engineering and its specialties—not execution of system security as a separate set of activities disconnected from systems engineering and other specialty engineering activities.

Engineering the Right Solutions for the Right Reasons

NASCAR is the entity that governs competition among race teams that engineer, operate, and sustain high-performance race cars designed to be extremely fast, able to operate in hostile racing environments, and able to protect the teams' most critical asset—the driver. The race cars are very different than the typical family car that carries your kids to school or makes the trip to the grocery store. Bigger, more powerful engines, larger tires, and additional safety features such as the head and neck safety (HANS) device are just a few items that result from the automobile engineering effort. In this example, the NASCAR team owner (the key stakeholder) wants to win races and at the same time provide the safest possible vehicle for the driver in accordance with rules, expectations, and constraints levied by NASCAR. Based on those stakeholder objectives, NASCAR rules, the specific conditions anticipated on the race track, and the strategy for how the team decides to compete, a set of requirements that include performance and safety are defined as part of the engineering process, and appropriate investments are made to produce a race car that meets those requirements. While the typical NASCAR race car is much more expensive than a family car, the additional expense is justified by the stakeholder mission and business objectives, strategy for competing, and willingness to preserve their most critical asset—the driver. Knowing the value of your assets and engineering to protect against asset loss and the consequences of such loss, given all types of hazards, threats, and uncertainty, are the focal points of the systems security engineering discipline.

2.1 SYSTEMS SECURITY ENGINEERING

Systems security engineering is a specialty engineering discipline of systems engineering that applies scientific, mathematical, engineering, and measurement principles, concepts, and methods to coordinate, orchestrate, and direct the activities of various security engineering specialties and other contributing engineering specialties to provide a fully integrated, system-level perspective of system security. Systems security engineering, as an integral part of systems engineering, helps to ensure that the appropriate security principles, concepts, methods, and practices are applied during the system life cycle to achieve stakeholder objectives for the protection of assets—across all forms of adversity characterized as disruptions, hazards, and threats. It also helps to reduce system defects that can lead to security vulnerability and as a result, reduces the susceptibility of the system to adversity. And finally, systems security engineering provides a sufficient base of *evidence* that supports claims that the desired level of trustworthiness has been achieved—that is, a level of trustworthiness that the agreed-upon asset protection needs of stakeholders can be adequately satisfied on a continuous basis despite such adversity.

---

[12] *Emergent properties* are typically qualitative in nature, are subjective in their nature and assessment, and require consensus agreement based on evidentiary analysis and reasoning.

The Power of Science and Engineering

When we drive across a bridge, we generally have a reasonable *expectation* that the bridge we are crossing will not collapse and will get us to our destination without incident. For bridge builders, it's all about the *physics*—equilibrium, static and dynamic loads, vibrations, and resonance. The science of physics combines with sound civil engineering principles and concepts to produce a final product that we deem adequately *trustworthy*, giving us a level of confidence that the bridge is fit-for-purpose.

For system developers, there are very similar fundamental principles in *mathematics, computer science*, and *systems/software engineering*, that when properly employed, provide the necessary and sufficient trustworthiness to give us that same level of confidence. Systems with an adequate level of trustworthiness cannot be achieved by applying best practices in cyber/security hygiene alone. Rather, it will take a significant and substantial investment in strengthening the underlying systems and system components by initiating multidisciplinary systems engineering efforts driven by well-defined security requirements, secure architectures and designs—efforts that have been proven to produce sound engineering-based solutions to complex and challenging systems security problems. Only under those circumstances, will we build and deploy systems that are adequately secure and exhibit a level of trustworthiness that is sufficient for the underlying purpose that the system was built.

Systems security engineering, as part of a multidisciplinary systems engineering effort:

- Defines stakeholder security objectives, protection needs and concerns, security requirements, and associated validation methods;

- Defines system security requirements and associated verification methods;

- Develops security views and viewpoints of the system architecture and design;

- Identifies and assesses vulnerabilities and susceptibility to life cycle disruptions, hazards, and threats;

- Designs proactive and reactive security functions encompassed within a balanced strategy to control asset loss and associated loss consequences;

- Provides security considerations to inform systems engineering efforts with the objective to reduce errors, flaws, and weakness that may constitute security vulnerability leading to unacceptable asset loss and consequences;

- Identifies, quantifies, and evaluates the costs/benefits of security functions and considerations to inform analysis of alternatives, engineering trade-offs, and risk treatment[13] decisions;

- Performs system security analyses in support of decision making, risk management, and engineering trades;

- Demonstrates through evidence-based reasoning, that security *claims* for the system have been satisfied;

---

[13] The term *risk treatment* as defined in [ISO 73], is used in [ISO/IEC/IEEE 15288].

- Provides evidence to substantiate claims for the trustworthiness of the system; and

- Leverages multiple security and other specialties to address all feasible solutions so as to deliver a trustworthy secure system.

Systems security engineering leverages many *security specialties* and focus areas that contribute to systems security engineering activities and tasks. These security specialties and focus areas include, for example: computer security; communications security; transmission security; anti-tamper protection; electronic emissions security; physical security; information, software, and hardware assurance; and technology specialties such as biometrics and cryptography. In addition, systems security engineering leverages contributions from other enabling engineering disciplines, specialties, and focus areas.[14] Figure 1 illustrates the relationship among systems engineering, systems security engineering, and the contributing security and other specialty engineering and focus areas.

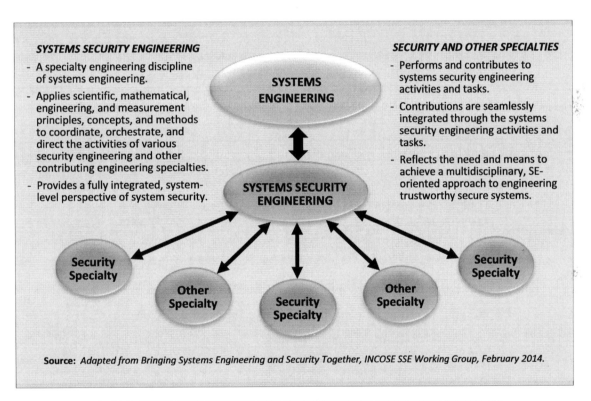

FIGURE 1: SYSTEMS ENGINEERING AND OTHER SPECIALITY ENGINEERING DISCIPLINES

The systems security engineering discipline provides the security perspective to systems engineering processes, activities, tasks, products, and artifacts. These processes, activities, and tasks are conducted in consideration of all system elements; the processes employed to acquire system elements and to develop, deliver, and sustain the system; the behavior of the system in all modes of operation; and the various forms of disruption, hazard, and threat events and conditions that constitute risk with respect to the intentional or unintentional loss of assets and associated consequences.

---

[14] Enabling engineering disciplines and specialties include, for example, human factors engineering (ergonomics), reliability, availability, maintainability (RAM) engineering, software engineering, and resilience engineering.

2.2 SYSTEM AND SYSTEM ELEMENTS

The term *system* defines a set of interacting elements (i.e., system elements) organized to achieve one or more stated purposes [ISO/IEC/IEEE 15288]. Each of the system elements is implemented to fulfill specified requirements. System elements include technology/machine elements, human elements, and physical/environmental elements. System elements may therefore be implemented via hardware, software, or firmware; physical structures or devices; or people, processes, and procedures. Individual system elements or combinations of system elements may satisfy system requirements. Interconnections between these system elements allow the elements to interact as necessary to produce capability as specified by the requirements. Finally, every system operates within an environment that has influence on the system and its operation.

For a large or complex system, a system element may be regarded as a system and will itself be composed of system elements. This hierarchical and context-dependent nature of the terms *system* and *system element* allows the term *system* to be used when referring to a discrete component or a complex, geographically distributed system-of-systems. Because the term system may apply across a continuum from composed elements to a discrete element, the context within which the term system is being used must be communicated and understood. Distinguishing context is important because one observer's system may be another observer's system element. Building on those two terms, the term *system-of-interest* is used to define the set of system elements, system element interconnections, and the environment that is the focus of the engineering effort.

The system-of-interest is supported by one or more *enabling systems* that provide support to the life cycle activities associate with the system-of-interest. Enabling systems are not necessarily delivered with the system-of-interest and do not necessarily exist in the operational environment of the system of interest. Finally, there are *other systems* that the system-of-interest interacts with in the operational environment. These systems may provide services to the system-of-interest (i.e., the system-of-interest is dependent on the other systems) or be the beneficiaries of services provided by the system-of-interest (i.e., other systems are dependent on the system-of-interest). Table 1 lists the system-related constructs that are foundational to systems security engineering.

TABLE 1: FOUNDATIONAL SYSTEM-RELATED ENGINEERING-BASED CONSTRUCTS

SYSTEM	Combination of interacting elements organized to achieve one or more stated purposes. *Examples include: general and special-purpose information systems; command, control, and communication systems; industrial/process control systems; weapons systems; medical devices and treatment systems; social networking systems; and financial, banking, and merchandising transaction systems.*
SYSTEM ELEMENT	Member of a set of elements that constitute a system. *Examples include: hardware; software; firmware; data; facilities; materials; humans; processes; and procedures.*
SYSTEM-OF-INTEREST	System that is the focus of the systems engineering effort.
ENABLING SYSTEM	System that supports a system-of-interest during its life cycle stages but does not necessarily contribute directly to its function during operation. *Examples include: modeling, simulation, and design tools; test scenario generators and test harnesses; training system and tools; software and firmware compilers; hardware design tools, and fabrication and manufacturing systems.*
OTHER SYSTEM	System that interacts with the system-of-interest in its operational environment. *Examples include: a global positioning system space vehicle being an "other system" interacting with a GPS receiver as the "system-of-interest."*
Source: *ISO/IEC/IEEE 15288: 2015*	

The engineering effort focuses on its particular system-of-interest and the systems elements and enabling systems that compose the system-of-interest. System elements of other systems may place constraints on the system-of-interest and, therefore, on the engineering of the system-of-interest. The engineering of the system-of-interest is informed by all constraints imposed by other systems unless the constraints are formally removed. The engineering effort must therefore be cognizant of all views of other systems regardless of the primary focus on the view that is the system-of-interest. Figure 2 illustrates the systems engineering view of the system-of-interest.

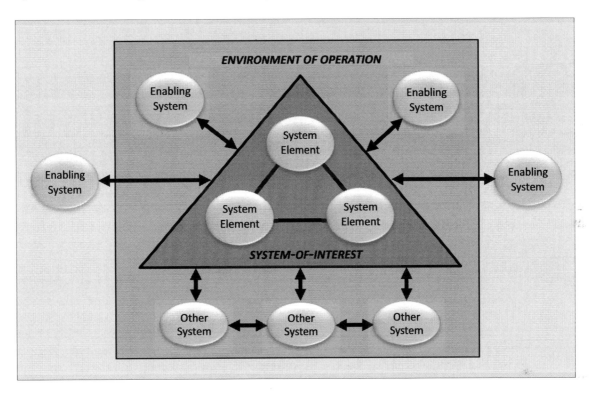

FIGURE 2: SYSTEMS ENGINEERING VIEW OF THE SYSTEM-OF-INTEREST

2.3 SYSTEM SECURITY PERSPECTIVE

Systems security engineering delivers systems deemed *adequately secure* by stakeholders. As such, the notion of security, system security, and adequate security must be established so as to provide the broader perspective of systems security engineering. For purposes of the systems security engineering considerations in this publication, security is defined as freedom from those conditions that can cause loss of assets with unacceptable consequences.[15] The fundamental relationships among assets, an asset-dependent interpretation of loss, and the corresponding loss consequences are central to any discussion of system security.

The term *asset* refers to an item of particular value to stakeholders. An asset may be tangible (e.g., a physical item such as hardware, firmware, computing platform, network device, or other technology component) or intangible (e.g., humans, data, information, software, capability,

---

[15] The definition of security and its foundational basis in *assets* and the consequences of asset *loss* is adapted from similar concepts defined by the National Aeronautics and Space Administration (NASA) for safety and system safety. This perspective better encompasses what security means in consideration of stakeholder concerns that go beyond the protection of data and information, and is therefore, fundamental to any determination of a system being trustworthy secure.

function, service, trademark, copyright, patent, intellectual property, image, or reputation).[16] The value of an asset is determined by stakeholders in consideration of loss concerns across the entire system life cycle. Such concerns include but are not limited to business or mission concerns. The meaning of loss and associated consequences varies based on the nature of the asset. For example, a data or information asset will have a different loss interpretation than would a capability or function. The value of an asset can also be represented in different ways to include criticality, irreplaceability, and the degree to which the assets are relied upon to achieve stakeholder objectives. From these characteristics, the appropriate protections are engineered to provide the requisite system security performance and effectiveness and to control, to the extent reasonable and practical, asset loss and the associated consequences.

Asset-Based Protection — Engineering for Success

Don't focus on what is *likely* to happen—but instead, focus on what *can* happen and be prepared. That is what systems security engineering means by adopting a proactive and reactive strategy in the form of a *concept of secure function* that addresses the spectrum of asset loss and associated consequences. This means proactively planning and designing to prevent the loss of an asset that you are not willing to accept; to be in a position to minimize the consequences should such a loss occur; and to be in an informed position to reactively recover from the loss when it does happen.

The term *protection*, in the context of systems security engineering, has a very broad scope and is primarily a control objective that applies across all asset types and corresponding consequences of loss. Thus, the system protection capability is a system control objective and a system design problem. The solution to the problem is optimized through a balanced proactive and reactive strategy that is not limited to *prevention*. The strategy also encompasses avoiding asset loss and consequences; detecting asset loss and consequences; minimizing (i.e., limiting, containing, or restricting) asset loss and consequences; responding to asset loss and consequences; recovering from asset loss and consequences; and forecasting or predicting asset loss and consequences.

With an established foundation of security in terms of asset, loss, and loss consequences, a secure system can be defined. A secure system is a system that for all of its identified states, modes, and transitions, is deemed to be secure. That is, the system provides protection sufficient to achieve freedom from those conditions that can cause a loss of assets with unacceptable consequences. It is important to note that the scope of security must be clearly defined by stakeholders in terms of the *assets to which security applies* and the *consequences against which security is assessed*.

Security specialties tend to view the cause of loss in terms of threats, with particular emphasis on the adversarial, intelligent nature of the threat. However, the specific causes of asset loss, and for which the consequences of asset loss are assessed, can arise from a variety of conditions and *events* related to adversity, typically referred to as disruptions, hazards, or threats. Regardless of the specific term used, the basis of asset loss constitutes all forms of intentional, unintentional, accidental, incidental, misuse, abuse, error, weakness, defect, fault, and/or failure events and associated conditions. The correlation between events and conditions and unacceptable asset loss consequences has several forms:

---

[16] The human is perhaps the most important and valuable of all intangible assets. Safety explicitly considers the human asset, and that same consideration is equally applicable to security.

- Events and conditions for which there is long-standing knowledge of their occurrence and the specific loss consequences that result;

- Events and conditions that might occur (e.g., anticipated, forecasted, or simply possible) and which would result in unacceptable consequences, or that may result in currently undefinable consequences, and for either case there is a reasoned basis to proactively address;

- Emergent events and conditions that result from the dynamic behaviors, interactions, and outcomes among system elements, including the specific case where good things combine to produce a loss;[17] and

- Specific loss consequences that can occur with uncertainty about the specific or forecast events and conditions that result in the loss consequences.

It is also the case that general uncertainty—that is, the limits to what we know and what we think we know, must be recognized, accepted, and applied across all of the forms identified above. This leads to the perspective about and concept of assurance, or having confidence about the ability of the system to remain trustworthy secure across all forms of adversity—driven by malicious intent, non-malicious intent, certainty, and uncertainty.

Other system aspects that systems security engineering brings into scope in the engineering of trustworthy secure systems are the technical performance, reliability, resilience, survivability, and sustainability of security functions and services, to include security function and service failure modes, behaviors, interactions, and outcomes. When combined together, the notion of protection integrates asset loss and the associated loss consequences into specific contexts across all system states, modes, and transitions. Therefore, any deviations from so called "good" or *secure states* are encompassed in the notion of protection against loss and loss consequences. That is, asset loss can be explicitly tied to the inability of the system to function as specified in its normal secure mode (irrespective of why this may be the case); the ability to operate in a by-design degraded or limited capacity secure mode, and to do so until such time that a secure recovery (i.e., trusted recovery) is possible (through methods such as restart, recovery, reconstitution, reconfiguration, adaptation, or failover) that reestablishes the system in its normal secure mode. These aspects of system security overlap with the concepts of adaptability, agility, reliability, resilience, safety, survivability, and sustainability, with the key differentiator that system security focuses on preserving some aspect of *secure function*.

Systems security is an emergent property of the system. This means that system security results from many things coming together to produce a state or condition that is free from asset loss and the resulting loss consequences. In addition, system security is rarely defined in its own context. Rather, system security is typically defined in the context of stakeholder concerns driven by business or mission needs or operational and performance objectives. System security may also be defined in the context of other emergent system properties including, for example, agility, maintainability, reliability, resilience, safety, scalability, and survivability. Conversely, the achievement of system security may constrain other emergent properties of the system, and may constrain mission or business objectives. It can be concluded, therefore, that systems security engineering can be realized only through multidisciplinary interaction and associated engineering

---

[17] Emergent behavior is a design objective of all systems (i.e., how the system elements combine to produce a particular outcome). However, the emergent behavior of a system can be desirable or undesirable. In addition, emergent behavior may be unspecified. Thus, there are cases where the system does precisely what it was designed to do, and is used only as intended, and the result is unspecified and undesirable behavior that produces a loss of assets. Further, that emergent behavior might be forced via an attack, or via cases of misuse or abuse of the system.

processes based on the predominate, contradicting, dependent, interacting, and conflicting nature of performance, effectiveness, and emergent system properties.

2.3.1 *Protection Capability and Security*

A *protection capability* represents the "many things that come together" in a planned manner to produce the emergent system security property. The protections must come together properly so as to do what the protections are supposed to do and to do nothing else (to include being made to do something else). Moreover, they must achieve this property despite the conditions mentioned previously that result in asset loss and associated consequences. Accordingly, there are two forms of protection capability:

- **Active Protection:** The security functions of the system that exhibit security protection behavior and therefore, have functional and performance attributes. These functions explicitly satisfy security requirements that address the behavior, utilization, and interaction of and among technology/machine, environment, human, and physical system elements.

- **Passive Protection:** The environment for the execution and construction of all security functions (both active protection and general system functionality). Passive protection includes architecture, design, and the rules that govern behavior, interaction, and utilization.

There is no system that can be engineered to be perfectly secure or absolutely trustworthy. That fact, coupled with the basic uncertainty that exists and the trade-offs that will be made routinely across contradicting, competing, and conflicting needs and constraints, necessitates that systems be engineered to achieve *adequate security*. Adequate security results from the *reasoned sum* of all system protections (both active and passive protections) for all system execution modes (e.g., initialization, operation, maintenance, training, shutdown); for all system states (e.g., secure, nonsecure, normal, degraded, recovery); and for all transitions that occur between system states and between system execution modes. Adequate security is a trade space decision or judgement driven by the objectives and priorities of stakeholders. Such decisions or judgements are based on weighing security protection, performance, and effectiveness against all other performance and effectiveness objectives and constraints. The foundation of the reasoning described above results from having well-defined security objectives and security requirements against which evidence about the system can be accumulated and assessed to produce confidence and to justify the conclusions of trustworthiness.

Adequate Security — A System Design Problem

As described in the Ware Report [Ware70], providing adequate security in a system is inherently a system design problem. It is achieved only through sound, purposeful engineering informed by the specialty discipline of systems security engineering. The concept of adequate security, therefore, is made explicit by "binding" together the following: defining asset loss and consequences as the primary target of security; establishing security as a protection control objective for the system; and recognizing that the achievement of the protection control objective (i.e., system security), is a system design problem that delivers trustworthy system function across all system elements.

2.3.2 System Security and Failure

In general, failure is defined as not meeting a specified requirement, objective, or performance measure. With respect to complexity, uncertainty, and security being an emergent property of a system, failure can be defined in terms of the *behavior* exhibited by the system, the *interactions* among the elements that compose the system, and the *outcomes* produced by the system. In this context, a system security failure is defined as not meeting the security-relevant requirements, objectives, and performance measures, to include exhibiting unspecified behavior, exhibiting unspecified interactions, or producing unspecified outcomes, where there is security-relevance.

The security perspective on failure helps to distinguish among the types of security failures for the purpose of system security analyses. Specifically, security failures can be forced or unforced, and regardless of the nature of the failure, the results constitute some manner of asset loss with associated *adverse consequences*. Forced security failures result from malicious activities of individuals with intent to cause harm. This includes attacks by intelligent adversaries and abuse activities of individuals that are properly part of the system—that is, the human system element. Unforced security failures result from non-malicious activities and events. This includes machine and technology errors, faults, and failures; human errors of omission and commission; and *incidents* and accidents across machine/technology and human system elements as well as those associated with physical, environmental, and disaster events.

Three additional considerations are relevant to security and its perspective of failure. First, security is defined and assessed in terms of asset loss concerns of stakeholders, and therefore security failure has to be assessed in a context that is broader than security. Second, system security must be assessed at the system level across all relevant informing aspects. Therefore, collaboration with non-security specialties is necessary to properly inform security-oriented failure analyses. Third, the events associated with security failure have historically been referred to as threats.

The system security perspective of failure recognizes that security failure can result from any event, condition, or circumstance that produces an adverse consequence. Therefore, in this document, the terms adversity, disruption, hazard, and threat are considered synonyms for "bad things that happen" that are of interest to systems security engineering. The security failure perspective is fundamental to addressing the "and does nothing else" aspect of system security relative to system behaviors, interactions, and outcomes. A system characteristic that is related to any discussion of system security failure is system modes and states.

2.3.3 Strategy for System Security

System security is optimized by engineering design based on a balanced proactive and reactive loss prevention strategy. A proactive loss strategy includes planned measures that are engineered to address what *can* happen rather than what *might* happen—to proactively identify and rid the system of weaknesses and defects that lead to security vulnerability; to proactively understand the certainty and uncertainty of threats, both of the adversarial and non-adversarial nature; and to put in place the means and methods to protect against adverse consequences. Proactive systems security engineering also includes planning for failure[18] regardless of whether the failure results

---

[18] The term *failure* in this sense is broadly interpreted as any deviation from specified behavior.

from adversarial or non-adversarial events, and to ensure that the system can be securely resilient to such events, and resilient otherwise.[19]

A reactive loss strategy assumes that despite the proactive planning and institution of means and methods to protect assets against adversarial and non-adversarial events and associated adverse consequences, unanticipated and otherwise unforeseen adverse consequences will occur. Systems security engineering enables options for more effective reactive response to such events, allowing response actions that include a mix of automated and human interaction.

The proactive and reactive strategies are combined and balanced across all assets, stakeholders, concerns, and objectives. To achieve such balance requires that security requirements elicitation and analysis be conducted to unambiguously and clearly ascertain the scope of security in terms of the assets to which security applies and the associated consequences or losses against which security is assessed.

Asset Protection Investments — A Real World Use Case

During the Cold War, the United States invested in a nuclear triad composed of strategic long-range bombers, ballistic missile submarines, and intercontinental ballistic missiles as part of its national defense strategy. This investment, which was arguably one of the costliest expenditures ever made by the United States Government, provided a protection capability for the nation that had an extremely low probability of ever being used. The rationale for making such a costly expenditure with such a low probability of use can be found in the concept of *asset valuation*. The asset in question, from a strategic perspective, was the Nation including the freedom of its citizens and the American way of life. The consequences of failing to provide an appropriate protection capability to defend the national security interests of the United States would have been severe and catastrophic. The design solution, in the form of a *composed set* of interrelated security functions (i.e., a long range bomber function, a ballistic missile submarine function, and an intercontinental ballistic missile function), were deemed "trustworthy" to provide adequate security to defend the national security interests of the United States. Thus, the value of assets is always based on the specific concerns of the relevant stakeholders—and the resulting subsequent investment in the capability to protect such assets is directly related to the value of the asset.

2.3.4 Beyond Verification and Validation – Demonstrating System Security

System security is defined as "freedom from those conditions that can cause a loss of assets with unacceptable consequences." As such, the specific scope of security must be clearly defined by stakeholders in terms of the *assets to which security applies* and the *consequences against which security is assessed*. This definition of security brings with it an inherently context-sensitive and subjective nature to any assertions or expectations about the system security objectives and the determination that those objectives have been achieved. No stakeholder can speak on behalf of all stakeholders regarding the ramifications or effect of the loss of stakeholder and system assets throughout the system life cycle. Moreover, system security being an emergent property of the

---

[19] The term *securely resilient* refers to the system's ability to preserve a secure state despite disruption, to include the system transitions between normal and degraded modes. Securely resilient is a primary objective of systems security engineering. The term *resilient otherwise* refers to security considerations applied to enable system operation despite disruption while not maintaining a secure mode, state, or transition; or only being able to provide for partial security within a given system mode, state, or transition.

system, is an outcome that results from and is assessed in terms of the composed results of the system element parts—system security is not determined relative to an assessment of any one part.[20] Therefore, the requirements and associated verification and validation methods alone do not suffice as the basis to deem a system as being secure. Such requirements and methods are necessary but not sufficient. What is necessary is the means to address the emergent property of security across the subjective and often contradicting, competing, and conflicting needs and beliefs of stakeholders, and to do so with a level of confidence that is commensurate with the asset loss consequences that are to be addressed.

This is achieved through diligent and targeted reasoning. The reasoning takes into account system capabilities, contributing system quantitative and qualitative factors, and how these capabilities and factors compose in the context of system security to produce an evidentiary base upon which analyses are conducted. These analyses, in turn, produce substantiated and reasoned conclusions that serve as the basis for consensus among stakeholders.[21] The ultimate objective is to be able to claim with sufficient confidence or assurance, that the system is adequately secure relative to all stakeholder's objectives, concerns, and associated constraints—and to do so in a manner that is meaningful to stakeholders and that can be recorded, traced, and evolved as variances occur throughout the system life cycle. There will never be absolute assurance, however, because of the inherent asymmetry in system security—that is, things can be declared insecure by observation, but there is no observation that allows one to declare an arbitrary system secure [Herley2016].

2.3.5 System Characteristics and System Security

The characteristics of systems that impact system security vary and can include, for example, the system type and function in terms of its primary purpose;[22] the system make-up in terms of its technology, mechanical, physical, and human elements; the modes and states within which the system delivers its functions and services; the *criticality* or importance of the system and its constituent functions and services; the sensitivity of data or information processed, stored, or transmitted; the consequence of loss, failure, or degradation relative to the ability of the system to execute correctly and to provide for its own protection (i.e., self-protection);[23] and monetary or other value. The system characteristics range from systems for which the impact of degradation, loss, or erroneous function are insignificant, to systems where the impact of degradation, loss, or erroneous function have significant monetary, life-threatening, reputational, or other unacceptable consequences. Systems can include, for example, general-purpose information systems; flight and transportation control systems; command, control, and communication systems; cyber-physical

---

[20] An individual function or mechanism can be verified and validated for correctness and for its specific quality and performance attributes. Those results inform the determination of system security but do not substitute for them.

[21] System security requirements development must be iterative with the involvement of stakeholders. Such development typically spans several life cycle processes as described in Chapter Three. The iterative development of system security requirements is necessary to address the natural evolution and maturation of the system as it proceeds from concept to design, and subsequently to its "as-built" forms.

[22] Some systems are in fact security-purposed systems. Such systems are dedicated to a specific security-oriented function and may be delivered as a fully independent security capability (e.g., surveillance system), incorporated as a system element within some system (e.g., cryptographic key management system), or attached to a system (e.g., sensor array on an aircraft).

[23] A foundational principle of system security states that the system must have the capability to execute correctly (i.e., establish and maintain integrity of execution); to protect itself and its assets; and to do so across all states and modes despite disruptions, hazards, and threats. *Self-protection* is a required capability and makes it possible for the system to deliver the required stakeholder capabilities —and to do so while protecting their assets against loss and consequences of loss. This represents an objective that is achieved to the extent possible given the constraints of cost, feasibility, and practicality. See Appendix F, *Security Design Principles*, for additional discussion of system self-protection.

systems; industrial/process control systems; medical devices and treatment systems; weapons systems; merchandising transaction, financial, and banking systems; entertainment systems, and social networking systems. Each system type has differences in terms of its system characteristics and how those characteristics impact the determination of adequate security.

Another set of system characteristics that impact system security is the nature of the system, the manner in which capability is delivered, and the assets required to deliver that capability and how they are utilized throughout the system life cycle. Capability may be delivered as a service, function, operation, or a combination thereof. The capability can be delivered fully by a single system or delivered as the emergent combined results of a system-of-systems (SoS). The services, functions, and operations may directly or indirectly interact with, control, or monitor physical, mechanical, hydraulic, or pneumatic devices, or other systems or capabilities, or provide the ability to create, manipulate, access, transmit, store, or share data and information. The common themes that underlie the challenges of system security include complexity, dynamicity, and interconnectedness; system elements based on automata, computation, and machine reliance on system-level data and control flows and operations that enable the system to function; and the susceptibility to adversity associated with hardware, software, and firmware-based technologies and their development, manufacturing, handling, and distribution throughout the life cycle.

2.3.6 Role of Systems Security Engineering

Systems security engineering ultimately performs security analyses with the appropriate fidelity and rigor to produce the evidence to substantiate claims that the system is adequately secure. The evidence spans the entire system life cycle and for all system life cycle concepts in terms of the following three roles:

- Engineering the security functions that provide system security capability;

- Engineering the security-driven constraints for all system functions; and

- Engineering and advising for the protection of data, information, technology, methods, and assets associated with the system throughout its life cycle.[24]

These roles require a systems security engineering presence in all systems engineering activities in order to establish a multidisciplinary security and specialty approach to engineering—resulting in sustainably trustworthy secure systems throughout the system life cycle.

Systems security engineering activities and tasks are based on foundational security principles, concepts, methods, and best practices and are intended to provide substantiated evidence-based confidence that security functions and their associated security mechanisms operate only as specified, are able to enforce *security policy*, produce the desired outcome, and warrant the trustworthiness that is required by stakeholders. The systems security engineering activities and tasks may exist as, supplement, or extend the parent systems engineering processes, activities, and tasks, or provide new security-specific methods, processes, activities, and tasks that directly address system security considerations and objectives. Chapter Three describes systems security engineering contributions to the life cycle processes found in ISO/IEC/IEEE 15288.[25]

---

[24] These assets typically provide some domain-specific advantage (e.g., competitive, combatant). They may constitute intellectual properly associated with how the system is engineered, how the system is manufactured or developed, how the system provides its capability, or the nature of the capability delivered and its performance.

[25] ISO/IEC/IEEE 15288 provides an engineering viewpoint and associated terminology for system life cycle processes. The standard does not define systems engineering processes. Accordingly, the use of the term *engineering processes* in this document refers to the engineering organization interpretation of the life cycle processes of ISO/IEC/IEEE 15288.

2.4 SYSTEMS SECURITY ENGINEERING FRAMEWORK

The *systems security engineering framework* [McEvilley15] provides a conceptual view of the
key contexts within which systems security engineering activities are conducted. The framework
defines, bounds, and focuses the systems security engineering activities and tasks, both technical
and nontechnical, towards the achievement of stakeholder *security objectives* and presents a
coherent, well-formed, evidence-based case that those objectives have been achieved.[26] The
framework is independent of system type and engineering or acquisition process model and is not
to be interpreted as a sequence of flows or process steps but rather as a set of interacting contexts,
each with its own checks and balances. The systems security engineering framework emphasizes
an integrated, holistic security perspective across all stages of the system life cycle and is applied
to satisfy the milestone objectives of each life cycle stage. Figure 3 provides an overview of the
systems security engineering framework and its key components.

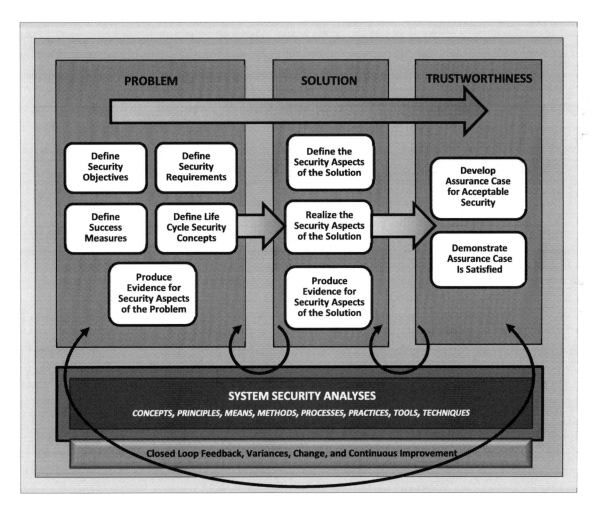

FIGURE 3: SYSTEMS SECURITY ENGINEERING FRAMEWORK

The framework defines three contexts within which the systems security engineering activities are
conducted. These are the *problem* context, the *solution* context, and the *trustworthiness* context.
Establishing the three contexts helps to ensure that the engineering of a system is driven by a
sufficiently complete understanding of the problem articulated in a set of stakeholder security

---

[26] Adapted from [NASA11].

objectives that reflect protection needs and security concerns—instead of by security solutions brought forth in the absence of consideration of the entire problem space and its associated constraints. Moreover, there is explicit focus and a set of activities to demonstrate the worthiness of the solution in providing adequate security across competing and often conflicting constraints.

The three contexts of the systems security engineering framework share a common foundational base of *system security analyses*. System security analyses produce data to support engineering and stakeholder decision making. Such analyses are differentiated for application within the problem, solution, and trustworthiness contexts and routinely employ concepts, principles, means, methods, processes, practices, tools, and techniques. System security analyses:

- Provide relevant data and technical interpretations of system issues from the system security perspective;

- Are differentiated in their application to align with the scope and objectives of where they are applied within the systems security engineering framework; and

- Are performed with a level of fidelity, rigor, and formality to produce data with a level of confidence that matches the assurance required by the stakeholders and engineering team.

System security analyses address important topic areas related to systems security engineering including, for example: architecture; assurance; behavior; cost; criticality; design; effectiveness; emergence; exposure; fit-for-purpose; life cycle concepts; penetration resistance; performance; privacy; protection needs; requirements; risk; security objectives; strength of function; security performance; threat; trades; uncertainty; vulnerability; verification; and validation.

The systems security engineering framework also includes a *closed loop feedback* for interactions among and between the three framework contexts and the requisite system security analyses to continuously identify and address variances as they are introduced into the engineering effort. The feedback loop also helps to achieve continuous process improvement for the system. Each of the framework contexts is described in the following sections.

Systems Security Engineering Framework – Why It Matters

Establishing problem, solution, and trustworthiness contexts as key components of a systems security engineering framework ensures that the *security* of a system is based on achieving a sufficiently complete understanding of the problem as defined by a set of stakeholder security objectives, security concerns, protection needs, and security requirements. This understanding is essential in order to develop effective security solutions—that is, a system that is sufficiently trustworthy and adequately secure to protect stakeholder's assets in terms of loss and the associated consequences.

2.4.1 The Problem Context

The *problem* context defines the basis for an acceptably and adequately secure system given the stakeholder's mission, capability, performance needs and concerns; the constraints imposed by stakeholder concerns related to cost, schedule, risk and loss tolerance; and other constraints associated with life cycle concepts for the system. The problem context enables the engineering team to focus attention on acquiring as complete an understanding of the stakeholder problem as practical; to explore all feasible solution class options; and to select the solution class option or options to be pursued. The problem context includes:

- Determining life cycle security concepts;[27]

- Defining security objectives;

- Defining security requirements; and

- Determining measures of success.

The security objectives are foundational in that they establish and scope what it means to be *adequately secure* in terms of protection against asset loss and the consequences of such asset loss. The security objectives have associated measures of success. The measures of success constitute specific and measureable criteria relative to operational performance measures and stakeholder concerns. Measures of success include both strength of protection and the level of assurance, or confidence, in the protection capability that has been engineered. The two combine to drive the development of security requirements and the development of assurance claims.

Life cycle security concepts are the processes, methods, and procedures associated with the system throughout its life cycle and provide distinct contexts for interpretation of system security. These concepts also serve to scope and bound attention in addressing protection needs and for broader security-informing considerations and constraints. Protection needs are determined based on the security objectives, life cycle concepts, and stakeholder concerns. The protection needs are subsequently transformed into stakeholder security requirements and associated constraints on system requirements, and the measures needed to validate that all requirements have been met. A well-defined and stakeholder-validated problem definition and context provides the foundation for all systems engineering and systems security engineering and supporting activities.

2.4.2 The Solution Context

The *solution* context transforms the stakeholder security requirements into design requirements for the system; addresses all security architecture, design, and related aspects necessary to realize a system that satisfies those requirements; and produces sufficient evidence to demonstrate that those requirements have been satisfied.[28] The solution context is based on a balanced proactive and reactive system security protection strategy[29] that exercises control over events, conditions, asset loss, and the consequence of asset loss to the degree possible, practicable, and acceptable to stakeholders. The solution context includes:

---

[27] The term *life cycle security concept* refers to all processes and activities associated with the system throughout the system life cycle, with specific security considerations. The term is an extension of the notion of *concept of operation* including, for example: processes and activities related to development; prototyping; analysis of alternatives; training; logistics; maintenance; sustainment; evolution; modernization; disposal; and refurbishment. Each life cycle concept has security considerations and constraints that must be fully integrated into the life cycle to ensure that security objectives for the system can be met. Life cycle security concepts include those applied broadly during acquisition and program management. Life cycle security concepts can affect such things as Requests for Information, Requests for Proposal, Statements of Work, source selections, development and test environments, operating environments and supporting infrastructures, supply chain, distribution, logistics, maintenance, training, and clearances/background checks.

[28] Security constraints are transformed and incorporated into system design requirements with metadata-tagging to identify security relevance.

[29] The system security protection strategy is consistent with the overall *concept of secure function*. The concept of secure function, defined during the problem context, constitutes a strategy for a proactive and reactive protection capability throughout the system life cycle. The strategy has the objective to provide freedom from specific concerns associated with asset loss and asset loss consequences.

- Defining the security aspects of the solution;

- Realizing the security aspects of the solution; and

- Producing evidence for the security aspects of the solution.

The security aspects of the solution include the development of the system protection strategy; the system security design requirements; the security architecture views and viewpoints; the security design; the security aspects, capabilities, and limitations in the system life cycle procedures; and the associated security performance verification measures. The security aspects of the solution are realized during the implementation of the system security design in accordance with the security architecture and in satisfaction of the security requirements. The evidence associated with the security aspects of the solution is obtained with a level of fidelity and degree of rigor that is influenced by the level of assurance[30] targeted by the security objectives. Assurance evidence is obtained from standard systems engineering verification methods (e.g., analysis, demonstration, inspection, and test) and from complementary validation methods applied against the stakeholder requirements.

2.4.3 The Trustworthiness Context

The *trustworthiness* context is a decision-making context that provides an evidence-based demonstration, through reasoning, that the system-of-interest is deemed trustworthy based upon a set of claims derived from security objectives. The trustworthiness context consists of:

- Developing and maintaining the assurance case; and

- Demonstrating that the assurance case is satisfied.

The trustworthiness context is grounded on the concept of an *assurance case*. An assurance case is a well-defined and structured set of arguments and a *body of evidence* showing that a system satisfies specific claims with respect to a given quality attribute.[31] Assurance cases also provide reasoned, auditable artifacts that support the contention that a claim or set of claims is satisfied, including systematic argumentation and its underlying evidence and explicit assumptions that support the claims [ISO/IEC 15026].

An assurance case is used to demonstrate that a system exhibits some complex emergent property such as safety, security, resiliency, reliability, or survivability. An effective security assurance case contains foundational security claims that are derived from stakeholder security objectives, credible and relevant evidence that substantiates the claims, and valid arguments that relate the various evidence to the supported security claims. The result provides a compelling statement that adequate security has been achieved and driven by stakeholder needs and expectations.

Assurance cases typically include supporting information such as assumptions, constraints, and any inferences that can affect the reasoning process. Subsequent to assurance case development, analyses by subject-matter experts determine that all security claims are substantiated by the evidence produced and the arguments that relate the evidence to the claims. For maximum effectiveness, the assurance cases must be maintained in response to variances throughout the engineering effort.

---

[30] *Assurance* is the measure of confidence associated with a given requirement. As the level of assurance increases, so does the scope, depth, and rigor associated with the methods and analyses conducted.

[31] Software Engineering Institute, Carnegie Mellon University.

The specific form of an assurance case and the level of rigor and formality in acquiring the evidence required by the assurance case is a trade space consideration. It involves the target (desired) level of assurance, the nature of the consequences for which assurance is sought, and the size and complexity of the dimensions that factor into the determination of trustworthiness. The assurance case itself is an engineering construct and accordingly, must be managed to ensure that the effort expended to produce the evidence is justified by the need for that evidence in making the trustworthiness determination. The assurance claims are the key trustworthiness factor and are developed from the security objectives and associated measures of success, independent of the realization of the system and its supporting evidence.

CHAPTER THREE

SYSTEM LIFE CYCLE PROCESSES

SYSTEM SECURITY IN SYSTEM LIFE CYCLE PROCESSES

This chapter describes the security considerations and contributions to system life cycle processes to produce the security outcomes that are necessary to achieve trustworthy secure systems. The security considerations and contributions are provided as systems security engineering activities and tasks and they are aligned with and developed as security extensions to the system life cycle processes in ISO/IEC/IEEE 15288, *Systems and software engineering – System life cycle processes*. The system life cycle processes are organized and grouped into four families. These include: Agreement Processes; Organization Project-Enabling Processes; Technical Management Processes; and Technical Processes. Figure 4 lists the system life cycle processes and illustrates their application across all stages of the system life cycle.

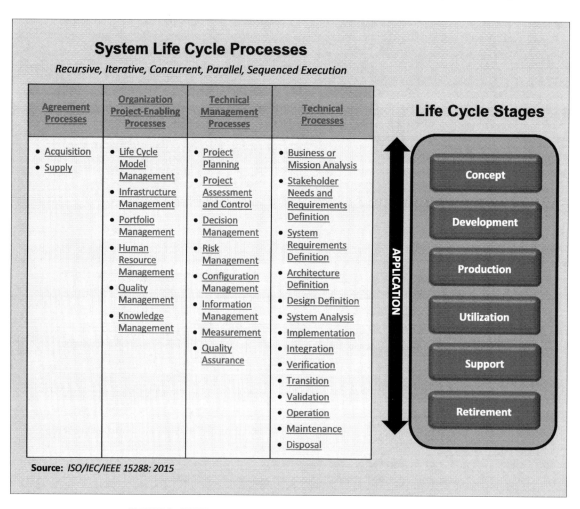

FIGURE 4: SYSTEM LIFE CYCLE PROCESSES AND LIFE CYCLE STAGES

The *systems security engineering* activities and tasks are grounded in security and *trust* principles and concepts, and leverage the principles, concepts, terms, and practices of systems engineering to facilitate consistency in their application as part of a systems engineering effort. Achieving the effective integration of systems security engineering into systems engineering requires all systems engineering activities to explicitly contain the system security activities and tasks identified by this publication. As such, all references to system life cycle processes explicitly include the systems security engineering activities and tasks. Moreover, any reference to a specific system life cycle process explicitly includes all of the systems security engineering activities and tasks defined for that process.

The system life cycle processes are *not* intended to be prescriptive in their execution and do not map explicitly to specific stages in the system life cycle. Rather, the system life cycle processes are conducted as needed to achieve specific systems engineering objectives. By design, the processes can be applied concurrently, iteratively, or recursively at any level in the structural hierarchy of a system, with the appropriate fidelity and rigor, and at any stage in the system life cycle, in accordance with acquisition, systems engineering, or other imposed process models.[32]

The processes are also intended to be *tailored* in their application, providing the needed flexibility and agility for optimized and efficient use across a wide variety of systems engineering efforts supporting diverse stakeholder communities of interest and sectors, system types, technologies, and trustworthiness objectives. Tailoring can include: altering the defined execution sequence of system life cycle processes for more effective application; supplementing the process activities in response to unique or specialized requirements or other circumstances; and completing the systems engineering effort without performing all of the individual processes.[33] Tailoring may be motivated by the stage of the system life cycle; the size, scope, and complexity of the system; specialized requirements; or the need to be able to accommodate specific methods, techniques, or technologies used to develop the system. Tailoring may also be appropriate in cases where the activities of different processes might overlap or interact in ways not defined in this document.[34]

Tailoring the system life cycle processes allows the engineering team to:

- Optimize the application of the processes in response to technological, programmatic, acquisition, process, procedural, system life cycle stage, or other objectives and constraints;

- Allow the concurrent application of the processes by sub-teams focused on different parts of the same engineering effort;

- Facilitate the application of the processes to conform with a variety of system development methodologies, processes, and models (e.g., agile, spiral, waterfall), recognizing that multiple such methodologies, processes, and models could be used on a single engineering effort; and

---

[32] Systems engineering and system life cycle processes do not map explicitly to specific stages in the system life cycle. Rather, the processes may occur in one or more stages of the life cycle depending on the particular process and the conditions associated with the systems engineering effort. For example, the *Maintenance* process includes activities that plan the maintenance strategy such that it is possible to identify constraints on the system design necessitated by how the maintenance will be performed once the system is operational. This example illustrates that the *Maintenance* process is conducted prior to or concurrent with the *Design Definition* process.

[33] *Tailoring* can occur either as part of the project planning process at the start of the systems security engineering effort or in an ad hoc manner at any time during the engineering effort—when situations and circumstances so dictate. Understanding the fundamentals of systems security engineering (i.e., the science underpinning the discipline) helps to inform the tailoring process whenever it occurs during the life cycle of the system. The INCOSE Systems Engineering Handbook provides additional guidance on how to tailor the systems engineering processes [INCOSE14].

[34] For example, the engineering team may need to initiate a system modification in a relatively short period to respond to a serious security incident. In this situation, the team may only informally consider each process rather than formally executing each process. It is essential that any system modifications continue to support stakeholder protection needs. Without this system-level perspective, modifications could fix one problem while introducing other problems.

- Accommodate the need for unanticipated or other event-driven execution of processes to resolve issues and respond to variances and changes that occur during the engineering effort.

Each of the system life cycle processes contains a set of system security *activities* and *tasks* that produce a set of security-oriented *outcomes*.[35] These outcomes combine to deliver a system and a corresponding body of evidence that serves as the basis to substantiate the security and the trustworthiness of the system; determine security risk across stakeholder concerns and with respect to the use of the system in support of mission or business objectives; help stakeholders decide which operational constraints are necessary to mitigate security risk; provide inputs to other processes associated with delivering the system; and support the system throughout the stages of its life cycle.[36] Each life cycle process description has the following format:

- **Purpose:** The purpose section identifies the primary goals and objectives of the process and provides a summary of the security-focused activities conducted during the process.

- **Outcomes:** The outcomes section describes the security-focused outcomes achieved by the completion of the process and the data generated by the process.[37]

- **Activities and Tasks:** The activities and tasks section provides a description of the security-oriented work performed during the process including the security-focused enhancements to the activities and tasks.

The activities and tasks may be repeated, in whole or in part, to resolve any problems, gaps, or issues identified. Likewise, there is not a rigid sequencing in the execution of system life cycle processes—activities and tasks may be combined across processes to achieve efficiencies as part of the tailoring effort. Any iteration and sequencing between the processes requires additional scrutiny to ensure that changes to the outcomes of previously executed processes are properly incorporated into the activities and tasks of the current process.

While the life cycle processes from ISO/IEC/IEEE 15288 are addressed in terms of systems security engineering, the activities and tasks in this publication are neither a restatement of those processes nor do they constitute a one-for-one mapping to those processes. This publication focuses on specific contributions to the process, and the activities and tasks are titled to reflect the security contributions. In some cases, activities and tasks have been added to address the range of outcomes appropriate for the achievement of trustworthy secure system objectives.

The descriptions of the system life cycle processes assume that sufficient time, funding, human, and material resources are available to ensure a complete application of the processes within a comprehensive systems engineering effort. The processes represent the "standard of excellence" within which tailoring is accomplished to achieve realistic, optimal, and cost-effective results within the constraints imposed on the engineering team.

---

[35] Outcomes from the systems engineering processes inform other systems engineering processes and can also serve to inform processes external to the engineering effort, such as the organizational life cycle processes of stakeholders and certification, authorization, or regulatory processes.

[36] The comprehensiveness, depth, fidelity, credibility, and relevance of the body of evidence are factors in helping to achieve the level of assurance sought by stakeholders. The objective is to have a body of evidence that is sufficient to convince stakeholders that their assurance needs are satisfied. The assurance level is an engineering trade space factor that must be planned for and executed with the appropriate fidelity and rigor. And doing so can drive cost and schedule.

[37] The data and information generated during the execution of a process is not necessarily produced in the form of a document. Such data and information can be conveyed in the most effective manner as set forth by stakeholders or the engineering team. Data and information produced during a particular process may flow into a subsequent process or support other processes that are associated with the systems security engineering process.

The following naming convention is established for the system life cycle processes. Each process is identified by a two-character designation (e.g., BA is the official designation for the *Business or Mission Analysis* process). Table 2 provides a listing of the system life cycle processes and their associated two-character designators.

TABLE 2: PROCESS NAMES AND DESIGNATORS

ID	PROCESS	ID	PROCESS
AQ	Acquisition	MS	Measurement
AR	Architecture Definition	OP	Operation
BA	Business or Mission Analysis	PA	Project Assessment and Control
CM	Configuration Management	PL	Project Planning
DE	Design Definition	PM	Portfolio Management
DM	Decision Management	QA	Quality Assurance
DS	Disposal	QM	Quality Management
HR	Human Resource Management	RM	Risk Management
IF	Infrastructure Management	SA	System Analysis
IM	Information Management	SN	Stakeholder Needs and Requirements Definition
IN	Integration	SP	Supply
IP	Implementation	SR	System Requirements Definition
KM	Knowledge Management	TR	Transition
LM	Life Cycle Model Management	VA	Validation
MA	Maintenance	VE	Verification

The security activities and tasks in each system life cycle process are uniquely identified using a two-character designation plus a numerical designation. For example, the first activity in the *Stakeholder Needs and Requirements Definition* process is designated SN-1. The first two tasks within SN-1 are designated SN-1.1 and SN-1.2 respectively. The identification of the security activities and tasks within each system life cycle process provides for precise referencing and traceability among the process elements. Each security task description within a security activity is supported by an *elaboration* section that provides additional information on considerations relevant to the successful execution of that task. A *references* section provides a list of pertinent publications associated with the elaboration of tasks and is a source of content for additional information. And finally, a *related publications* section provides a list of documents that are related to the topic being addressed but should not necessarily be considered a source for further elaboration. The following example illustrates the second task in the second activity of the *Stakeholder Needs and Requirements Definition* process:

BA-2.2 Define the security aspects and considerations of the mission, business, or operational problem or opportunity.

Elaboration: Information is elicited from stakeholders to acquire an understanding of the mission, business, or operational problem or opportunity from a system security perspective. Information items that can have security implications and that can affect the requirements generation process are described in Appendix G.

The remaining sections in this chapter describe the security contributions, considerations, and outcomes for the thirty system life cycle processes defined in ISO/IEC/IEEE 15288.

Systems Engineering Throughout the Life Cycle

Systems engineering execution of life cycle processes occurs throughout the life cycle of the system. In that regard, the systems engineering objectives for the *Operation* (**OP**), *Maintenance* (**MA**), and *Disposal* (**DS**) processes are not to prescribe the day-to-day operations, maintenance, or disposal activities of organizations. Nor are field engineering teams or personnel responsible for the execution of operations, maintenance, or disposal activities. Rather, the systems engineering objectives for these processes are to accomplish the engineering component of planning for the operations, maintenance, and disposal life cycle stages of the system. The systems engineering execution of these processes results in determining capabilities and constraints to inform the system requirements, architecture, and design, and to inform the development of best practices, procedures, and training in support of operational, maintenance, sustainment, and other life cycle support organizations.

Field engineering teams work alongside the operations, maintenance, and other life cycle support organizations to assist in the collection of data for continued improvement and to support the investigation and analysis of events and circumstances associated with failures, incidents, attacks, accidents, and other situations where there is a demonstrated or suspected nonconformance to the system or its specified behavior. The field engineering teams also help to identify performance deficiencies, gaps, and opportunities for modernization and enhancement. Field engineering teams may also assist in the installation of planned modifications, upgrades, or enhancements to the system. The field engineering team applies all required technical and non-technical processes as necessary, while addressing field engineering issues. The teams also consult with and provide feedback to developmental engineering teams. This helps to ensure that the lessons learned in the field are properly communicated to guide and inform any future development engineering efforts and that the relevant improvements and modifications being made on future systems can be effectively employed to systems in the field.

3.1 AGREEMENT PROCESSES

This section contains the two ISO/IEC/IEEE 15288 *agreement* processes with extensions for systems security engineering. The processes are:

- Acquisition (AQ); and

- Supply Process (SP).

3.1.1 Acquisition Process

Purpose

"The purpose of the Acquisition process is to obtain a product or service in accordance with the acquirer's requirements."

ISO/IEC/IEEE 15288-2015. Reprinted with permission from IEEE, Copyright IEEE 2015, All rights reserved.

Systems Security Engineering Purpose

Systems security engineering, as part of the *Acquisition* process, ensures that the acquirer's protection needs and security concerns are addressed by the acquirer's requirements used to obtain a *product* or *service*.

Systems Security Engineering Outcomes

- Security considerations are addressed by the acquisition strategy.

- A request for a supplier to provide a product or service includes security considerations.

- Security considerations are included in the criteria for selecting a supplier.

- An agreement between the acquirer and the supplier that contains security considerations is established.

- A product or service complying with the security aspects of the agreement is accepted.

- Acquirer security obligations defined in the agreement are satisfied.

Systems Security Engineering Activities and Tasks

AQ-1   PREPARE FOR SECURITY ASPECTS OF THE ACQUISITION

    AQ-1.1 Define the security aspects for how the acquisition will be conducted.

    Elaboration: The security aspects include how security objectives, protection needs, and security concerns are achieved by the acquisition strategy. Security concerns and considerations impact and are impacted by the objectives and scope of the engineering effort; the *life cycle models* to be used; the acquisition activities, milestones, gates, and associated review and approval criteria; the protection of data, information, and material assets; risk and issues mitigation; the selection of suppliers; and acceptance conditions to include demonstrations of compliance or conformance to laws, directives, regulations, policies, or other criteria. The acquisition strategy may describe life cycle models; liabilities; methods or processes; levels of criticality; levels of trustworthiness and assurance; and priority of relevant trade factors.

    AQ-1.2 Prepare a request for a product or service that includes the security requirements.

    Elaboration: The security requirements are integrated with and provided as part of the stakeholder requirements or system requirements depending on the type of acquisition approach and specifics of the product or service required. The security requirements are developed by application of the requirements engineering approach described in the acquisition strategy. This approach achieves the outcomes of the *Stakeholder Needs and Requirements Definition* and *System Requirements Definition* processes. The request includes security criteria for the business practices to which the supplier is to comply, a list of bidders with adequate security qualifications, and the security criteria that will be used to select the supplier.

References: ISO/IEC/IEEE 15288, Section 6.1.1.3 a); ISO/IEC 15026; ISO/IEC 27036.

Related Publications: ISO/IEC 12207, Section 6.1.1.3.1; ISO/IEC 21827.

AQ-2   ADVERTISE THE ACQUISITION AND SELECT THE SUPPLIER TO CONFORM WITH THE SECURITY ASPECTS OF THE ACQUISITION

> **AQ-2.1** Communicate the request for a product or service to potential suppliers consistent with security requirements.

Elaboration: All forms of communications and interactions associated with the advertisement of acquisition requests (i.e., the solicitation) are to be conducted with adequate protection of data, information, material, technology, and human assets. This includes protection concerns of data and information sensitivity and privacy; knowledge of stakeholder organizations and personnel; the nature, timing, schedule, performance, and other characteristics of the acquisition; and intellectual property and technologies. Communication with potential suppliers includes subcontractors and other supporting organizations to those suppliers.

> **AQ-2.2** Select one or more suppliers that meet the security criteria.

Elaboration: Subject-matter experts with relevant security expertise participate in the supplier selection process. The subject-matter experts make selection recommendations and rankings based on the strengths and weaknesses of the candidate supplier's ability to deliver the requested product or service in satisfaction of the stated security requirements and secure business practice criteria. The subject-matter experts also provide justification to support the recommendations provided. Supplier selection includes subcontractors and other supporting organizations to the supplier.

References: ISO/IEC/IEEE 15288, Section 6.1.1.3 b); ISO/IEC 15026; ISO/IEC 27036.

Related Publications: ISO/IEC 12207, Section 6.1.1.3.2, Section 6.1.1.3.3; ISO/IEC 21827.

AQ-3   ESTABLISH AND MAINTAIN THE SECURITY ASPECTS OF AGREEMENTS

> **AQ-3.1** Develop an agreement with the supplier to satisfy the security aspects of acquiring the product or service and supplier acceptance criteria.

Elaboration: The security aspects of the agreement address business practice security expectations and constraints including, for example: configuration management, risk reporting, reporting of security measures, and security measure analysis; security requirements; secure development; security verification; security validation; security acceptance procedures and criteria to include regulatory body acceptance, authorization, and approval; procedures for transport, handling, delivery, and storage; security and privacy protections and restrictions on the use, dissemination, and destruction of data, information and intellectual property; security-relevant exception-handling procedures and criteria; agreement change management procedures; and agreement termination procedures. The security aspects of the agreement also include application of all of the above to subcontractors and other supporting organizations to the supplier.

> **AQ-3.2** Identify and evaluate the security impact of necessary changes to the agreement.

Elaboration: Necessary changes to agreements may be identified by the acquirer or the supplier. The basis for the agreement change may or may not be security-related. However, there may be security-related impact regardless of the basis for the change. A security-related evaluation of the needed change identifies any *security relevance* and determines impact in terms of schedule, cost, plans, technical capability, quality, assurance, and trustworthiness.

AQ-3.3 Negotiate and institute changes to the agreement with the supplier to address identified security impacts.

Elaboration: Changes are captured in relevant agreements. The security aspects of the initial agreement and of all agreement revisions are negotiated in the context of the identified security impacts and other needs of the acquirer, with consideration of the feasibility of delivering an acceptable product or service within associated constraints. The security-relevant results are captured in project plans and communicated to all affected parties and stakeholders.

References: ISO/IEC/IEEE 15288, Section 6.1.1.3 c); ISO/IEC 15026; ISO/IEC 27036.

Related Publications: ISO/IEC 12207, Section 6.1.1.3.4; ISO/IEC 21827.

AQ-4   MONITOR THE SECURITY ASPECTS OF AGREEMENTS

AQ-4.1 Assess the execution of the security aspects of the agreement.

Elaboration: Adherence to the security aspects of agreements is to be confirmed on a continuing basis to ensure that all parties are meeting their security responsibilities. Necessary corrective actions and adjustments are made to address any nonconformances or deficiencies identified. The *Project Assessment and Control* process is used to evaluate projected cost, schedule, performance, and the impact of undesirable security-related outcomes that are identified. The *Risk Management* process identifies associated risks and provides recommendations for risk treatment.

AQ-4.2 Provide data needed by the supplier in a secure manner in order to achieve timely resolution of issues.

Elaboration: Agreement execution issues may require specific data for timely and effective response action by the supplier. The issue to be resolved may or may not be security-relevant. However, the data provided to the supplier must be appropriately protected throughout all forms and manner of its communications to the supplier. The nature of the acquisition, stakeholders involved, sensitivity and proprietary aspects of data, to include privacy concerns all factor into the method of secure provision of data to the supplier.

References: ISO/IEC/IEEE 15288, Section 6.1.1.3 d); ISO/IEC 27036.

Related Publications: ISO/IEC 12207, Section 6.1.1.3.5; ISO/IEC 21827.

AQ-5   ACCEPT THE PRODUCT OR SERVICE

AQ-5.1 Confirm that the delivered product or service complies with the security aspects of the agreement.

Elaboration: The confirmation is informed by security evidence accumulated throughout the period of performance specified by the agreement. The security evidence is to be indicative of the activities performed, changes made, and results achieved, and is sufficient to confirm compliance with the security aspects of the agreement. All technical processes produce evidence in support of the confirmation that the delivered product or service complies with the security aspects of the agreement.

AQ-5.2 Accept the product or service from the supplier or other party, as directed by the security criteria in the agreement.

Elaboration: Security considerations may impact the manner in which the product or service is accepted and transitioned from the supplier or other party to the acquirer or the acquirer's designated representative. The *Transition*, *Operation*, and *Validation* processes provide for security in transition and acceptance.

References: ISO/IEC/IEEE 15288, Section 6.1.1.3 e); ISO/IEC 27036.

Related Publications: ISO/IEC 12207, Section 6.1.1.3.6; ISO/IEC 21827.

3.1.2 Supply Process

Purpose

"The purpose of the Supply process is to provide an acquirer with a product or service that meets agreed requirements."

ISO/IEC/IEEE 15288-2015. Reprinted with permission from IEEE, Copyright IEEE 2015, All rights reserved.

Systems Security Engineering Purpose

Systems security engineering, as part of the *Supply* process, ensures that a product or service provided to an acquirer provides the security functions and services while meeting all security concerns and constraints expressed by the acquirer's requirements.

Systems Security Engineering Outcomes

- The acquirer's security needs are matched to the capability of products and services that can satisfy those needs.

- Security criteria are addressed by the supply strategy.

- A response to the acquirer addresses the security criteria in the acquirer's request.

- Security criteria are addressed in an agreement to supply a product or service.

- A product or service that satisfies the security criteria in the agreement is supplied.

- Supplier security obligations defined in the agreement are satisfied.

Systems Security Engineering Activities and Tasks

SP-1   PREPARE FOR SECURITY ASPECTS OF THE SUPPLY

SP-1.1   Identify the security aspects of the acquirer's need for a product or service.

Elaboration: Any need for a product or service is likely to have security aspects associated with it or the acquirer may have an explicit need for a security product or service. The security need is identified based on explicit security criteria in the request and through derivation of such criteria where it is not explicit. A determination is made if the security need matches that which can be provided. The *Business or Mission Analysis* process can be used to guide the identification of need and to explicitly capture security criteria in the request.

SP-1.2   Define the security aspects of the supply strategy.

Elaboration: The security aspects of the supply strategy include how stakeholder security objectives, protection needs, and security concerns are achieved by the supply strategy. Security concerns and considerations impact and are impacted by the objectives and scope of the product or service to be delivered; the methods, processes, and tools used to deliver it; the life cycle models to be used; the acquisition activities, milestones, gates, and the associated review and approval criteria; the protection of data, information, and material assets; risk and issues mitigation; the selection of subcontractors and supporting organizations, materials, and resources; and compliance with acceptance conditions. The supply strategy may identify or describe life cycle models; liabilities; methods or processes; levels of criticality; levels of assurance and trustworthiness; and priority of relevant trade factors.

References: ISO/IEC/IEEE 15288, Section 6.1.2.3 a); ISO/IEC 15026; ISO/IEC 27036.

Related Publications: ISO/IEC 12207, Section 6.1.2.3.1; ISO/IEC 21827.

SP-2   RESPOND TO A SOLICITATION

SP-2.1   Evaluate a request for a product or service with respect to the feasibility of satisfying the security criteria.

Elaboration: The security criteria may require specific human resources, capabilities, methods, technologies, techniques, or tools to deliver an acceptable product or service with the desired level of assurance and trustworthiness. The evaluation considers these factors to determine what must be done to satisfy the request and the feasibility of doing so.

SP-2.2   Prepare a response that satisfies the security criteria expressed in the solicitation.

Elaboration: The response should include constraints on feasibility of satisfying the security criteria and security-driven constraints on satisfying other aspect of the solicitation. Acceptance of the response may be based on negotiation that optimizes the agreement across security criteria and associated constraints that impact feasibility of delivering an acceptance product or service.

References: ISO/IEC/IEEE 15288, Section 6.1.2.3 b); ISO/IEC 15026; ISO/IEC 27036.

Related Publications: ISO/IEC 12207, Section 6.1.2.3.2; ISO/IEC 21827.

SP-3   ESTABLISH AND MAINTAIN THE SECURITY ASPECTS OF AGREEMENTS

SP-3.1   Develop an agreement with the acquirer to satisfy the security aspects of the product or service and security acceptance criteria.

Elaboration: The security aspects of the agreement address business practice security expectations and constraints including, for example: configuration management, risk reporting, reporting of security measures, and security measure analysis; security requirements; secure development; security verification; security validation; security acceptance procedures and criteria to include regulatory body acceptance, authorization, and approval; procedures for transport, handling, delivery, and storage; security and privacy protections and restrictions on the use, dissemination, and destruction of data, information and intellectual property; security-relevant exception-handling procedures and criteria; agreement change management procedures; and agreement termination procedures. The security aspects of the agreement also include application of all of the above to the plans for use of subcontractors and other supporting organizations.

SP-3.2   Identify and evaluate the security impact of necessary changes to the agreement.

Elaboration: Necessary changes to agreements may be identified by the acquirer or the supplier. The basis for the agreement change may or may not be security-related. However, there may be security-related impact regardless of the basis for the change. A security-related evaluation of the needed change identifies any security relevance and determines impact in terms of plans, schedule, cost, technical capability, quality, assurance, and trustworthiness.

SP-3.3   Negotiate and institute changes to the agreement with the acquirer to address identified security impacts.

Elaboration: Changes are captured in relevant agreements. The security aspects of the initial agreement and of all agreement revisions are negotiated in the context of the identified security impacts and other needs of the acquirer, with consideration of the feasibility of delivering an acceptable product or service within associated constraints. The security-relevant results are captured in project plans and communicated to all affected parties and stakeholders.

References: ISO/IEC/IEEE 15288, Section 6.1.2.3 c); ISO/IEC 15026; ISO/IEC 27036.

Related Publications: ISO/IEC 12207, Section 6.1.2.3.3; ISO/IEC 21827.

SP-4   EXECUTE THE SECURITY ASPECTS OF AGREEMENTS

SP-4.1   Execute the security aspects of the agreement according to the engineering project plans.

Elaboration: The security aspects of the agreement are executed as a fully integrated component of all technical and nontechnical engineering activities as outlined by engineering project plans.

SP-4.2   Assess the execution of the security aspects of the agreement.

Elaboration: Adherence to the security aspects of agreements is to be confirmed on a continuing basis to ensure that all parties are meeting their security responsibilities. Necessary corrective actions and adjustments are made to address any nonconformance or deficiencies identified. The *Project Assessment and Control* process is used to evaluate projected cost, schedule, performance, and the impact of undesirable security-related outcomes that are identified. The *Risk Management* process identifies associated risks and provides recommendations for risk treatment.

References: ISO/IEC/IEEE 15288, Section 6.1.2.3 d); ISO/IEC 27036.

Related Publications: ISO/IEC 12207, Section 6.1.2.3.4; ISO/IEC 21827.

SP-5   DELIVER AND SUPPORT THE SECURITY ASPECTS OF THE PRODUCT OR SERVICE

SP-5.1   Deliver the product or service in accordance with the security aspects and considerations in the agreement with the acquirer.

Elaboration: The delivery of the product or service is to follow agreed-upon procedures and methods for the protection of the product or service at all times when it is out of the possession of the supplier.

SP-5.2   Provide security assistance to the acquirer as stated in the agreement.

Elaboration: Systems security engineering assistance and support continues throughout operations, sustainment, and disposal of the system.

SP-5.3   Transfer the responsibility for the product or service to the acquirer or other party, as directed by the security aspects and considerations in the agreement.

Elaboration: There should be confirmation that there are no outstanding security-relevant issues that prevent transfer of responsibility for the product or service to the acquirer, and confirmation that any agreement termination actions have been taken. This includes the return of sensitive, proprietary, or classified information and material assets shared as part of the agreement.

References: ISO/IEC/IEEE 15288, Section 6.1.2.3 e); ISO/IEC 27036.

Related Publications: ISO/IEC 12207, Section 6.1.2.3.5; ISO/IEC 21827.

3.2 ORGANIZATIONAL PROJECT-ENABLING PROCESSES

This section contains the six ISO/IEC/IEEE 15288 *organizational project-enabling* processes with extensions for systems security engineering. The processes are:

- Life Cycle Model Management (LM);

- Infrastructure Management (IF);

- Portfolio Management (PM);

- Human Resource Management (HR);

- Quality Management (QM); and

- Knowledge Management (KM).

3.2.1 Life Cycle Model Management Process

Purpose

"The purpose of the Life Cycle Model Management process is to define, maintain, and assure availability of policies, life cycle processes, life cycle models, and procedures for use by the organization with respect to the scope of this International Standard."

ISO/IEC/IEEE 15288-2015. Reprinted with permission from IEEE, Copyright IEEE 2015, All rights reserved.

Systems Security Engineering Purpose

Systems security engineering, as part of the *Life Cycle Model Management* process, identifies and assesses the security needs and considerations for life cycle policies, procedures, processes, and models that are capable of being applied using effective proven methods and tools to achieve assurance and trustworthiness objectives.

Systems Security Engineering Outcomes

- Security considerations are captured in organizational policies and procedures for the management and deployment of life cycle models and processes.

- Security responsibility, accountability, and authority for and within life cycle policies, procedures, processes, and models are defined.

- Security needs and considerations for life cycle models and processes for use by the organization are assessed.

- Security needs and considerations inform the implementation of prioritized process, model, and procedure improvements.

Systems Security Engineering Activities and Tasks

LM-1   ESTABLISH THE SECURITY ASPECTS OF THE PROCESS

> **LM-1.1** Establish policies and procedures for process management and deployment that are consistent with the security aspects of organizational strategies.

> **Elaboration:** The policies and procedures may be explicit to security or may have security-informing aspects. Organizational strategies are to include security objectives and considerations that aid in determining the most effective means to ensure that policies and procedures are consistent.

> **LM-1.2** Define the security roles, responsibilities, and authorities to facilitate implementation of the security aspects of processes and the strategic management of life cycles.

> **Elaboration:** Appendix E provides information on roles and responsibilities.

> **LM-1.3** Define the security aspects of the business criteria that control progression through the life cycle.

> **Elaboration:** Security criteria must inform gates, checkpoints, and entry and exit criteria for key milestones and decision points used to control the progression of the engineering project through

the stages in the system life cycle. This ensures that the security objectives, success measures, concerns, and considerations are explicitly part of all life cycle decision making.

LM-1.4 Establish the security criteria of standard life cycle models for the organization.

Elaboration: Security criteria is identified for a standard life cycle model and for each of its constituent stage models. The security criteria are used to reflect the security purpose, outcomes, and level of assurance of each stage. The security criteria also address tailoring needs to optimize the standard model to suit the specific needs of the engineering project for delivering a specific system of interest to meet assurance, trustworthiness objectives, and identified constraints.

References: ISO/IEC/IEEE 15288, Section 6.2.1.3 a); ISO/IEC 15026.

Related Publications: ISO/IEC 12207, Section 6.2.1.3.1; ISO/IEC 21827; National Cybersecurity Workforce Framework; DoD Directive 8140.01.

LM-2 ASSESS THE SECURITY ASPECTS OF THE PROCESS

LM-2.1 Monitor and analyze the security aspects of process execution across the organization.

Elaboration: Monitoring and analysis identifies security-relevant trends regarding the efficiency and effectiveness of the process in achieving the intent of the engineering organization policies and complying with relevant laws, regulations, directives, or policies. The scope of monitoring includes the security-specific process execution methods and the process execution of methods that are not producing any specific security outcome but must operate effectively within security-oriented constraints. The security aspects monitored include those aspects associated with levels of assurance.

LM-2.2 Conduct periodic reviews of the security aspects of the life cycle models used by the projects.

Elaboration: Security reviews include the suitability, adequacy, and effectiveness expectations that are a function of the level of assurance, and apply to the methods of execution as well as to the criteria that control progression at milestones, gates, and decision points.

LM-2.3 Identify security improvement opportunities from assessment results.

Elaboration: Security improvement opportunities may be identified in one assurance context but translate to a need for improvement in others. The specific nature of the opportunity may therefore be a function of the level of assurance.

References: ISO/IEC/IEEE 15288, Section 6.2.1.3 b); ISO/IEC 15026.

Related Publications: ISO/IEC 12207, Section 6.2.1.3.2; ISO/IEC 21827.

LM-3 IMPROVE THE SECURITY ASPECTS OF THE PROCESS

LM-3.1 Prioritize and plan for security improvement opportunities.

Elaboration: The prioritization and planning for security improvements may be informed by the level of assurance in addition to the impact of not effecting the improvement relative to other considerations and concerns.

LM-3.2 Implement security improvement opportunities and inform appropriate stakeholders.

Elaboration: Regulatory, acceptance, and other such stakeholders may need to be informed of security-related improvements. This interaction is guided by agreements and any exchange of information is to be in accordance with criteria identified by the *Information Management* process.

References: ISO/IEC/IEEE 15288, Section 6.2.1.3 c); ISO/IEC 15026.

Related Publications: ISO/IEC 12207, Section 6.2.1.3.3; ISO/IEC 21827.

3.2.2 *Infrastructure Management Process*

Purpose

"The purpose of the Infrastructure Management process is to provide the infrastructure and services to projects to support organization and project objectives throughout the life cycle."

ISO/IEC/IEEE 15288-2015. Reprinted with permission from IEEE, Copyright IEEE 2015, All rights reserved.

Systems Security Engineering Purpose

Systems security engineering, as part of the *Infrastructure Management* process, provides the basis to ensure that the infrastructure and services supporting the organizational and project objectives are adequate to address protection needs, considerations, and concerns. The process addresses the security aspects of the facilities, tools, communications, and information technology assets used to support the engineering project.

Systems Security Engineering Outcomes

• The security requirements for the infrastructure are defined.

• The security capabilities and constraints of infrastructure elements are identified and specified.

• Infrastructure elements are developed or acquired to satisfy infrastructure security requirements.

• A secure infrastructure is available.

Systems Security Engineering Activities and Tasks

IF-1   ESTABLISH THE SECURE INFRASTRUCTURE

    IF-1.1   Define the infrastructure security requirements.

    Elaboration: The infrastructure includes facilities, tools, hardware, software, firmware, services, personnel, and standards used to engineer the system-of-interest. The enabling systems of the system-of-interest may be part of the infrastructure and may also be produced by the same infrastructure. Therefore, they are subject to the same level of trustworthiness and risk thresholds as the system-of-interest. Infrastructure protection needs, associated constraints, and assurance and trustworthiness objectives for the infrastructure are defined and driven by the project assets and the associated asset loss consequences in consideration of disruptions, hazards, and threats. The protection needs are transformed into security requirements for the infrastructure and associated security constraints that inform all infrastructure requirements. The technical processes are used to provide a secure infrastructure in accordance with engineering organizational and project strategic plans and policies. In addition, the infrastructure security requirements and security constraints are informed by the protection needs for project data and information to include stakeholder data and information used by the project. The results of the *Information Management* process along with the results of the other technical processes are leveraged by this task.

    IF-1.2   Identify, obtain, and provide the infrastructure resources and services that provide security functions and services that are adequate to securely implement and support projects.

Elaboration: Infrastructure security requirements and associated security constraints are used to identify, obtain, and provide all infrastructure resources. Infrastructure resources may be subject to security constraints although only some infrastructure resources actually provide or support a security function or service.

References: ISO/IEC/IEEE 15288, Section 6.2.2.3 a); ISO/IEC 15026; ISO/IEC 27036.

Related Publications: ISO/IEC 12207, Section 6.2.2.3.1, Section 6.2.2.3.2; ISO/IEC 21827.

IF-2   MAINTAIN THE SECURE INFRASTRUCTURE

IF-2.1   Evaluate the degree to which delivered infrastructure resources satisfy project protection needs.

Elaboration: The method of evaluation and success criteria are identified as part of defining the infrastructure security requirements. Evaluation may be based on methods used for verification and validation, to include methods for delivery, acceptance, assembly, and checkout. The scope of evaluation includes facilities, personnel, procedures, and processes. The *Transition*, *Verification* and *Validation* processes may be used to conduct evaluation of the degree of effectiveness.

IF-2.2   Identify and provide security improvements or changes to the infrastructure resources as the project requirements change.

Elaboration: Infrastructure security functions and services must be properly matched to project needs and expectations to ensure coverage, compatibility, absence of conflict, and effectiveness. Variances in project requirements must be proactively addressed to ensure that the infrastructure is able to securely support specified projects without any gaps in security coverage or effectiveness. Projects subject to laws, regulations, directives, or policies may be delayed by the inability of the infrastructure to mandate security requirements. Any mismatch between project security needs and the security provided by infrastructure resources may result in vulnerability that may not be necessarily known or understood.

References: ISO/IEC/IEEE 15288, Section 6.2.2.3 b); ISO/IEC 15026; ISO/IEC 27036.

Related Publications: ISO/IEC 12207, Section 6.2.2.3.3; ISO/IEC 21827.

3.2.3 *Portfolio Management Process*

Purpose

"The purpose of the Portfolio Management process is to initiate and sustain necessary, sufficient, and suitable projects in order to meet the strategic objectives of the organization."

ISO/IEC/IEEE 15288-2015. Reprinted with permission from IEEE, Copyright IEEE 2015, All rights reserved.

Systems Security Engineering Purpose

Systems security engineering, as part of the *Portfolio Management* process, ensures that security considerations are a factor in the management of the portfolio of organizational projects, and security considerations are used in the assessment of projects to confirm that the projects justify continued investment.

Systems Security Engineering Outcomes

- Business venture opportunities, investments, or necessities are qualified, prioritized, and selected in consideration of security objectives.

- The security objectives of projects are identified.

- Resources and budgets for the security aspects of each project are allocated.

- Project management responsibilities, accountability, and authorities for security are defined.

- Projects meeting the security criteria in agreements and stakeholder security requirements are sustained.

- Projects not meeting the security criteria in agreements or not satisfying stakeholder security requirements are redirected or terminated.

- Projects that are closed satisfy all security criteria in agreements and all stakeholder security requirements.

Systems Security Engineering Activities and Tasks

PM-1   DEFINE AND AUTHORIZE THE SECURITY ASPECTS OF PROJECTS

> **PM-1.1** Identify potential new or modified security capabilities or security aspects of missions or business opportunities.
>
> **Elaboration:** There are two aspects of security that must be considered. First, there is a basic need for across-the-board consideration of security in all project matters. Second, the primary project objective may be to address the need for a new or modified security capability, product, or security service. The *Business or Mission Analysis* and *Stakeholder Needs and Requirements Definition* are leveraged in determining security-oriented needs and opportunities of the portfolio of projects, which are then managed through this process.
>
> **PM-1.2** Prioritize, select, and establish new business opportunities, ventures, or undertakings with consideration for security objectives and concerns.

Elaboration: The *Decision Management* and *System Analysis* processes are used to analyze the security aspects of alternatives and make decisions regarding the prioritization, selection, and establishment of new business opportunities, ventures, or undertakings.

PM-1.3 Define the security aspects of projects, accountabilities, and authorities.

Elaboration: The security aspects are defined as constraints and considerations for all projects to ensure that there is defined accountability and authority to execute projects with security in mind. The security aspects may also include specific security-oriented projects where the project has the objective to deliver a security capability, function, or service. The security aspects also include the constraints expressed in laws, regulations, directives, or organizational policies.

PM-1.4 Identify the security aspects of goals, objectives, and outcomes of each project.

Elaboration: Security aspects include those that define, constrain, or inform goals, objectives, and outcomes of each project. Specific security-driven objectives and constraints include level of assurance and risk thresholds.

PM-1.5 Identify and allocate resources for the achievement of the security aspects of project goals and objectives.

Elaboration: Security aspects will include meeting any proprietary, sensitivity, and privacy criteria associated with the nature of the project and the regulatory aspects of the environment in which it operates.

PM-1.6 Identify the security aspects of any multi-project interfaces and dependencies to be managed or supported by each project.

Elaboration: Projects tend to operate as a system and there are security needs and considerations associated with inter-project behavior, interfaces, interactions, and outcomes. Shared resources in the form of enabling systems, data and information, and services facilitate effective and efficient inter-project execution. The security aspects are identified to help ensure that effective security functions, methods, and mechanisms are put in place to securely achieve multi-project interaction.

PM-1.7 Specify the security aspects of project reporting requirements and review milestones that govern the execution of each project.

Elaboration: The security aspects of reporting requirements apply throughout the execution of the project. The *Project Planning* and *Life Cycle Model Management* processes are used to determine the security aspects relative to project execution. The security aspects of reporting requirements may be specified by laws, regulations, directives, or organizational policies.

PM-1.8 Authorize each project to commence execution with consideration of the security aspects of project plans.

Elaboration: Execution of project plans should be dependent on a determination that security considerations have been adequately addressed and properly captured by the security aspects in project plans.

References: ISO/IEC/IEEE 15288, Section 6.2.3.3 a); ISO/IEC 15026.

Related Publications: ISO/IEC 12207, Section 6.2.3.3.1; ISO/IEC 21827.

PM-2   EVALUATE THE SECURITY ASPECTS OF THE PORTFOLIO OF PROJECTS

PM-2.1 Evaluate the security aspects of projects to confirm ongoing viability.

Elaboration: Confirming the ongoing viability of a project from a security perspective includes determining that the project is making substantiated and measurable progress toward achieving established security goals and objectives; the project is complying with security directives; the project is being conducted with adherence to the security aspects of life cycle policies, processes, and procedures, and to explicit security policies, processes, and procedures; and that the needs for security functions and services provided by the project remain viable, practical, and provide an acceptable investment benefit.

PM-2.2 Continue or redirect projects that are satisfactorily progressing or can be expected to progress satisfactorily by appropriate redirection in consideration of project security aspects.

Elaboration: The action taken to continue executing a project with no changes or to take action to redirect a project should be dependent on a determination that security objectives and goals remain viable and are being achieved or may be achieved through appropriate redirection.

References: ISO/IEC/IEEE 15288, Section 6.2.3.3 b).

Related Publications: ISO/IEC 12207, Section 6.2.3.3.2; ISO/IEC 21827.

PM-3 TERMINATE PROJECTS

PM-3.1 Cancel or suspend projects whose security-driven disadvantages or security-driven risks to the organization outweigh the benefits of continued investments.

Elaboration: The *Decision Management* process, informed by the *System Analysis* and *Risk Management* processes, determines whether projects are to be cancelled or suspended due to security concerns.

PM-3.2 After completion of agreements for products or services, act to close the projects in accordance with established security criteria, constraints, and considerations.

Elaboration: The security criteria, constraints, and considerations are captured in agreements, organizational policies and procedures, and relevant laws, regulations, directives, or policies.

References: ISO/IEC/IEEE 15288, Section 6.2.3.3 c).

Related Publications: ISO/IEC 12207, Section 6.2.3.3.3; ISO/IEC 21827.

3.2.4 Human Resource Management Process

Purpose

"The purpose of the Human Resource Management process is to provide the organization with necessary human resources and to maintain their competencies, consistent with business needs."

ISO/IEC/IEEE 15288-2015. Reprinted with permission from IEEE, Copyright IEEE 2015, All rights reserved.

Systems Security Engineering Purpose

Systems security engineering, as part of the _Human Resource Management_ process, defines the security criteria for the qualification, assessment, selection, and ongoing training of skilled and experienced personnel qualified to perform the security aspects of life cycle processes to achieve organization, project, and stakeholder security objectives.

Systems Security Engineering Outcomes

- Systems security engineering skills required by projects are identified.

- Individuals with systems security engineering skills are provided to projects.

- Systems security engineering skills of personnel are developed, maintained, or enhanced.

Systems Security Engineering Activities and Tasks

HR-1   IDENTIFY SYSTEMS SECURITY ENGINEERING SKILLS

   HR-1.1 Identify systems security engineering skills needed based on current and expected projects.

   Elaboration: Systems security engineering skills include foundational skills that span systems engineering, security specialties, security technologies, and other contributing specialties. These skills address qualifications for the development of trustworthy secure systems as well as the secure operation, sustainment, and support of those systems.

   HR-1.2 Identify existing systems security engineering skills of personnel.

   Elaboration: Skills identified include all relevant systems engineering and specialty security engineering, technology, and related skills.

   References: ISO/IEC/IEEE 15288, Section 6.2.4.3 a).

   Related Publications: ISO/IEC 12207, Section 6.2.4.3.1; National Cybersecurity Workforce Framework; DoD Directive 8140.01; ISO/IEC 27034-1, (SDL) Section A.9.1.

HR-2   DEVELOP SYSTEMS SECURITY ENGINEERING SKILLS

   HR-2.1 Establish a plan for systems security engineering skills development.

   Elaboration: The plan addresses foundational systems security engineering skills development to build core and specialty competencies, and to grow competencies in core and specialty areas identified by gap analyses between the existing personnel skills and identified needs. The plan includes, for example, the types and levels of training; training sequences; learning paths and flows; training categories of personnel; and prerequisites for training.

HR-2.2 Obtain systems security engineering training, education, or mentoring resources.

Elaboration: Systems security engineering training, education, and mentoring resources include, for example, degree programs; continuing education and training programs; and professional certifications. Resources may be developed or provided by the organization or through external parties.

HR-2.3 Provide and document records of systems security engineering skills development.

Elaboration: None.

References: ISO/IEC/IEEE 15288, Section 6.2.4.3 b).

Related Publications: ISO/IEC 12207, Section 6.2.4.3.2; ISO/IEC 27034-1, (SDL) Section A.9.1.

HR-3 ACQUIRE AND PROVIDE SYSTEMS SECURITY ENGINEERING SKILLS TO PROJECTS

HR-3.1 Obtain qualified systems security engineering personnel to meet project needs.

Elaboration: Criteria for recruitment is determined by project-identified needs for skills that span the technical and nontechnical processes of systems engineering, with depth in security and related specialties. The criterion balance between systems engineering breadth and security specialty depth is determined by the roles and responsibilities associated with the project need. Another criterion is the level of assurance at which the systems security engineering is to be conducted.

HR-3.2 Maintain and manage the pool of skilled systems security engineering personnel to staff ongoing projects.

Elaboration: This includes ensuring that skills are managed and maintained to match assurance levels and other expectations that differentiate how staff go about performing their duties on a project. Maintaining skills with these security considerations allows better resource utilization across a variety of projects and within the changing needs in the execution of a single project.

HR-3.3 Make personnel assignments based on the specific systems security engineering needs of the project and staff development needs.

Elaboration: Matching an individual to a project is based on a combination of project need and the need for staff development, exposure, and growth. Effective performance in a systems security engineering capacity is achieved through a balance of systems engineering breadth and security specialty depth, with additional consideration for the level of assurance needed. Personnel require exposure and time to acquire experience and to grow into the role of working effectively across multiple security and non-security specialties on an engineering team.

References: ISO/IEC/IEEE 15288, Section 6.2.4.3 c).

Related Publications: ISO/IEC 12207, Section 6.2.4.3.3; National Cybersecurity Workforce Framework.

3.2.5 *Quality Management Process*

Purpose

"The purpose of the Quality Management process is to assure that products, services, and implementations of the quality management process meet organizational and project quality objectives and achieve customer satisfaction."

ISO/IEC/IEEE 15288-2015. Reprinted with permission from IEEE, Copyright IEEE 2015, All rights reserved.

Systems Security Engineering Purpose

Systems security engineering, as part of the *Quality Management* process, defines security quality objectives and the criteria used to determine that those objectives are met by products, services, and implementations of the quality management process.

Systems Security Engineering Outcomes

- Organizational security quality objectives are defined and implemented.

- Organizational security quality management policies, standards, and procedures are defined and implemented.

- Security quality evaluation criteria and methods are established.

- Resources, data, and information are provided to projects to support the operation and monitoring of project security quality assurance activities.

- Accountability and authority for security quality management are defined.

- Appropriate action is taken when security quality objectives are not achieved.

- Security quality management policies and procedures are improved based upon project and organization results.

Systems Security Engineering Activities and Tasks

QM-1   PLAN SECURITY QUALITY MANAGEMENT

> **QM-1.1** Establish security quality management objectives.
>
> **Elaboration:** Security quality management objectives are informed by the strategy for *customer* satisfaction and the types of products, services, and technologies provided and utilized. These objectives are calibrated as a function of the assurance and trustworthiness objectives targeted for the delivered products and services.
>
> **QM-1.2** Establish security quality management policies, standards, and procedures.
>
> **Elaboration:** Security quality management policies, standards, and procedures include security considerations across all security-based and security-informed technical and nontechnical engineering activities and the products and services realized by those engineering activities. The security considerations are oriented toward achievement of security quality objectives.
>
> **QM-1.3** Define responsibilities and authority for the implementation of security quality management.

Elaboration: Explicit responsibility and authority for security quality management is necessary to effectively integrate security considerations into all aspects of the quality management program. These include responsibility and authority for required interaction with regulatory and approval stakeholders. The authority for security quality management is often assigned to organizations with independence from project management.

QM-1.4 Define security quality evaluation criteria and methods.

Elaboration: Security quality evaluation criteria and methods transform the overarching security quality objectives into criteria and methods that are applied comprehensively across all aspects of quality management. In some cases, quality management is oriented to specific security products and services. In other cases, it is oriented to security considerations for all products and services.

QM-1.5 Provide resources, data, and information for security quality management.

Elaboration: Resources, data, and information to support security quality management are informed by the security quality management objectives; the assurance and trustworthiness objectives targeted for delivered products and services; and the technologies included in those products and services. The resources for security quality management are often assigned to organizations with a level of independence from project management.

References: ISO/IEC/IEEE 15288, Section 6.2.5.3 a); ISO/IEC 15026; ISO 9001.

Related Publications: ISO/IEC 12207, Section 6.2.5.3.1.

QM-2 ASSESS SECURITY QUALITY MANAGEMENT

  QM-2.1 Obtain and analyze quality assurance evaluation results in accordance with the defined security quality evaluation criteria.

  Elaboration: The *Quality Assurance* process is used to obtain data and information for the conduct the security quality assurance evaluation.

  QM-2.2 Assess customer security quality satisfaction.

  Elaboration: Customer security quality satisfaction is assessed across all stakeholders to include regulatory, authorization, and approval stakeholders.

  QM-2.3 Conduct periodic reviews of project quality assurance activities for compliance with the security quality management policies, standards, and procedures.

  Elaboration: Project quality assurance reviews are performed in accordance with project plans, agreements, and periodic reviews within the engineering organization. The reviews target the specific contexts and objectives of security quality.

  QM-2.4 Monitor the status of security quality improvements on processes, products, and services.

  Elaboration: Monitoring includes determining the effectiveness, constraints, and impacts of the security improvements on other aspects of quality management.

  References: ISO/IEC/IEEE 15288, Section 6.2.5.3 b); ISO/IEC 15026; ISO 9001.

  Related Publications: ISO/IEC 12207, Section 6.2.5.3.1.

QM-3 PERFORM SECURITY QUALITY MANAGEMENT CORRECTIVE AND PREVENTIVE ACTIONS

  QM-3.1 Plan corrective actions when security quality management objectives are not achieved.

Elaboration: The need for corrective action is addressed by the *Project Planning* and *Project Assessment and Control* processes, which in turn may require corrective or improvement action by technical and other nontechnical processes.

QM-3.2 Plan preventive actions when there is a sufficient risk that security quality management objectives will not be achieved.

Elaboration: The need for preventive action is addressed by the *Project Planning* and *Project Assessment and Control* processes, which in turn may require proactive corrective or improvement action by technical and other nontechnical processes.

QM-3.3 Monitor security quality management corrective and preventive actions to completion and inform relevant stakeholders.

Elaboration: Security quality improvement results are communicated to relevant customer, regulatory, and approval stakeholders. The results are also communicated within the engineering organization to ensure consistency and repeatability across projects.

References: ISO/IEC/IEEE 15288, Section 6.2.5.3 c); ISO/IEC 15026; ISO 9001.

Related Publications: ISO/IEC 12207, Section 6.2.5.3.2.

3.2.6 Knowledge Management Process

Purpose

"The purpose of the Knowledge Management process is to create the capability and assets that enable the organization to exploit opportunities to reapply existing knowledge."

ISO/IEC/IEEE 15288-2015. Reprinted with permission from IEEE, Copyright IEEE 2015, All rights reserved.

Systems Security Engineering Purpose

Systems security engineering, as part of the *Knowledge Management* process, identifies, obtains, maintains, and manages the security knowledge and skills needed to enable the organization to exploit opportunities and to reapply existing security knowledge.

Systems Security Engineering Outcomes

- A taxonomy for the application of security knowledge assets is identified.

- Organizational security knowledge, skills, and knowledge assets are developed or acquired.

- Organizational security knowledge, skills, and knowledge assets are available.

- Security knowledge management usage data is gathered and analyzed.

Systems Security Engineering Activities and Tasks

KM-1   PLAN SECURITY KNOWLEDGE MANAGEMENT

KM-1.1 Define the security aspects of the knowledge management strategy.

Elaboration: The security aspects of the strategy include those that address security content deemed appropriate for knowledge management and those that address the concerns to securely utilize all knowledge and knowledge management resources. Security content includes, for example: the identification of security knowledge domains and associated types of technologies, specialties, methods, patterns, architectures, techniques, tools, and their potential for the reapplication of knowledge; plans for obtaining and maintaining security knowledge, skills, and knowledge assets for their useful life; and the criteria for accepting, qualifying, and retiring security knowledge, skills, and security knowledge assets. The security aspects in the secure utilization of knowledge and knowledge management resources include collection, storage, retrieval, dissemination, access, use, and disposal of knowledge assets. Security aspects also address security concerns for internal and external sharing of organizational, stakeholder, acquirer, and business partner knowledge assets. This includes sensitive, privacy, and classified information and information knowledge assets. Information sharing is subject to intellectual property and non-disclosure agreements, and any classified, sensitive, privacy, and other governing laws, regulations, policies, and directives.

KM-1.2 Identify the security knowledge, skills, and knowledge assets to be managed.

Elaboration: Security knowledge, skills, and knowledge assets are those external to the organization that inform effective execution of the technical and nontechnical processes and those produced by the execution of technical and nontechnical activities and tasks and that reflect lessons learned.

KM-1.3 Identify projects that can benefit from the application of the security knowledge, skills, and knowledge assets.

Elaboration: None.

References: ISO/IEC/IEEE 15288, Section 6.2.6.3 a).

Related Publications: ISO/IEC 12207, Section 6.2.4.3.4; ISO/IEC 21827; National Cybersecurity Workforce Framework; DoD Directive 8140.01.

KM-2   SHARE SECURITY KNOWLEDGE AND SKILLS THROUGHOUT THE ORGANIZATION

KM-2.1 Establish and maintain a classification for capturing and sharing security knowledge and skills.

Elaboration: Classification of knowledge differentiates among the levels of requisite knowledge, skill, and ability expectations to comprehend and apply knowledge; to communicate knowledge; and to use knowledge in directing the activities of others. Considerations include, for example, the breadth, depth, relevance, and level of knowledge.

KM-2.2 Capture or acquire security knowledge and skills.

Elaboration: None.

KM-2.3 Share security knowledge and skills across the organization.

Elaboration: Body of knowledge repositories, education, training, and collaboration methods facilitate effective and efficient knowledge sharing. The *Human Resource Management* process is used to establish needs and to institute methods for sharing knowledge and skills.

References: ISO/IEC/IEEE 15288, Section 6.2.6.3 b).

Related Publications: ISO/IEC 12207, Section 6.2.4.3.4; ISO/IEC 21827.

KM-3   SHARE SECURITY KNOWLEDGE ASSETS THROUGHOUT THE ORGANIZATION

KM-3.1 Establish a taxonomy to organize security knowledge assets.

Elaboration: The taxonomy includes, for example: security knowledge domains, boundaries, and relationships; security domain models of common and different features, capabilities, architecture, patterns, concepts, functions, or security strength of mechanism; security assurance and trust; and the limitations and constraints that govern use of knowledge assets. The taxonomy helps to enable identifying the needed knowledge assets, determining the relationships with other knowledge assets, and determining the proper application of the knowledge asset within its constraints and limitations.

KM-3.2 Develop or acquire security knowledge assets.

Elaboration: Security knowledge assets include, for example, security reference architectures, security viewpoints, and security views; security evaluation criteria; trusted code libraries; security design characteristics; security architecture and design patterns; security design documentation; security training and awareness materials, and security lessons learned.

KM-3.3 Securely share knowledge assets across the organization.

Elaboration: All knowledge, skills, and knowledge assets are accessed, utilized, and shared in accordance with established agreements and governing laws, regulations, policies, and directives. Sharing may occur across the organization and external to the organization with stakeholders, acquirers, contractors, and business or mission partners.

References: ISO/IEC/IEEE 15288, Section 6.2.6.3 c); ISO/IEC/IEEE 42010.

Related Publications: ISO/IEC 12207, Section 6.2.4.3.4; ISO/IEC 21827.

KM-4 MANAGE SECURITY KNOWLEDGE, SKILLS, AND KNOWLEDGE ASSETS

KM-4.1 Maintain security knowledge, skills, and knowledge assets.

Elaboration: Security knowledge, skills, and knowledge assets are maintained in body of knowledge repositories and collaboration resources.

KM-4.2 Monitor and record the use of security knowledge, skills, and knowledge assets.

Elaboration: Monitoring and recording the use of security-relevant knowledge, skills, and knowledge assets support and inform assessments to ascertain the value and investment return on maintaining security knowledge, skills, and knowledge asset items.

KM-4.3 Periodically reassess the currency of the security aspects of technology and market needs of the security knowledge assets.

Elaboration: Periodic assessment results support action to ensure consistency between the demand for security methods, processes, tools, and technologies and the knowledge required to properly utilize and employ them. Outdated and otherwise unneeded security knowledge, skills, and knowledge assets are removed from knowledge repositories and collaboration resources and securely retained for historical reference or securely disposed of or destroyed.

References: ISO/IEC/IEEE 15288, Section 6.2.6.3 d).

Related Publications: ISO/IEC 12207, Section 6.2.4.3.4; ISO/IEC 21827.

3.3 TECHNICAL MANAGEMENT PROCESSES

This section contains the eight ISO/IEC/IEEE 15288 *technical management* processes with extensions for systems security engineering. The processes are:

- Project Planning (PL);

- Project Assessment and Control (PA);

- Decision Management (DM);

- Risk Management (RM);

- Configuration Management (CM);

- Information Management (IM);

- Measurement (MS); and

- Quality Assurance (QA).

3.3.1 *Project Planning Process*

Purpose

"The purpose of the Project Planning process is to produce and coordinate effective and workable plans."

ISO/IEC/IEEE 15288-2015. Reprinted with permission from IEEE, Copyright IEEE 2015, All rights reserved.

Systems Security Engineering Purpose

Systems security engineering, as part of the *Project Planning* process, produces and coordinates the security aspects of project plans; develops the security scope of the technical and management activities; and identifies security planning outputs, tasks, deliverables, achievement criteria, and the resources needed to accomplish security tasks.

Systems Security Engineering Outcomes

- Security objectives and the security aspects of project plans are defined.

- Systems security engineering roles, responsibilities, accountabilities, and authorities are defined.

- Resources and services necessary to achieve the security objectives of the project are formally requested and committed.

- Plans for the execution of the security aspects of the project are activated.

Systems Security Engineering Activities and Tasks

PL-1   DEFINE THE SECURITY ASPECTS OF THE PROJECT

    PL-1.1   Identify the security objectives and security constraints for the project.

    Elaboration: Security objectives and constraints encompass quality, cost, time, risk and loss thresholds and tolerances, assurance, trustworthiness, and regulatory and customer stakeholder satisfaction. The objectives and constraints are captured at a level of detail that permits selection, tailoring, and implementation of the appropriate processes, activities, and tasks.

    PL-1.2   Define the security aspects of the project scope as established in agreements.

    Elaboration: The security aspects of the project scope include meeting the security expectations of stakeholders and the secure execution of all project plans. The security aspects also include the stages of the system life cycle within which the project is conducted and all relevant activities and tasks are to be performed, to include the planning, assessment, and control aspects of meeting the project objectives.

    PL-1.3   Define and maintain a security view of the life cycle model and its constituent stages.

    Elaboration: The selected life cycle model for the project produces security-relevant and security-driven outcomes and artifacts. Some of these outcomes and artifacts build upon each other with results that accrue over time and others are associated with specific *life cycle stages*. The security view includes security-oriented milestone/gate entry, exit, and review criteria.

PL-1.4   Identify the security activities and tasks of the work breakdown structure.

Elaboration: The work breakdown structure includes security activities and tasks to ensure that security considerations, concerns, and risks are seamlessly addressed by the project. Some aspects of security require explicit security-oriented activities and tasks that produce security outcomes, while others are security-informing in the achievement of other project outcomes.

PL-1.5   Define and maintain the security aspects of processes that will be applied on the project.

Elaboration: The conduct of the project is tailored to achieve the stated project objectives through execution of processes associated with the chosen life cycle model. Tailoring guidance is provided in ISO/IEC/IEEE 15288, Annex A. Tailoring includes defining the entry criteria; inputs; process activity and task sequencing constraints; process concurrency; measures of effectiveness and performance attributes; and scope and cost parameters. Security considerations inform all of the above.

References: ISO/IEC/IEEE 15288, Section 6.3.1.3 a), Annex A; ISO/IEC 15026; ISO/IEC 27036; ISO/IEC TR 24748-1.

Related Publications: ISO/IEC 12207, Section 6.3.1.3.1; ISO/IEC 21827.

PL-2   PLAN THE SECURITY ASPECTS OF THE PROJECT AND TECHNICAL MANAGEMENT

PL-2.1   Define and maintain the security aspects of a project schedule based on management and technical objectives and work estimates.

Elaboration: The security aspects of a project include the security needs and constraints that affect the duration, relationship, dependencies, and sequence of activities. The security aspects also include security subject-matter resources employed in reviews and security risk considerations that impact timely completion of the project.

PL-2.2   Define the security achievement criteria and major dependencies on external inputs and outputs for life cycle stage decision gates.

Elaboration: Explicit definition of security achievement criteria and dependences for each life cycle stage ensures that security considerations are fully captured in decisions regarding progress of the project. The security achievement criteria include the criteria that are defined by regulatory, certification, evaluation, and other approval authorities.

PL-2.3   Define the security-related costs for the project and plan the budget informed by those projected costs.

Elaboration: Security-related costs are a function of the materials, enabling systems, services, infrastructures, and human resources required to conduct systems security engineering activities and tasks throughout the system life cycle.

PL-2.4   Define the systems security engineering roles, responsibilities, accountabilities, and authorities.

Elaboration: Defining systems security engineering roles, responsibilities, accountabilities, and authorities serves to ensure that the definition of project organization and structure accounts for the security needs and resources to accomplish project objectives. Security-relevant decision making and approval authorities are also defined for the project based on governing laws, regulations, or policies. These security-relevant authorities include, for example, security design authorizations or approvals; authorizations to test the system security; and authorizations to operate the system and to accept the identified residual risks. Appendix E provides additional information on systems security engineering roles and responsibilities. The *Human Resource*

Management process is used to define the knowledge, skills, and abilities required to support the engineering effort.

PL-2.5   Define the security aspects of infrastructure and services required.

Elaboration: Infrastructure and services support and enable achievement of project objectives. The security aspects of infrastructure and services include the specific protection capabilities, capacities, facilities, tools, communications, information technology, and related assets. The *Infrastructure Management* and *Information Management* processes are used to support all infrastructure and associated information protection needs and capabilities.

PL-2.6   Plan the security aspects of acquisition of materials and enabling systems and services supplied from outside the project.

Elaboration: Security-enabling systems and services to be acquired externally are identified and addressed in acquisition plans. The acquisition of any enabling systems or services from external sources is planned to ensure that security considerations and security concerns are addressed.

PL-2.7   Generate and communicate a plan for the project and technical management and execution, including reviews that address all security considerations.

Elaboration: The security considerations and the planning to address those considerations are captured as part of the Systems Engineering Management Plan. Related plans include software development, hardware development, or other engineering plans. Each related plan includes the appropriate security-relevant activities and tasks.

References: ISO/IEC/IEEE 15288, Section 6.3.1.3 b); ISO/IEC 27036; ISO/IEC/IEEE 16326.

Related Publications: ISO/IEC 12207, Section 6.3.1.3.2; ISO/IEC 21827.

PL-3   ACTIVATE THE SECURITY ASPECTS OF THE PROJECT

PL-3.1   Obtain authorization for the security aspects of the project.

Elaboration: There may be specialized security authorizations associated with the project that must be obtained prior to activating the project. These authorizations may be based on or derived from laws, regulations, directives, policies, or agreements.

PL-3.2   Submit requests and obtain commitments for the resources required to perform the security aspects of the project.

Elaboration: Obtaining commitments for specialized security services provided by human and material resources may require formal submission requests. Such requests need to be submitted with sufficient lead time that it will not impact the timely activation of the project.

PL-3.3   Implement the security aspects of the project plan.

Elaboration: The implementation of the security aspects of the project plan occurs through the execution of the processes, activities, and tasks in the project plan. The *Project Assessment and Control* process has the responsibility to direct and manage the implementation of project plans.

References: ISO/IEC/IEEE 15288, Section 6.3.1.3 c).

Related Publications: ISO/IEC 12207, Section 6.3.1.3.3; ISO/IEC 21827.

3.3.2 Project Assessment and Control Process

Purpose

"The purpose of the Project Assessment and Control process is to assess if the plans are aligned and feasible; determine the status of the project, technical and process performance; and direct execution to help ensure that the performance is according to plans and schedules, within projected budgets, to satisfy technical objectives."

ISO/IEC/IEEE 15288-2015. Reprinted with permission from IEEE, Copyright IEEE 2015, All rights reserved.

Systems Security Engineering Purpose

Systems security engineering, as part of the *Project Assessment and Control* process, evaluates the progress and achievements of the security aspects of project plans, and communicates the need for specific management action to resolve any identified variances that could affect the overall ability of the project to satisfy security technical objectives. Systems security engineering redirects the activities of security-focused resources as needed, in order to correct the identified security deviations and variations in support of other technical management processes and/or technical processes.

Systems Security Engineering Outcomes

- The security aspects of performance measures or assessment results are available.
- The adequacy of security-relevant roles, responsibilities, accountabilities, and authorities is assessed.
- The adequacy of resources allocated to the security aspects of the project is assessed.
- The security aspects of technical progress reviews are performed.
- Deviations in the security aspects of project performance from plans are investigated and analyzed.
- Lessons learned are recorded to help inform and guide future projects and activities within projects.
- Affected stakeholders are informed of the security aspects of project status.
- Corrective action is defined and directed, when the security aspects of project achievement are not meeting targets.
- The security aspects of project replanning are initiated, as necessary.
- The security aspects of project action to progress (or not) from one scheduled milestone or event to the next is authorized.
- Project security objectives are achieved.

Systems Security Engineering Activities and Tasks

PA-1   PLAN FOR THE SECURITY ASPECTS OF PROJECT ASSESSMENT AND CONTROL

   PA-1.1   Define the security aspects of the project assessment strategy.

Elaboration: The security aspects of the project assessment strategy include, for example, security assessment methods and activities; security assessment performance criteria; security assessment time frames and sequencing; project technical and management reviews; and any technical reviews required by regulatory, certification, and related authorization entities. The security aspects also include conducting project assessment strategy activities securely with respect to protection of project and stakeholder data and information and the interactions of participants involved in the reviews. The scope of the strategy includes enabling systems and the security concerns associated with protecting data, information, technology, intellectual property, and capabilities associated with the project.

PA-1.2 Define the security aspects of the project control strategy.

Elaboration: The security aspects of the project control strategy include actions taken to address situations when project or technical achievement is not meeting planned security targets. Security-oriented actions can include replanning, reallocation of personnel, enabling systems and services, infrastructures, or tools. The security aspects also include conducting project control strategy activities securely with respect to protection of project and stakeholder data and information and the interactions of participants involved in the reviews. The scope of the strategy includes enabling systems and the security concerns associated with protecting data, information, technology, intellectual property, and capabilities associated with the project.

References: ISO/IEC/IEEE 15288, Section 6.3.2.3 a); ISO/IEC 15026.

Related Publications: ISO/IEC 21827.

PA-2   ASSESS THE SECURITY ASPECTS OF THE PROJECT

PA-2.1 Assess the alignment of the security aspects of project objectives and plans with the project context.

Elaboration: The project context may be determined by life cycle stage or activity within a stage, as defined by the life cycle model used by the project. The assessment is based on project context, and the assessment results provide a basis to determine what action, if any, is required to achieve the security aspects associated with that project context.

PA-2.2 Assess the security aspects of the management and technical plans against objectives to determine adequacy and feasibility.

Elaboration: Consideration is given to the adequacy and feasibility of the security constraints to which all management and technical plans must adhere. In addition, consideration is also given to the adequacy and sufficiency of the management and technical plans oriented to a specific system security capability.

PA-2.3 Assess the security aspects of the project and its technical status against appropriate plans to determine actual and projected cost, schedule, and performance variances.

Elaboration: The security aspects of management and technical plans will impact the cost and schedule, and are to be considered in the assessment of security performance variances and the security impact on system performance and those variances.

PA-2.4 Assess the adequacy of the security roles, responsibilities, accountabilities, and authorities associated with the project.

Elaboration: None.

PA-2.5 Assess the adequacy and availability of resources allocated to the security aspects of the project.

Elaboration: Resources allocated to the security aspects of the project are composed of various security specialties and other contributing specialties. The assessment determines the adequacy and availability of qualified individuals.

PA-2.6 Assess progress using measured security achievement and milestone completion.

Elaboration: Security achievement criteria are defined by the assessment and control strategy. All assessments of achievement-based progress and milestone completion are to include the relevant security achievement and milestone completion criteria.

PA-2.7 Conduct required management and technical reviews, audits, and inspections with full consideration for the security aspects of the project.

Elaboration: The reviews, audits, and inspections are security-focused or security-informed. Reviews, audits, and inspections may involve stakeholders representing regulatory, certification, authorization, or equivalent organizations. The reviews are formal or informal, and serve to determine readiness to proceed to the next milestone of the project or stage of the life cycle.

PA-2.8 Monitor the security aspects of critical processes and new technologies.

Elaboration: The security aspects of critical processes are not limited to security-focused processes and the security aspects of new technologies are not limited to security technologies. Monitoring attention is given to security maturity and insertion of technology, and particularly for NDI system elements selected for insertion. The *Design Definition* process is leveraged to identify NDI items and other identified technology solutions. The *System Analysis* process is used to provide data for monitoring of the security aspects of NDI.

PA-2.9 Analyze security measurement results and make recommendations.

Elaboration: The *System Analysis* and *Measurement* processes are used to define and analyze the measurement results.

PA-2.10 Record and provide security status and security findings from the assessment tasks.

Elaboration: The results from all of the security assessment tasks are compared against project strategy, plans, goals, and objectives. Security status and findings are determined, recorded, and reported as designated in agreements, regulations, policies, and procedures.

PA-2.11 Monitor the security aspects of process execution within the project.

Elaboration: The security aspects of process execution include all life cycle processes that are used by the engineering effort. Monitoring includes the analysis of process security measures and the review of security-relevant trends with respect to project objectives. Improvement actions identified are handled by the *Quality Assurance* and *Life Cycle Model Management* processes.

References: ISO/IEC/IEEE 15288, Section 6.3.2.3 b); ISO/IEC 15026.

Related Publications: ISO/IEC 12207, Section 6.3.2.3.1, Section 6.3.2.3.3; ISO/IEC 21827.

PA-3   CONTROL THE SECURITY ASPECTS OF THE PROJECT

PA-3.1 Initiate the actions needed to address identified security issues.

Elaboration: Security-oriented actions are taken to address situations when project or technical achievement is not meeting planned security targets. These actions include corrective, preventive, and problem resolution actions. The security-oriented actions may require replanning, reallocation of personnel, enabling systems and services, infrastructures, or tools. Actions taken may also impact the cost, schedule or technical scope or definition of the project, or may require change to the execution of the life cycle processes.

PA-3.2 Initiate the security aspects of necessary project replanning.

Elaboration: Security-oriented project replanning is necessary when the action required to address identified security issues cannot be accomplished within the project context, scope, definition, and breakdown of roles, responsibilities, and authorities as they are defined and assigned. Additional considerations for project replanning include the need for different or additional human, material, and enabling system resources, services, and capabilities that are beyond what has been defined by the project plan and strategy.

PA-3.3 Initiate change actions when there is a contractual change to cost, time, or quality due to the security impact of an acquirer or supplier request.

Elaboration: The security impact of a requested contractual change is not necessarily obvious for the case where the request is not security-driven or security-oriented. The *System Analysis*, *Risk Management*, and *Decision Management* processes are used to analyze change requests and decide on the appropriate change actions to address an identified security impact. The determination and handling of contractual changes is accomplished by the *Acquisition* and *Supply* processes.

PA-3.4 Recommend the project to proceed toward the next milestone or event, if justified, based on the achievement of security objectives and performance measures.

Elaboration: The recommendation to proceed is based on adequate satisfaction of the security objectives, and the achievement and performance criteria defined by the assessment and control strategy. The recommendation may be dependent on concurrence or the recommendations provided by regulatory, certification, authorization, or equivalent organizations.

References: ISO/IEC/IEEE 15288, Section 6.3.2.3 c); ISO/IEC 27036.

Related Publications: ISO/IEC 12207, Section 6.3.2.3.2, Section 6.3.2.3.4; ISO/IEC 21827.

3.3.3 Decision Management Process

Purpose

"The purpose of the Decision Management process is to provide a structured, analytical framework for objectively identifying, characterizing and evaluating a set of alternatives for a decision at any point in the life cycle and select the most beneficial course of action."

ISO/IEC/IEEE 15288-2015. Reprinted with permission from IEEE, Copyright IEEE 2015, All rights reserved.

Systems Security Engineering Purpose

Systems security engineering, as part of the *Decision Management* process, identifies, analyzes, characterizes, and evaluates a set of security-based and security-informed alternatives for a decision, and recommends the most beneficial course of security-based or security-informed action. Systems security engineering leverages a variety of disciplines and associated bodies of knowledge to identify the alternatives that provide the preferred outcomes for decision situations. Each alternative is assessed against decision criteria that includes security-focused criteria such as vulnerability; susceptibility to disruptions, hazards, or threats; assurance; strength of function or mechanism; security regulatory criteria; thresholds for loss and risk; and the general criteria that includes cost and schedule impact, programmatic constraints, regulatory implications, technical performance characteristics, critical quality characteristics, and risk.

Systems Security Engineering Outcomes

- The security aspects of the decision management strategy are established.

- The security aspects of decisions requiring alternative analysis are identified.

- Security-based decisions requiring alternative analysis are identified.

- The security aspects of alternative courses of action are identified and evaluated.

- A preferred course of action informed by or driven by security considerations is selected.

- The security aspects of a resolution, of the decision rationale, and of the assumptions are identified.

Systems Security Engineering Activities and Tasks

DM-1 PREPARE FOR DECISIONS WITH SECURITY IMPLICATIONS

> **DM-1.1** Define the security aspects of the decision management strategy.
>
> **Elaboration:** The security aspects of the decision management strategy include: the security-related roles, responsibilities, accountabilities, and authorities; security decision categories and an associated prioritization scheme to support the decision based on results of assessments, technical trade-offs, a problem to be solved, an action needed in response to risk exceeding the acceptable threshold, entry/exit gate progression, or in response to a new opportunity; security-specific criteria driven by technology and security performance and effectiveness such as strength of function/mechanism; degree of rigor and formality to achieve assurance and trustworthiness objectives; and regulatory stakeholders that are impacted by decisions.

DM-1.2 Identify the security aspects of the circumstances and need for a decision.

Elaboration: The security aspects of the circumstances and need for a decision provide a security interpretation of the problem or opportunity and the proposed alternative courses of action. The security aspects include the prioritization between security aspects and other critical quality aspects of the decision. Security aspects are recorded, categorized, traced to other aspects, and reported.

DM-1.3 Involve stakeholders with relevant security expertise in the decision making in order to draw on their experience and knowledge.

Elaboration: Subject-matter experts include security and other specialty knowledge, skills, experience, and expertise. The specific skills are determined by the security-informing or security-focused aspects of the decision, as the need and circumstances of the decision may not be security-based. Subject-matter experts may be delegates representing stakeholder interests.

References: ISO/IEC/IEEE 15288, Section 6.3.3.3 a).

Related Publications: ISO/IEC 12207, Section 6.3.3.3.1; ISO/IEC 21827.

DM-2   ANALYZE THE SECURITY ASPECTS OF DECISION INFORMATION

DM-2.1 Select and declare the security aspects of the decision management strategy for each decision.

Elaboration: The decision management strategy for a decision includes the security-defined rigor, formality, and the analysis methods, processes, and tools required to evaluate the alternatives. The data to inform the analysis and the data to be produced by the analysis are also identified. These aspects of the strategy may be determined or constrained by decision security objectives such as strength of function/mechanism, assurance, and trustworthiness.

DM-2.2 Determine the desired security outcomes and measurable security selection criteria.

Elaboration: This includes desired values for quantifiable security criteria and threshold values that determine acceptability for results. This also includes determination of qualitative security criteria and threshold boundaries to enable reasoning about analysis results and to determine acceptability for results. The *System Analysis* process is used to determine security outcomes and security selection criteria. The *Risk Management* process is used to establish risk thresholds.

DM-2.3 Identify the security aspects of the trade space and alternatives.

Elaboration: The security aspects of the trade space include those aspects that drive the decisions, those aspects that inform the decisions, and those aspects that are impacted by the decisions. In addition, the security aspects are assessed to reduce the size of the trade space to a manageable number for the cases where numerous alternatives exist. This reduction may be necessitated by cost, schedule, or resource constraints associated with the decision.

DM-2.4 Evaluate each alternative against the security evaluation criteria.

Elaboration: The *System Analysis* process is used to produce data to evaluate each alternative. The process is also used to conduct assessments that support decisions to establish the security evaluation criteria and associated thresholds and sensitivities of values. The security evaluation criteria may be defined by or informed by regulatory bodies.

References: ISO/IEC/IEEE 15288, Section 6.3.3.3 b).

Related Publications: ISO/IEC 12207, Section 6.3.3.3.2; ISO/IEC 21827.

DM-3 MAKE AND MANAGE SECURITY DECISIONS

DM-3.1 Determine preferred alternative for each security-informed and security-based decision.

Elaboration: The strategy for the decision contains the criteria to guide evaluation and selection of the preferred alternative.

DM-3.2 Record the security-informed or security-based resolution, decision rationale, and assumptions.

Elaboration: Security-informed resolutions are those resolutions that have security considerations, constraints, and assumptions associated with the decision made. Security-based resolutions are those resolutions that address a specific security function or service issue and that have other considerations, constraints, and assumptions associated with the decision made. All aspects are recorded and metadata tagged to the decision for traceability in the event of change. The nature of the recording and metadata tagging depends on whether the resolution is security-informed or security-based.

DM-3.3 Record, track, evaluate, and report the security aspects of security-informed and security-based decisions.

Elaboration: The recording, tracking, evaluation, and reporting of the security aspects of security-informed and security-based decisions is conducted in accordance with agreements, organizational procedures, and regulations, and includes recording the decision results, which may be to defer the decision. Tracking and evaluation enables confirmation that problems have been closed or require continued attention, and identifies trends and issues and their resolution. The reporting informs stakeholders of decision results and is accomplished as stipulated in agreements. The *Information Management* process is used to report decision results to stakeholders.

References: ISO/IEC/IEEE 15288, Section 6.3.3.3 c).

Related Publications: ISO/IEC 12207, Section 6.3.3.3.3; ISO/IEC 21827.

3.3.4 Risk Management Process

Purpose

"The purpose of the Risk Management process is to identify, analyze, treat and monitor the risks continually."

ISO/IEC/IEEE 15288-2015. Reprinted with permission from IEEE, Copyright IEEE 2015, All rights reserved.

Systems Security Engineering Purpose

Systems security engineering, as part of the *Risk Management* process, identifies, analyzes, treats, and monitors security risks for all identified contexts within the risk profile. The risk management process is an ongoing process for systematically addressing security risk throughout the life cycle of a system. Security risk is defined as the effect of uncertainty on objectives pertaining to asset loss and the associated consequences.[38]

Systems Security Engineering Outcomes

- The security aspects of the risk management strategy are defined.

- Security risks are identified and analyzed.

- Security risk treatment options are identified, prioritized, and selected.

- Appropriate security risk treatment is implemented.

- Security risks are evaluated on an ongoing basis to assess changes in status and progress in security risk treatment.

- Security risks are recorded and maintained in the risk profile.

Systems Security Engineering Activities and Tasks

RM-1 PLAN SECURITY RISK MANAGEMENT

RM-1.1 Define the security aspects of the risk management strategy.

Elaboration: Security risk is managed collaboratively as one of many dimensions of risk management. The security aspects of the risk management strategy provide the security viewpoints of risk and include all life cycle concepts, processes, and methods. These are the contexts that inform and bound the analyses for the security aspects of risk management. The security contexts for risk management are typically embodied in strategic plans, policies, and roadmaps. Other contexts in which risk is managed (i.e., reliability, availability, maintainability; resilience; safety; and survivability) must also be considered to ensure that the proper relationships are established in terms of which risk concerns take priority over other risk concerns and which risk concerns inform the other concerns.

RM-1.2 Define and record the security context of the risk management process.

---

[38] Adapted from ISO Guide 73:2009 which defines risk as the effect of uncertainty on objectives. Furthermore, risk can be either positive or negative.

Elaboration: The security context includes stakeholders' perspectives and concerns, technical and programmatic risk categories, assurance, trustworthiness, and asset classes, types, and associated loss consequences. Security risk contexts also include system normal and contingency modes of operation; other system modes and states (e.g., maintenance mode, training mode, test mode); and the business or mission operations and process modes and states. Security risk contexts consider security impact of not pursuing an opportunity and the security risk of not achieving the effects provided by the opportunity.

References: ISO/IEC/IEEE 15288, Section 6.3.4.3 a); ISO/IEC 15026; ISO 31000.

Related Publications: ISO/IEC 12207, Section 6.3.4.3.1; ISO/IEC 21827.

RM-2   MANAGE THE SECURITY ASPECTS OF THE RISK PROFILE

RM-2.1 Define and record the security risk thresholds and conditions under which a level of risk may be accepted.

Elaboration: Security risk thresholds and conditions that constitute acceptable risk are defined for representative or specific asset classes and types and correlated to the details of the contexts for which risk decisions are made. Risk thresholds may vary across stakeholders, across the contexts of security risk, and across system modes and states relative to business or mission modes and states. These risk thresholds and conditions reflect the security risk tolerance of stakeholders.

RM-2.2 Establish and maintain the security aspects of the risk profile.

Elaboration: The risk profile contains all data associated with each risk. The security aspects of the risk profile capture all security data associated with each risk. The risk profile is dynamic in nature and is updated in response to variances and other factors that change the state of a risk. The risk profile enables traceability of security risk across all dimensions in which it is identified, analyzed, treated, and monitored.

RM-2.3 Provide the security aspects of the risk profile to stakeholders based on their needs.

Elaboration: The security aspects of the risk profile support security risk-informed decision making by stakeholders and the engineering team throughout the system life cycle. The security risk aspects are provided to appropriate stakeholders as stated in agreements and when necessary in support of risk and other trade space decisions. The *Information Management* process is used to determine the form in which the security risk aspects are provided and protected so as to satisfy the needs of stakeholders.

References: ISO/IEC/IEEE 15288, Section 6.3.4.3 b); ISO 31000; ISO/IEC 16085.

Related Publications: ISO/IEC 12207, Section 6.3.4.3.2; ISO/IEC 21827.

RM-3   ANALYZE SECURITY RISK

RM-3.1 Identify security risks in the categories described in the security risk management context.

Elaboration: The security risks are identified relative to those events that might create, enhance, prevent, degrade, accelerate, or delay the achievement of objectives. The identification of security risks is informed by the results of a variety of differentiated system security analyses that includes many factors such as threat, vulnerability, protection needs, strength of mechanism, misuse, abuse, human factors, and assurance. The *System Analysis* process is leveraged to provide the data that support the identification of security risks.

RM-3.2 Estimate the likelihood of occurrence and consequences of each identified security risk.

Elaboration: The *likelihood* of occurrence and the consequence of each identified security risk are estimated using available hazard and threat data across the spectrum of events and incidents that have occurred, reasoned speculation of events and incidents, and forecast of potential hazards and threat events. Reasonable limits of certainty must be taken into account with respect to the confidence level in data, expertise, and experience. The uncertainty regarding likelihood of occurrence should not rule out risk should the consequence be sufficient to warrant risk treatment considerations. Assumptions are a key scoping and framing attribute used in determining the likelihood of occurrence.

Data regarding the consequences of each identified security risk is available from the assessment of stakeholder protection needs and results of security requirements elicitation and analysis. The *System Analysis* process is used to provide data required to support the estimation of likelihood of occurrence and consequences of identified risks, and is used to identify appropriate subject-matter expertise that solicits, captures, assesses, and records estimation of likelihood. This expertise includes knowledge of assumptions, hazards, or actual threat information (e.g., historical data on attacks, disaster events, distribution, supplier, and supply chain issues; information on specific adversary capabilities, intentions, and targeting); technology and business or mission process issues that include faults, failures, and errors, or activity that includes misuse and abuse cases; cost and schedule; and material and human resource factors.

RM-3.3 Evaluate each security risk against its security risk thresholds.

Elaboration: The evaluation of security risk produces a prioritization and categorization of identified risks. The evaluation is based on criteria associated with the security risk thresholds established by stakeholders. The *System Analysis* process is used to conduct analysis and provide the data that supports the evaluation of each security risk against its risk thresholds.

RM-3.4 Define risk treatment strategies and measures for each security risk that does not meet its security risk threshold.

Elaboration: The feasibility of alternative risk treatment strategies and measures are defined with consideration of cost, schedule, operational and technical performance impact, ability to achieve target levels of assurance, strength of mechanism, and the effectiveness in security risk reduction. The *System Analysis* process is used to provide the data that substantiates the feasibility of each recommended alternative risk treatment strategy and measure to include any supporting positive and negative effects.

References: ISO/IEC/IEEE 15288, Section 6.3.4.3 c); ISO/IEC 15026; ISO 31000; ISO/IEC 16085.

Related Publications: ISO/IEC 12207, Section 6.3.4.3.3; ISO/IEC 21827.

RM-4   TREAT SECURITY RISK

RM-4.1 Identify recommended alternatives for security risk treatment.

Elaboration: An analysis is conducted to select those security risk treatment alternatives that are considered for risk treatment. The *Decision Management* process is used to decide which defined security risk treatment alternatives are recommended to stakeholders.

RM-4.2 Implement the security risk treatment alternatives selected by stakeholders.

Elaboration: The implementation of each security risk treatment leverages all required technical processes. The *Project Planning* and *Project Assessment and Control* processes address the resources and schedule impact of the risk treatment options selected and ensure that the required technical activities are conducted to accomplish the selected risk treatment.

RM-4.3 Identify and monitor those security risks accepted by stakeholders to determine if any future risk treatment actions are necessary.

Elaboration: The security risk posture reflected in the risks accepted by stakeholders may change over time due to variances in the events, conditions, and circumstances upon which the decision to accept the risk is based. These security risks are monitored to detect trends and circumstances that move the risk outside of the threshold of acceptance. Additionally, unintended consequences of other risk treatment measures may alter the risk posture of the accepted risks. In particular, the security concern that only specified behavior be realized by the system requires that monitoring of all accepted risks be accomplished with confidence that the accepted risk remains within the acceptance threshold.

RM-4.4 Coordinate management action for the identified security risk treatments.

Elaboration: Security risk treatment may require specific attention to both active and passive mechanisms but may also require specific attention to non-security functions and processes of the system. Proper coordination is necessary to ensure the effectiveness of the identified security risk treatments. The *Project Planning* and *Project Assessment and Control* processes are used to help ensure that all relevant impacted entities within the engineering and stakeholder organizations are involved in a coordinated manner to achieve proper implementation of security risk treatments.

References: ISO/IEC/IEEE 15288, Section 6.3.4.3 d); ISO 31000; ISO/IEC 16085.

Related Publications: ISO/IEC 12207, Section 6.3.4.3.4; ISO/IEC 21827.

RM-5   MONITOR SECURITY RISK

RM-5.1 Continually monitor all risks and the security risk management context for changes and evaluate the security risks when their state has changed.

Elaboration: All risks are continually monitored for changes that result in security risk, a change to a treated security risk, or change to the security risk management context. Evaluation of risk detects cases and trends that are indicative of a change in the relationship between a treated security risk and its acceptance threshold, or a change in an accepted risk and its threshold criteria for acceptance. Additionally, changes in the security risk management context may alter the acceptance threshold or effectiveness of risk treatment.

RM-5.2 Implement and monitor measures to evaluate the effectiveness of security risk treatments.

Elaboration: The evaluation of implemented security risk treatments includes consideration of the impacts on other operational and technical performance objectives, and the impact of other system functions and behavior on the effectiveness of security risk treatments. The monitoring measures must also be qualified in terms of their ability to support the effectiveness evaluation with the appropriate precision, accuracy, and level of assurance.

RM-5.3 Monitor on an ongoing basis, the emergence of new security risks and sources of risk throughout the life cycle.

Elaboration: The complex nature of systems, system interactions, and behavior coupled with the uncertainty associated with disruptive hazard and threat events is of particular concern in terms of emerging and emergent security risks. This is a full life cycle concern across stakeholders, their concerns, and all methods and processes associated with the life cycle concepts of the system.

References: ISO/IEC/IEEE 15288, Section 6.3.4.3 e); ISO/IEC 15026; ISO 31000; ISO/IEC 16085.

Related Publications: ISO/IEC 12207, Section 6.3.4.3.5; ISO/IEC 21827.

3.3.5 Configuration Management Process

Purpose

"The purpose of [the] Configuration Management [process] is to manage and control system elements and configurations over the life cycle."

ISO/IEC/IEEE 15288-2015. Reprinted with permission from IEEE, Copyright IEEE 2015, All rights reserved.

Systems Security Engineering Purpose

Systems security engineering, as part of the *Configuration Management* process, ensures that security considerations are addressed in the management and the control of system elements, configurations, and associated data and information over the system life cycle.

Systems Security Engineering Outcomes

- The security aspects of the configuration management strategy are defined.

- The security aspects of *configuration items* are identified and managed.

- Security criteria are included in configuration *baselines*.

- Changes to items under configuration management are securely controlled.

- Security aspects are included in configuration status information.

- Completed configuration audits include security criteria.

- The security aspects of system releases and deliveries are controlled and approved.

Systems Security Engineering Activities and Tasks

CM-1   PLAN FOR THE SECURITY ASPECTS OF CONFIGURATION MANAGEMENT

>   **CM-1.1** Define the security aspects of a configuration management strategy.

>   **Elaboration:** These include, for example: security-relevant roles, responsibilities, accountabilities, and authorities; criteria for secure disposition of, access to, release of, and control of changes to configuration items; security parameters or other considerations for definition and establishment of baselines; security considerations, criteria, and constraints for the locations, conditions, and environment of storage; the storage media and its storage constraints; security criteria or events for commencing configuration control and maintaining baselines of evolving configurations; security criteria and constraints for change management, including security-focused configuration control boards, regulatory and emergency change requests, and security-informed procedures for change management; security audit strategy and the responsibilities for assessing continual integration of the configuration definition information; and the secure coordination of configuration management activities across the set of acquirer, supplier, subcontractor, logistics, supply chain, and other organizations that have impact on achieving configuration management objectives.

>   **CM-1.2** Define the approach for the secure archive and retrieval for configuration items, configuration management artifacts, data, and information.

Elaboration: This approach includes authorized knowledge of, access to, use of, changes to, and retention time frames for configuration items, configuration management artifacts, data, and information; and is to be consistent with relevant regulations, directives, policies, and agreements.

References: ISO/IEC/IEEE 15288, Section 6.3.5.3 a); ISO 10007; IEEE 828; ANSI/EIA 649B.

Related Publications: ISO/IEC 12207, Section 6.3.5.3.1, Section 7.2.2.3.1; ISO/IEC 21827.

CM-2   PERFORM THE SECURITY ASPECTS OF CONFIGURATION IDENTIFICATION

> **CM-2.1** Identify the security aspects of system elements and information items that are configuration items.

Elaboration: The security aspects of system elements and information items help to inform the identification and labeling of items that are placed under configuration management and that are subject to formal review and configuration audits. The configuration items may serve specific *security function* or may have security relevance. Configuration items include requirements, architecture, and design artifacts; product and system elements; information items; and baselines. Security considerations for configuration items may be defined in regulations, directives, policies, or agreements.

> **CM-2.2** Identify the security aspects of the hierarchy and structure of system information.

Elaboration: The security aspects of the hierarchy and structure of system information may reflect or be associated with the hierarchy and structure of the system and its decomposition into system elements and constituent components.

> **CM-2.3** Establish the security nomenclature for system, system element, and information item identifiers.

Elaboration: Explicit security marking, labels, and metadata tagging of information items and identifiers enables unambiguous recognition and traceability to system, system element, baseline, and other configuration items, and the correlation to the secure methods for handling configuration items.

> **CM-2.4** Define the security aspects of baseline identification throughout the system life cycle.

Elaboration: The security criteria used to define and identify baselines support unambiguous association and traceability of baseline items to their system configuration context. The criteria are determined in accordance with relevant standards and technology, regulatory, or product sector conventions.

> **CM-2.5** Obtain acquirer and supplier agreement for security aspects to establish a baseline.

Elaboration: Agreement on the security aspects of baselines considers expectations and constraints on the set of acquirer, supplier, logistics, and supply chain organizations involved, and how those considerations are to be addressed in accordance with the configuration management strategy.

References: ISO/IEC/IEEE 15288, Section 6.3.5.3 b); ISO/IEC 27036.

Related Publications: ISO/IEC 12207, Section 6.3.5.3.2, Section 7.2.2.3.2; ISO/IEC 21827.

CM-3   PERFORM SECURITY CONFIGURATION CHANGE MANAGEMENT

> **CM-3.1** Identify security aspects of requests for change and requests for variance.

Elaboration: The request for change or variance can be based on reasons other than security and without an obvious relevance to security. Requests for change and variance are therefore reviewed to identify any security aspects. A request for variance is also referred to as a request for deviation, waiver, or concession.

CM-3.2 Determine the security aspects of action to coordinate, evaluate, and disposition requests for change or requests for variance.

Elaboration: The security aspects identified are coordinated and evaluated across all impacted performance and effectiveness evaluation criteria, and the criteria of project plans, cost, benefits, risks, quality, and schedule. The security aspects inform disposition action to approve or deny the request for variance, or may require revision to the request for variance as a specific condition for approval. The security aspects are evaluated to determine any security-driven impacts and impacts on security, and to identify any security-relevant dependencies between individual requests.

CM-3.3 Incorporate security aspects in requests submitted for review and approval.

Elaboration: Security aspects are to support the review and approval of the request. These aspects may serve to justify a security-driven change or to confirm that the security-relevant impact of a general request is nonexistent or acceptable. Such requests are generally submitted for evaluation by a Configuration Control Board that makes the approval decision based on need and impact.

CM-3.4 Track and manage the security aspects of approved changes to the baseline, requests for change, and requests for variance.

Elaboration: Security considerations factor into the prioritization and scheduling of approved requests and pending requests not yet approved. Approved changes are made by the technical processes, and verified and validated by the *Verification* and *Validation* processes. Requests for change or variance are closed out after confirming successful completion of the request, or after it is determined that the change or variance is no longer justified.

References: ISO/IEC/IEEE 15288, Section 6.3.5.3 c).

Related Publications: ISO/IEC 12207, Section 6.3.5.3.2, Section 7.2.2.3.3; ISO/IEC 21827.

CM-4   PERFORM SECURITY CONFIGURATION STATUS ACCOUNTING

CM-4.1 Develop and maintain security-relevant configuration management status information for system elements, baselines, approved changes, and releases.

Elaboration: Security-relevant configuration management status information supports decision making within and across system elements, baselines, approved changes, and releases. The security-relevant status information is maintained to reflect the security aspects of the hierarchy and structure of system information. This information also includes certification, accreditation, authorization, or approval decisions associated with a system element, baseline, or release.

CM-4.2 Capture, store, and report security-relevant configuration management data.

Elaboration: Capturing, storing, and reporting security-relevant configuration management data is done to preserve, protect, and ensure the correctness, integrity, timeliness, and confidentiality of such data and configuration items. The configuration data and associated records are maintained throughout the life cycle of the system, and are securely destroyed, disposed of, or archived in accordance with agreements and regulatory constraints.

References: ISO/IEC/IEEE 15288, Section 6.3.5.3 d).

Related Publications: ISO/IEC 12207, Section 7.2.2.3.4; ISO/IEC 21827.

CM-5   PERFORM SECURITY CONFIGURATION EVALUATION

CM-5.1 Identify the need for security-focused configuration management audits.

Elaboration: Security considerations are included in all configuration management audits to address relevant security concerns. These security-focused audits include technical and non-technical concerns specific to security functions and services and the associated technical, administrative, and user information guidance and artifacts.

CM-5.2 Verify that the system configuration satisfies the security-relevant configuration requirements.

Elaboration: Security requirements and security metadata-tagged requirements, constraints, waivers, and variances are compared against the security results of verification activities to identify differences, gaps, and other issues. The *Verification* process provides data used by this task.

CM-5.3 Monitor the security aspects of incorporation of approved configuration changes.

Elaboration: Security aspects to monitor include security function and service performance and effectiveness; desirable and undesirable emergent behavior and outcomes; and susceptibility to disruptions, hazards, and threats. The security aspects may result as by products and side effects of approved changes, to include those approved changes with no obvious security relevance.

CM-5.4 Assess whether the system meets baseline security functional and performance capabilities.

Elaboration: The system elements that provide security functions and services identified by the baseline undergoing assessment are verified; variances and deficiencies are identified; and risks are identified. All system elements identified by the baseline are assessed to identify any security-relevant variances and deficiencies. The *Verification* process is used to conduct the verification activities and to provide data to support risk identification. This assessment may be referred to as a Functional Configuration Audit.

CM-5.5 Assess whether the system conforms to the security aspects of the operational and configuration information items.

Elaboration: The configuration of the validated system is assessed against baseline configuration items to identify security-relevant discrepancies, variances, and deficiencies. This assessment may be referred to as a Physical Configuration Audit.

CM-5.6 Record the security aspects of configuration management audit results and disposition actions.

Elaboration: None.

References: ISO/IEC/IEEE 15288, Section 6.3.5.3 e).

Related Publications: ISO/IEC 12207, Section 7.2.2.3.5; ISO/IEC 21827.

CM-6 PERFORM THE SECURITY ASPECTS OF RELEASE CONTROL

CM-6.1 Approve the security aspects of system releases and deliveries.

Elaboration: The purpose of the system release is to authorize the use of the system for a specific purpose and the release may be contingent on explicit use restrictions. The security aspects of release control identify the security-relevant restrictions, if any, associated with the authorization to use the specified system configuration. System releases generally include a set of changes accomplished by the technical processes and verified and/or validated by the *Verification* and *Validation* processes. The security aspects of release control are dependent on the security-focused results of the verified and validated changes, to include security analyses for assurance and trustworthiness. The *System Analysis*, *Risk Management*, *Decision Management*, and *Transition* processes are used to address release control authorization as part of other considerations that contribute to the release decision.

CM-6.2 Track and manage the security aspects of system releases.

Elaboration: System elements and associated information items are securely handled, stored, packaged, and delivered in accordance with agreements and relevant security policies of the organizations involved. Tracking and managing the security aspects of system releases includes maintaining and correlating copies of configuration items relative to the identified baselines, variances, deviations, and concessions.

References: ISO/IEC/IEEE 15288, Section 6.3.5.3 f).

Related Publications: ISO/IEC 12207, Section 7.2.2.3.6; ISO/IEC 21827.

3.3.6 Information Management Process

> ### Purpose
>
> "The purpose of the Information Management process is to generate, obtain, confirm, transform, retain, retrieve, disseminate and dispose of information to designated stakeholders."
>
> *ISO/IEC/IEEE 15288-2015. Reprinted with permission from IEEE, Copyright IEEE 2015, All rights reserved.*

Systems Security Engineering Purpose

Systems security engineering, as part of the *Information Management* process, ensures that all stakeholder protection needs and all associated security considerations, constraints, and concerns are adequately addressed by the information management process.

Systems Security Engineering Outcomes

- Protections for information to be managed are identified.

- Information representations are defined with consideration of security aspects.

- Information is securely obtained, developed, transformed, stored, validated, presented, and disposed.

- The security aspects of information status are identified.

- Information is available to designated stakeholders in compliance with authorized access, use, and dissemination criteria.

Systems Security Engineering Activities and Tasks

IM-1   PREPARE FOR THE SECURITY ASPECTS OF INFORMATION MANAGEMENT

IM-1.1   Define the security aspects of the information management strategy.

Elaboration: The security aspects of the information management strategy describe the approach for protecting stakeholder, technical, agreement, and other information for the duration of the engineering project and until such time that information may be disposed or is no longer required to be protected. The security aspects address security and privacy concerns, and the rights for all program, technical, sensitive, proprietary, intellectual property, and other specified information types associated with the program. The security aspects of the strategy are to conform with any applicable laws, policies, directives, regulations, agreement restrictions, and patents.

IM-1.2   Define protections for information items that will be managed.

Elaboration: The types of security functions and the strength of security mechanisms needed for individual information items or classes of information items are determined by the *Business or Mission Analysis, Stakeholder Needs and Requirements Definition*, and *Agreement* processes. Laws, policies, directives, regulations, and/or patents may dictate specific types and strength of protection, and the constraints regarding information access, dissemination, use, storage, handling, transmission, disposal, declassification, and destruction.

IM-1.3   Designate authorities and responsibilities for the security aspects of information management.

Elaboration: Security-relevant authorities include those of the organization with responsibility to plan, execute, and monitor compliance with and the effectiveness of the information management strategy. Additional authorities may be identified that include personnel representing legislative, regulatory, and other stakeholders.

IM-1.4   Define protections for specific information item content, formats, and structure.

Elaboration: Information exists in many forms (e.g., audio, visual, textual, graphical, numerical) and may be provided using a variety of mediums (e.g., electronic, printed, magnetic, optical). The protection technology and methods are defined to match and be effective relative to the form and medium used. Specific consideration is given to protections when information is transferred across forms or across mediums.

IM-1.5   Define the security aspects of information maintenance actions.

Elaboration: The security aspects of information maintenance are to maintain the in-place information protections to at least the specified level of protection and strength during all actions to maintain the information in useable form. The security aspects apply to all resources (e.g., methods, processes, tools) used to perform maintenance actions, including those actions that transform the information from one form to another or to move information from one medium to another. Resources that are used to support information maintenance actions are to be placed under configuration control and are addressed by the *Configuration Management* process.

References: ISO/IEC/IEEE 15288, Section 6.3.6.3 a).

Related Publications: ISO/IEC 12207, Section 6.3.6.3.1; ISO/IEC 21827.

IM-2   PERFORM THE SECURITY ASPECTS OF INFORMATION MANAGEMENT

IM-2.1   Securely obtain, develop, or transform the identified information items.

Elaboration: Information items are generated by all life cycle processes and are securely captured in the form suitable for use by stakeholders as outlined by the security aspects of the information management strategy and in accordance with the protection technology, methods, and strength defined for the information item type or class.

IM-2.2   Securely maintain information items and their storage records, and record the security status of information.

Elaboration: Information and associated storage records are securely maintained as outlined by the security aspects of the information management strategy and in accordance with the protection technology, methods, and strength defined for the information item type or class. Records of the actions are kept and protected in the same manner as the information items to which they are associated.

IM-2.3   Securely publish, distribute, or provide access to information and information items to designated stakeholders.

Elaboration: Information is provided to stakeholders as outlined by the publishing and distribution security aspects of the information management strategy and in accordance with the protection technology, methods, and strength defined for the information or information items.

IM-2.4   Securely archive designated information.

Elaboration: Information is designated for archive in accordance with project closure, audit, and knowledge retention purposes. The information management strategy establishes the protection technology, methods, and strength defined for the information or information items to be placed in archive. Secure retention of information items continues in accordance with the protection criteria and associated expiration dates defined by agreements, organizational policy, or legislative or regulatory bodies.

IM-2.5 Securely dispose of unwanted or invalid information or information that has not been validated.

Elaboration: Secure retention criteria include the manner of declassification/desensitizing, disposal, or destruction of the information item and/or its retention medium. The *Disposal* process is used to dispose of information and its associated storage medium in a secure manner.

References: ISO/IEC/IEEE 15288, Section 6.3.6.3 b).

Related Publications: ISO/IEC 12207, Section 6.3.6.3.2; ISO/IEC 21827.

3.3.7 *Measurement Process*

Purpose

"The purpose of the Measurement process is to collect, analyze, and report objective data and information to support effective management and demonstrate the quality of the products, services, and processes."

ISO/IEC/IEEE 15288-2015. Reprinted with permission from IEEE, Copyright IEEE 2015, All rights reserved.

Systems Security Engineering Purpose

Systems security engineering, as part of the *Measurement* process, collects, analyzes, and reports security-relevant data and information to support effective management and to demonstrate the quality of the products, services, and processes.

Systems Security Engineering Outcomes

- Security-relevant information needs are identified.

- An appropriate set of security measures, based on the security-relevant information needs, are identified or developed.

- Required security-relevant data is collected, verified, and stored.

- Security-relevant data is analyzed and the results interpreted.

- Security-relevant information items provide information that support decisions.

Systems Security Engineering Activities and Tasks

MS-1   PREPARE FOR SECURITY MEASUREMENT

    MS-1.1 Define the security aspects of the measurement strategy.

    Elaboration: None.

    MS-1.2 Describe the characteristics of the organization that are relevant to security measurement.

    Elaboration: None.

    MS-1.3 Identify and prioritize the security-relevant information needs.

    Elaboration: None.

    MS-1.4 Select and specify measures that satisfy the security-relevant information needs.

    Elaboration: None.

    MS-1.5 Define procedures for the collection, analysis, access, and reporting of security-relevant data.

    Elaboration: None.

MS-1.6 Define criteria for evaluating the security-relevant information items and the process used for the security aspects of measurement.

Elaboration: None.

MS-1.7 Identify, plan for, and obtain enabling systems or services to support the security aspects of measurement.

Elaboration: None.

References: ISO/IEC/IEEE 15288, Section 6.3.7.3 a); ISO/IEC 15939; ISO 9001.

Related Publications: ISO/IEC 12207, Section 6.3.7.3.1.

MS-2 PERFORM SECURITY MEASUREMENT

MS-2.1 Integrate procedures for the generation, collection, analysis, and reporting of security-relevant data into the relevant processes.

Elaboration: None.

MS-2.2 Collect, store, and verify security-relevant data.

Elaboration: None.

MS-2.3 Analyze security-relevant data and develop security-informed information items.

Elaboration: None.

MS-2.4 Record security measurement results and inform the measurement users.

Elaboration: Security measurement results are provided to relevant stakeholders and project personnel to support decision making, risk management, and to initiate corrective action and improvements.

References: ISO/IEC/IEEE 15288, Section 6.3.7.3 b); ISO/IEC 15939; ISO 9001.

Related Publications: ISO/IEC 12207, Section 6.3.7.3.2, Section 6.3.7.3.3.

3.3.8 Quality Assurance Process

Purpose

"The purpose of the Quality Assurance process is to help ensure the effective application of the organization's Quality Management process to the project."

ISO/IEC/IEEE 15288-2015. Reprinted with permission from IEEE, Copyright IEEE 2015, All rights reserved.

Systems Security Engineering Purpose

Systems security engineering, as part of the *Quality Assurance* process, conducts proactive security quality assurance analyses throughout the project to ensure the effective application of the security aspects of the *Quality Management* process and to provide a level of confidence that the product or service delivered will be of the desired security quality.

Systems Security Engineering Outcomes

- The security aspects of the quality assurance strategy are established.

- The security aspects of the project quality assurance procedures are defined and implemented.

- Criteria and methods for the security aspects of quality assurance evaluations are defined.

- The evaluations of the products, services, and processes of the project are performed, consistent with security quality management policies, procedures, and requirements.

- Security results of evaluations are provided to relevant stakeholders.

- Security-relevant incidents are resolved.

- Prioritized security-relevant problems are treated.

Systems Security Engineering Activities and Tasks

QA-1   PREPARE FOR SECURITY QUALITY ASSURANCE

> **QA-1.1** Define the security aspects of the quality assurance strategy.
>
> **Elaboration:** The security aspects of the quality assurance strategy are informed by and consistent with the quality management policies, objectives, and procedures as they are applied to security-oriented products and services and across all products and services. These security aspects include: project security quality assurance procedures; security roles, responsibilities, accountabilities, and authorities; security activities oriented to each life cycle engineering process; security activities appropriate to each supplier and subcontractor; required security-oriented verification, validation, monitoring, measurement, inspection, and test activities specific to the product or service; security criteria for product or service acceptance; and security evaluation criteria and methods for process, product, and service evaluations.
>
> **QA-1.2** Establish independence of security quality assurance from other life cycle processes.
>
> **Elaboration:** Considerations and expectations for security quality assurance independence may be imposed by regulatory and other acceptance stakeholders, or by agreements.
>
> **References:** ISO/IEC/IEEE 15288, Section 6.3.8.3 a); ISO/IEC 15408; ISO/IEC 15026.

Related Publications: ISO/IEC 12207, Section 7.2.3.3.1.

QA-2   PERFORM PRODUCT OR SERVICE SECURITY EVALUATIONS

QA-2.1 Evaluate products and services for conformance to established security criteria, contracts, standards, and regulations.

Elaboration: Product or service security evaluations include the system and security quality requirements that are derived from the *Stakeholder Needs and Requirements Definition* and *System Requirements Definition* processes and must conform to relevant criteria, contracts, standards, and regulations.

QA-2.2 Perform the security aspects of verification and validation of the outputs of the life cycle processes to determine conformance to specified security requirements.

Elaboration: The security requirements include security metadata-tagged requirements that contain or are informed by security constraints.

References: ISO/IEC/IEEE 15288, Section 6.3.8.3 b); ISO/IEC 15026.

Related Publications: ISO/IEC 12207, Section 7.2.3.3.2.

QA-3   PERFORM PROCESS SECURITY EVALUATIONS

QA-3.1 Evaluate project life cycle processes for conformance to established security criteria, contracts, standards, and regulations.

Elaboration: Process security evaluations include the system and security quality requirements that are derived from the *Life Cycle Model Management* and *Project Planning* processes.

QA-3.2 Evaluate tools and environments that support or automate the process for conformance to established security criteria, contracts, standards, and regulations.

Elaboration: Security evaluations of tools and environments include enabling systems and the security quality requirements that are derived from the *Infrastructure Management* and *Project Planning* processes.

QA-3.3 Evaluate supplier processes for conformance to process security requirements.

Elaboration: Security evaluations include supplier processes, constraints, and quality criteria that are derived from agreements. Supplier processes include distribution, logistics, and supply chain.

References: ISO/IEC/IEEE 15288, Section 6.3.8.3 c); ISO/IEC 15026; ISO/IEC 27036.

Related Publications: ISO/IEC 12207, Section 7.2.3.3.3.

QA-4   MANAGE QUALITY ASSURANCE SECURITY RECORDS AND REPORTS

QA-4.1 Create records and reports related to the security aspects of quality assurance activities.

Elaboration: Records and reports conform to organizational, regulatory, and project requirements, to include protection requirements as determined by the *Information Management* process.

QA-4.2 Securely maintain, store, and distribute records and reports.

Elaboration: The *Information Management* process determines the criteria and constraints used.

QA-4.3 Identify the security aspects of incidents and problems associated with product, service, and process evaluations.

Elaboration: The security aspects of incidents and problems are identified and subsequently traced to the relevant product or service, and to the process undergoing evaluation and the entity that is responsible for performing the process.

References: ISO/IEC/IEEE 15288, Section 6.3.8.3 d); ISO/IEC 15026.

Related Publications: ISO/IEC 12207, Section 7.2.3.3.4.

QA-5 TREAT SECURITY INCIDENTS AND PROBLEMS

QA-5.1 The security aspects of incidents are recorded, analyzed, and classified.

Elaboration: The classification of incidents is a security-informed categorization that is relative to all other incidents. This categorization is different from a security-based sensitivity classification, where such classification is warranted.

QA-5.2 The security aspects of incidents are resolved or elevated to problems.

Elaboration: Problems are also referred to as nonconformities that, if left untreated, could cause the project to fail to meets its requirements.

QA-5.3 The security aspects of problems are recorded, analyzed, and classified.

Elaboration: The classification of problems is a security-informed categorization that is relative to all other problems. This categorization is different from a security-based sensitivity classification, where such is warranted.

QA-5.4 Treatments for the security aspects of problems are prioritized and implementation is tracked.

Elaboration: The prioritization of treatments takes into account security-specific issues and their relative prioritization, as well as the consideration of security as an informing aspect of general problem prioritization. Tracking the security aspects of problem resolution includes attention to problems where the security relevance is not necessarily obvious and identifies implementation results that constitute additional security concerns or fail to address the identified security aspects.

QA-5.5 Trends in the security aspects of incidents and problems are noted and analyzed.

Elaboration: Trends include the security-driven impact on all incidents and problems and non-security aspects of incidents and problems and how they impact security considerations and objectives.

QA-5.6 Stakeholders are informed of the status of the security aspects of incidents and problems.

Elaboration: Incident and problem status is communicated to relevant customer, regulatory, and approval stakeholders in accordance with agreements, regulations, and policies. The *Information Management* process determines the information protection methods to be used in all stakeholder interactions.

QA-5.7 The security aspects of incidents and problems are tracked to closure.

Elaboration: Tracking the security aspects of incidents and problems includes tracking incidents and problems where the security relevance is not necessarily obvious and identifies treatment results that constitute additional security concerns or fail to address the identified security aspects.

References: ISO/IEC/IEEE 15288, Section 6.3.8.3 e); ISO/IEC TR 24748-1; ISO/IEC 15026.

Related Publications: None.

3.4 TECHNICAL PROCESSES

This section contains the fourteen ISO/IEC/IEEE 15288 *technical* processes with extensions for systems security engineering. The processes are:

- Business or Mission Analysis Process (BA);

- Stakeholder Needs and Requirements Definition Process (SN);

- System Requirements Definition Process (SR);

- Architecture Definition Process (AR);

- Design Definition Process (DE);

- System Analysis Process (SA);

- Implementation Process (IP);

- Integration Process (IN);

- Verification Process (VE);

- Transition Process (TR);

- Validation Process (VA);

- Operation Process (OP);

- Maintenance Process (MA); and

- Disposal Process (DS).

3.4.1 Business or Mission Analysis Process

Purpose

"The purpose of the Business or Mission Analysis process is to define the business or mission problem or opportunity, characterize the solution space, and determine potential solution class(es) that could address a problem or take advantage of an opportunity."

ISO/IEC/IEEE 15288-2015. Reprinted with permission from IEEE, Copyright IEEE 2015, All rights reserved.

Systems Security Engineering Purpose

Systems security engineering, as part of the *Business or Mission Analysis* process, analyzes business or mission problems or opportunities in the context and viewpoint of security factors. This analysis helps the engineering team to understand the scope, basis, and drivers of the business or mission problems or opportunities and ascertain the asset loss consequences that present security and protection issues associated with those problems or opportunities. Systems security engineering ascertains the security objectives, concerns, considerations, limitations, and constraints that are used in the identification and selection of a preferred solution from a group of candidate alternative solutions. This process may be invoked at any time during the engineering effort in response to changes made by stakeholders or to plan future business or mission solutions and modernizations in response to new problems or opportunities. This process is accomplished in close coordination with the *Stakeholder Needs and Requirements Definition* process.

Systems Security Engineering Outcomes

- The security aspects of the problem or opportunity space are defined.

- The security aspects of the solution space are characterized.

- The concerns, constraints, limitations, and other security considerations that can affect potential solutions are defined.

- Preliminary concepts for the security aspects of system life cycle concepts are defined.

- Alternative solution classes that take into account security objectives, considerations, concerns, limitations, and constraints are identified.

- Candidate and preferred alternative solution classes are identified, analyzed, and selected to explicitly account for security objectives, considerations, concerns, limitations, and constraints.

- Any enabling systems or services needed to achieve the security aspects of business or mission analysis are available.

- Security-relevant traceability of the business or mission problems and opportunities and the preferred alternative solution classes is established.

Systems Security Engineering Activities and Tasks

BA-1   PREPARE FOR THE SECURITY ASPECTS OF BUSINESS OR MISSION ANALYSIS

    BA-1.1   Identify stakeholders who will contribute to the identification and assessment of any mission, business, or operational problems or opportunities.

Elaboration: These stakeholders encompass all individuals, organizations, representatives, and delegates with concerns across the life cycle of the system.

BA-1.2   Review organizational problems and opportunities with respect to desired security objectives.

Elaboration: This review examines organizational problems or opportunities and the security objectives that must be considered to address those problems or opportunities from the business or mission perspective. The review also includes any gaps in the existing systems or services related to protection or security capability that would preclude the organization from achieving the identified security objectives.

BA-1.3   Define the security aspects of the business or mission analysis strategy.

Elaboration: Security aspects of the business or mission strategy analysis are used to inform the definition of the problem space, characterization of the solution space, and selection of a solution class.

BA-1.4   Identify, plan for, and obtain access to enabling systems or services to support the security aspects of the business or mission analysis process.

Elaboration: Specific enabling systems and services may be required to support the security aspects of the business or mission analysis process. These enabling systems and services are relied upon to provide the capability to realize and support the system-of-interest, and therefore impact the trustworthiness of the system. The business or mission analysis-oriented security concerns for enabling systems and services used to support the business or mission analysis process must be determined and captured as security requirements and as security-driven constraints for the interfaces and interactions with the system-of-interest. The *Validation* process is used to confirm that enabling systems and services achieve their intended use and do so with an appropriate level of trustworthiness.

References: ISO/IEC/IEEE 15288, Section 6.4.1.3 a).

Related Publications: FIPS Publication 199; NIST SP 800-37.

BA-2   DEFINE THE SECURITY ASPECTS OF THE PROBLEM OR OPPORTUNITY SPACE

BA-2.1   Analyze the problems or opportunities in the context of the security objectives and measures of success to be achieved.

Elaboration: The security objectives that are part of any solution determine what it means to be adequately secure. These objectives also address the scope of security for the system including the assets requiring protection and the consequences or impacts against which security is assessed. Measures of success establish the trustworthiness of the system in terms of the specific and measureable criteria relative to the operational performance measures and the stated security objectives. These measures include both strength of protection and the level of assurance, or confidence, in the protection capability. The results of the analyses inform decisions on the suitability and feasibility of alternative options to be pursued.

BA-2.2   Define the security aspects and considerations of the mission, business, or operational problem or opportunity.

Elaboration: Information is elicited from stakeholders to acquire an understanding of the mission, business, or operational problem or opportunity from a system security perspective. Information items that can have security implications and that can affect the requirements generation process are described in Appendix G.

References: ISO/IEC/IEEE 15288, Section 6.4.1.3 b); ISO/IEC 15026.

Related Publications: FIPS Publication 199; NIST SP 800-37.

BA-3 CHARACTERIZE THE SECURITY ASPECTS OF THE SOLUTION SPACE

BA-3.1 Define the security aspects of the preliminary operational concepts and other concepts in life cycle stages.

Elaboration: Security considerations are defined relative to all preliminary life cycle concepts including, for example: acquisition, development, engineering, manufacturing, production; deployment and operation; sustainment and support (training, maintenance, logistics, supply, and distribution); disposal and retirement; and any other life cycle concept for which security aspects are necessarily a part of or inform secure execution and achievement of security objectives. Specific security operational concepts include, for example: modes of secure operation; security-related operational scenarios and use cases; or secure usage within a mission area or line of business. Security considerations are integrated into all identified life cycle concepts and used to support feasibility analysis and evaluation of candidate alternative solution classes.

BA-3.2 Identify alternative solution classes that can achieve the security objectives within limitations, constraints, and other considerations.

Elaboration: Relevant security issues or concerns related to the candidate alternative solution classes are identified and recorded. In addition, any security-related limitations or constraints on life cycle concepts or the engineering of each alternative solution class are examined.

References: ISO/IEC/IEEE 15288, Sections 6.4.1.3 c); ISO/IEC 42010; ISO/IEC TR 24748-1.

Related Publications: FIPS Publication 199; NIST SP 800-37.

BA-4 EVALUATE AND SELECT SOLUTION CLASSES

BA-4.1 Assess each alternative solution class taking into account the security objectives, limitations, constraints, and other relevant security considerations.

Elaboration: Security aspects are one of many decision criteria used to assess each alternative solution class. Security assessments may be accomplished in combination with or as a separate informing assessment of the non-security decision criteria. The *System Analysis* process is used to perform the security analyses required to inform the alternative solution assessments.

BA-4.2 Select the preferred alternative solution class (or classes) based on the identified security objectives, trade space factors, and other criteria defined by the organization.

Elaboration: Stakeholder assessments of each solution class are carried out in consideration of all relevant criteria. Data to inform the selection decision-making process is provided by the *Risk Management* and *System Analysis* processes, and the *Validation* process ensures the preferred alternative solution class(es) fit in the context of the proposed business or mission strategy. The *Decision Management* process is employed to evaluate alternatives and to select the preferred alternative solution class or classes.

References: ISO/IEC/IEEE 15288, Sections 6.4.1.3 d).

Related Publications: NIST SP 800-37.

BA-5 MANAGE THE SECURITY ASPECTS OF BUSINESS OR MISSION ANALYSIS

BA-5.1 Maintain traceability of the security aspects of business or mission analysis.

Elaboration: Bidirectional traceability is maintained between all identified security aspects and supporting security data associated with the business or mission problems and opportunities; the proposed solution class or classes; the organizational strategy; stakeholder protection needs and security requirements; and system analysis results.

BA-5.2   Provide security-relevant information items required for business or mission analysis to baselines.

Elaboration: Security aspects are captured in various artifacts that are maintained in an identified baseline for the life cycle of the system. The security-relevant configuration items from this process are identified and incorporated into engineering baselines so that they may be produced and made available as required throughout the system life cycle. The *Configuration Management* process manages the baseline and the artifacts identified by this process. The *Information Management* process determines the appropriate forms of information and protections for the information that is provided to stakeholders.

References: ISO/IEC/IEEE 15288, Sections 6.4.1.3 e).

Related Publications: NIST SP 800-37.

3.4.2 Stakeholder Needs and Requirements Definition Process

Purpose

"The purpose of the Stakeholder Needs and Requirements Definition process is to define the stakeholder requirements for a system that can provide the capabilities needed by users and other stakeholders in a defined environment."

ISO/IEC/IEEE 15288-2015. Reprinted with permission from IEEE, Copyright IEEE 2015, All rights reserved.

Systems Security Engineering Purpose

Systems security engineering, as part of the *Stakeholder Needs and Requirements Definition* process, defines the stakeholder security requirements that include the protection capability, security characteristics, and security-driven constraints for the system, so as to securely provide the capabilities needed by users and other stakeholders.[39] Systems security engineering performs requirements elicitation and analysis activities to identify stakeholder life cycle protection needs for all assets associated with the system-of-interest, its enabling systems, and for the interactions with other systems; determines the consequence of asset loss relative to the identified assets; and assesses the susceptibility of those assets to adversity in the form of disruptions, hazards, and threats. The stakeholder security requirements are the reference against which the protection capability is validated, and against which the system is deemed suitable for use. This process is accomplished in close coordination with the *Business or Mission Analysis* process.

Systems Security Engineering Outcomes

- The ssecurity interests and concerns of stakeholders of the system are identified.

- Required security characteristics and security context for the secure use of capabilities for all system life cycle concepts in all system life cycle stages, are defined.

- Stakeholder assets and assets classes are identified.

- Asset susceptibility to adversity and uncertainty is determined.

- Asset protection priorities and protection assurances are determined.

- Stakeholder protection needs are defined and prioritized.

- Security-driven and security-informed constraints on a system are identified.

- Stakeholder protection needs are transformed into stakeholder security requirements.

- Security-oriented performance measures are defined.

- Stakeholder agreement that their protection needs and expectations are adequately reflected in the security requirements is achieved.

- Any enabling systems or services needed to support the security aspects of stakeholder needs and requirements definition are available.

---

[39] Security characteristics and constraints may be expressed as security-driven or security-informed performance requirements or constraints. Metadata tagging is used to support traceability of requirements to their security-driven and security-informed basis.

- Asset protection data associated with protection needs and stakeholder security requirements is recorded as part of the system requirements.

- Traceability of stakeholder security requirements, stakeholders, protection needs, and asset protection data is established.

Systems Security Engineering Activities and Tasks

SN-1   PREPARE FOR STAKEHOLDER PROTECTION NEEDS AND SECURITY REQUIREMENTS DEFINITION

> **SN-1.1**   Identify the stakeholders who have a security interest in the system throughout its life cycle.

Elaboration: Stakeholders include persons, groups, and organizations (or a designated delegate thereof) that impact the system or are impacted by the system, including the protection aspects of the system. Stakeholders are identified, including their security interest and specific roles and responsibilities relative to the systems engineering effort. Key stakeholders are those stakeholders that have decision-making responsibility associated with life cycle concepts; program planning, control, and execution; acquisition and life cycle milestones; engineering trades; risk management; system acceptance; and trustworthiness. Key stakeholders and their associated decision-making authority are correlated to each of the engineering activities performed in each life cycle stage.

> **SN-1.2**   Define the stakeholder protection needs and security requirements definition strategy.

Elaboration: This strategy addresses the elicitation activities, methods, and techniques used to acquire information from stakeholders and the security analyses conducted to help identify, disambiguate, and otherwise enable an accurate and complete transformation of protection needs into verifiable security requirements. The strategy strives to achieve stakeholder consensus on a common set of security requirements and system assurance objectives.

> **SN-1.3**   Identify, plan for, and obtain access to enabling systems or services to support the security aspects of the stakeholder needs and requirements definition process.

Elaboration: Specific enabling systems and services may be required to support the security aspects of the stakeholder needs and requirements definition process. These enabling systems and services are relied upon to provide the capability to realize and support the system-of-interest, and therefore impact the trustworthiness of the system. The stakeholder needs and requirements definition-oriented security concerns for enabling systems and services used to support the stakeholder needs and requirements definition process must be determined and captured as security requirements and as security-driven constraints for the interfaces and interactions with the system-of-interest. The *Validation* process is used to confirm that enabling systems and services achieve their intended use and do so with an appropriate level of trustworthiness.

References: ISO/IEC/IEEE 15288, Section 6.4.2.3 a); ISO/IEC 15026.

Related Publications: ISO/IEC 12207, Section 6.4.1.3.1; ISO/IEC 21827; ISO/IEC 27001; ISO/IEC 27002; FIPS Publication 199; FIPS Publication 200; NIST SP 800-37; NIST SP 800-53.

SN-2   DEFINE STAKEHOLDER PROTECTION NEEDS

> **SN-2.1**   Define the security context of use across all preliminary life cycle concepts.

Elaboration: A context-of-use description provides a security perspective or security view of an existing, intended, implemented, or deployed system. The description includes security-relevant information about the users and other stakeholder groups, the characteristics of each group, the goals of the users, the tasks of the users, and the environment in which the system is used. The context-of-use description also provides a collection of data for the analysis, specification, design, and evaluation of a system from the security perspective of the various user groups and other stakeholders.

SN-2.2 Identify stakeholder assets and asset classes.

Elaboration: Assets include all tangible and intangible assets. The assets and asset classes are identified in consideration of all stakeholders and all contexts in which assets are used by the system-of-interest. This includes the business or mission; the enabling systems of the system-of-interest; the other systems that interact with the system-of-interest; and stakeholders whose assets are utilized by the business or mission and/or by the system-of-interest.

Tangible assets are physical in nature and include the physical elements of the environment of operation (e.g., structures, facilities, utility infrastructures) and hardware elements of components, mechanisms, systems, networks, and telecommunications infrastructure. Intangible assets, in contrast, are not physical in nature and include business or mission processes, functions, data, information, firmware, software, personnel, and services. Data and information assets include data and information required to execute business or mission functions, deliver services, and for system management and operation; sensitive data and information (e.g., classified information, controlled unclassified information, proprietary data, trade secrets, privacy information, critical program information, and intellectual property); and all forms of documentation associated with the system. Intangible assets also include the image and reputation of an organization.

SN-2.3 Prioritize assets based on the adverse consequence of asset loss.

Elaboration: The meaning of loss has to be defined for each asset to enable a determination of loss consequence. Loss consequences constitute a continuum that spans partial to total loss relative to the asset. The consequence of losing an asset is determined relative to the specific concerns of stakeholders. For example, interpretations of the loss of data or information may include loss of possession, destruction, or loss of precision or accuracy. The loss of a function or service may be interpreted as a loss of accessibility, loss of control, loss of the ability to deliver normal function, performance, or behavior, or a limited loss of ability resulting in a level of degradation of function, performance, or behavior. The prioritization of assets is based on the stakeholder assessment of acceptance of the adverse consequence of loss. This may be reflected in terms of asset value, criticality, importance, cost of replacement, impact on image or reputation, or trust by users or business/mission partners or collaborating organizations. The priority translates to precedence in allocating resources, determining strength of mechanisms, and defining levels of assurance.

SN-2.4 Determine asset susceptibility to adversity and uncertainty.

Elaboration: Adversity includes all forms of potential disruptions, threats, and hazards across all technology/machine, human, physical, and environment forms. Adversity consists of the events and preexisting or emergent conditions that combine to produce the loss of assets and associated adverse consequences to stakeholders. Adversity comes in malicious and non-malicious forms and can emanate from a variety of sources across a broad spectrum including, for example, simple or sophisticated attacks (cyber, electronic, physical, social); human error (commission or omission); abuse and misuse; accidents and incidents; component fault and failure; and natural or man-made disasters.

The identification and assessment of adversity characterizes the events and conditions that are anticipated throughout the life cycle of the system and correlates them to the asset loss concerns of stakeholders. The correlation of asset susceptibility to adversity with loss consequence takes into account what is known, what is possible, what is likely, and what is uncertain. Uncertainty about the manner in which a particular asset loss consequence might occur is not grounds to dismiss such a consequence. Uncertainty as it relates to adversity, is addressed by considerations of those situations where there are known consequences that can be forecast and deemed unacceptable and for which there is an absence of specific credible knowledge of an adverse event-to-consequence relationship, or for which there is insufficient basis to forecast such a relationship. There are also limits on what specific knowledge is obtainable and consequently, adverse consequences can occur for reasons unknown until the event manifests itself. Nonetheless, the adverse impact can be minimized and the uncertainty-to-consequence relationship addressed as part of the determination of susceptibility to threats. The *System Analysis* process supports this activity by providing information used in identifying and correlating adversity to consequence.

SN-2.5   Identify stakeholder protection needs.

Elaboration: Stakeholder protection needs are identified in terms of the loss consequences realized by stakeholder relative to assets and the events that produce the loss consequences. Protection needs should be identified in a manner consistent with how stakeholders manage the assets. The protection needs are identified in dimensions that are consistent with the loss concerns (e.g., loss of control, loss of ownership, loss as in destruction) so as to account for varying needs across varying concerns. The *Business and Mission Analysis* process is leveraged by this activity to help ensure consistency in statement and interpretation of factors that impact the identification of protection needs.

SN-2.6   Prioritize and down-select the stakeholder protection needs.

Elaboration: Stakeholders must decide on the prioritization of protection needs and on the down-select of assets that warrant protection. These stakeholder decisions are informed by the results of security-focused analyses. The *System Analysis* and *Decision Management* processes are used to support the analysis of the competing protection needs and the decisions required to prioritize those needs and make the final selection.

SN-2.7   Define the stakeholder protection needs and rationale.

Elaboration: Stakeholder protection needs are an informal expression of the protection capability required in the system. The protection needs include the security characteristics of the system and the security behavior of the system in its intended operational environment and across all life cycle stages and life cycle concepts. The protection needs reflect the relative priorities of stakeholders, the results of negotiations among stakeholders in response to conflicts, contradictions, opposing priorities, and objectives, and therefore are inherently subjective. The protection needs and rationale are captured to ensure the reasoning, assumptions, and constraints associated with those needs are available should the basis of the decisions or the objectives that drive the definition of the protection needs, change.

References: ISO/IEC/IEEE 15288, Section 6.4.2.3 b); ISO/IEC 15026; ISO/IEC 25010; ISO TS 18152; ISO/IEC 25063.

Related Publications: ISO/IEC 21827; ISO/IEC 27001; ISO/IEC 27002; FIPS Publication 199; FIPS Publication 200; NIST SP 800-37; NIST SP 800-53.

SN-3   DEVELOP THE SECURITY ASPECTS OF OPERATIONAL AND OTHER LIFE CYCLE CONCEPTS

SN-3.1   Define a representative set of scenarios to identify all required protection capabilities and security measures that correspond to anticipated operational and other life cycle concepts.

Elaboration: Scenarios are used to analyze the operation of the system in its security context of use. The scenarios are developed to reflect how the system behaves in the intended environment of operation to determine if additional protection needs or requirements that have not been explicitly identified or addressed are necessary. The scenarios bring together the real-world human-machine-environment behavior and interactions to include the behavior driven or influenced by regulatory and other mandated expectations. The scenarios facilitate the identification of protection gaps or deficiencies. Such gaps and deficiencies in protection capability can result in the definition of additional or modified protection needs or security requirements. Scenarios can also help to identify security-driven changes to life cycle concepts.

SN-3.2   Identify the security-relevant interaction between users and the system.

Elaboration: The security-relevant interactions between users (human element) and system (machine element) informs protection needs and security requirements for all life cycle concepts and across all normal, abnormal, or otherwise defined system modes and states.

References: ISO/IEC/IEEE 15288, Section 6.4.2.3 c); ISO/IEC 15026; ISO 9241; ISO TS 18152; ISO/IEC 25060; ISO/IEC/IEEE 29148.

Related Publications: ISO/IEC 21827; ISO/IEC 27001; ISO/IEC 27002; FIPS Publication 199; FIPS Publication 200; NIST SP 800-37; NIST SP 800-53.

SN-4   TRANSFORM STAKEHOLDER PROTECTION NEEDS INTO SECURITY REQUIREMENTS

SN-4.1   Identify the security-oriented constraints on a system solution.

Elaboration: The realization of prioritized protection needs may result in security constraints being levied on the system solution. These constraints include both security-driven constraints, whereby the constraints are derived directly from the protection capability, and security-informed constraints which serve to reduce vulnerabilities in the system. Additionally, the level of assurance associated with an identified protection need may impose constraints that must be adhered to and thereby constrain the trade space for relevant aspects of the system solution.

SN-4.2   Identify the stakeholder security requirements and security functions.

Elaboration: The stakeholder security requirements and security functions are the formal expression of the critical quality characteristics of the system for security and assurance.

SN-4.3   Define stakeholder security requirements, consistent with life cycle concepts, scenarios, interactions, constraints, and critical quality characteristics.

Elaboration: Stakeholder security requirements constitute the formal expression of stakeholder protection needs across all system life cycle stages, inclusive of enabling systems, services, and interacting systems, all associated system life cycle processes, and all protections for assets associated with the system.

SN-4.4   Apply security metadata tagging to identify stakeholder security requirements and security-driven constraints.

Elaboration: Security metadata tagging is employed to identify stakeholder security requirements and stakeholder requirements that contain security constraints. Metadata tagging provides an accurate security view of all stakeholder requirements and supports preservation of the security view of the stakeholder requirements as variances occur. Metadata tagging also supports analysis of consistency and completeness across interrelated viewpoints and views of the system.

References: ISO/IEC/IEEE 15288, Section 6.4.2.3 d); ISO/IEC 15026; ISO/IEC 25030.

Related Publications: ISO/IEC 12207, Section 6.4.1.3.2; ISO/IEC 21827; ISO/IEC 27001; ISO/IEC 27002; FIPS Publication 200; NIST SP 800-37; NIST SP 800-53; ISO/IEC 15408; ISO/IEC 27034-1, (SDL) Section A.9.2.

SN-5   ANALYZE STAKEHOLDER SECURITY REQUIREMENTS

SN-5.1   Analyze the complete set of stakeholder security requirements.

Elaboration: Stakeholder security requirements are analyzed for completeness, consistency, and clarity. Identified issues are resolved with the appropriate stakeholders to ensure consistency and compatibility among all requirements. Stakeholders must weigh their intent to achieve a specific operational capability against the cost of the security measures required to protect all assets that are associated with that operational capability. Cost concerns include: financial; human/material resource availability and suitability; schedule; development, operations, sustainment, and training; and assurance and practicality. Stakeholders may decide to remove requirements in response to issues identified. Such change in requirements must be assessed for impact to related requirements and to overall objectives. Any change to stakeholder requirements signifies the need to reassess protection needs and determine if any subsequent changes are required to the stakeholder security requirements.

SN-5.2 Define critical security-relevant performance and assurance measures that enable the assessment of technical achievement.

Elaboration: Each stakeholder security requirement must be satisfied within specified operational performance measures. Each stakeholder security requirement must have validation and assurance measures defined.

SN-5.3 Validate that stakeholder protection needs and expectations have been adequately captured and expressed by the analyzed security requirements.

Elaboration: Stakeholders must provide consensus agreement that they understand and are satisfied that the security requirements derived from the stakeholder protection needs are an accurate and complete representation of their protection needs, expectations, and concerns.

SN-5.4 Resolve stakeholder security requirements issues.

Elaboration: Identified issues are resolved to ensure that all impacted stakeholders are in agreement that their individual and collective protection needs, expectations, and concerns are addressed. Any changes to the stakeholder security requirements are subjected to analyses to ensure that the entire set of security requirements is internally consistent and also consistent with stakeholder requirements.

References: ISO/IEC/IEEE 15288, Section 6.4.2.3 e); ISO/IEC 15026; ISO/IEC 15939; ISO/IEC/IEEE 29148; INCOSE TP-2003-020-01.

Related Publications: ISO/IEC 12207, Section 6.4.1.3.3; ISO/IEC 21827; ISO/IEC 27001; ISO/IEC 27002; FIPS Publication 200; NIST SP 800-37; NIST SP 800-53.

SN-6 MANAGE STAKEHOLDER PROTECTION NEEDS AND SECURITY REQUIREMENTS DEFINITION

SN-6.1 Obtain explicit agreement on the stakeholder security requirements.

Elaboration: Concurrence on the security requirements is obtained from stakeholders with a security interest in the system. Issues of nonconcurrence are resolved through the established decision-making processes based on the type of the nonconcurrence and can include, for example, cost, schedule, performance, effectiveness, and capability.

SN-6.2 Record asset protection data.

Elaboration: All data associated with the identification of stakeholder protection needs is recorded along with engineering data produced by requirements elicitation and analysis activities for the system. For each asset, data collected should reflect the role of the asset, the consequence of loss of the asset, the importance of the asset (e.g., criticality, sensitivity, or value), the exposure of the asset, the protections required for the asset, and the priority of the asset. Asset protection data also provides an asset protection management view that is useful to inform life cycle protection concepts captured in policies and procedures.

SN-6.3 Maintain traceability between stakeholder protection needs and stakeholder security requirements.

Elaboration: Traceability is maintained between the stakeholder requirements, the stakeholder protection needs, the stakeholders, and the supporting information used in the analyses and development of stakeholder security requirements.

SN-6.4 Provide security-relevant information items required for stakeholder needs and requirements definition to baselines.

Elaboration: Security aspects are captured in various artifacts that are maintained in an identified baseline for the life cycle of the system. The security-relevant configuration items from this process are identified and incorporated into engineering baselines so that they may be produced and made available as required throughout the system life cycle. The *Configuration Management* process manages the baseline and the artifacts identified by this process. The *Information Management* process determines the appropriate forms of information and protections for the information that is provided to stakeholders.

References: ISO/IEC/IEEE 15288, Section 6.4.2.3 f).

Related Publications: ISO/IEC 12207, Section 6.4.1.3.4, Section 6.4.1.3.5; ISO/IEC 21827; NIST SP 800-37.

3.4.3 System Requirements Definition Process

Purpose

"The purpose of the System Requirements Definition process is to transform the stakeholder, user-oriented view of desired capabilities into a technical view of a solution that meets the operational needs of the user."

ISO/IEC/IEEE 15288-2015. Reprinted with permission from IEEE, Copyright IEEE 2015, All rights reserved.

Systems Security Engineering Purpose

Systems security engineering, as part of the *System Requirements Definition* process, transforms the stakeholder security requirements into the system requirements that reflect a technical security view of the system. This security view of the system relates to the security protection capability, security-driven constraints, security criticality of the system, security quality characteristics, level of assurance, and risk. Systems security engineering also refines the security aspects of system life cycle concepts to correspond to the selected solution. In addition, it ensures that the security aspects of verification activities are clearly specified in order to obtain the required evidence with the appropriate fidelity and rigor to substantiate assurance claims and to enable a determination of trustworthiness. The system security requirements, security-driven constraints captured in system requirements, and the security aspects of life cycle concepts provide the basis for architecture and design definition, implementation and integration, and all in-process verification activities. The definition of system requirements from a technical security view is conducted in synchronization with the *Architecture Definition* and *Design Definition* processes.

Systems Security Engineering Outcomes

- The system security description, including the security aspects of system interfaces, functions, and boundaries for a system solution is defined.

- System security requirements and security-driven design constraints are defined.

- Security performance measures are defined.

- System security requirements and associated security-driven constraints are analyzed.

- Any enabling systems or services needed for the security aspects of system requirements definition are available.

- Traceability of system security requirements and associated constraints to stakeholder security requirements is established.

Security Engineering Activities and Tasks

SR-1   PREPARE FOR SYSTEM SECURITY REQUIREMENTS DEFINITION

      SR-1.1   Define the security aspects of the functional boundary of the system in terms of the security behavior and security properties to be provided.

      Elaboration: The system functional boundary provides the basis for the security perspective relative to all interactions and behavior with enabling systems, other systems, and the physical environment. The security behavior and security properties to be realized at the functional boundary consider the characteristics of the capability provided or utilized, the characteristics of the entity that interacts with the system-of-interest at the function boundary, and the level of assurance associated with the capability. The security aspects of the functional boundary may be physical or virtual.

SR-1.2 Define the security domains of the system and their correlation to the functional boundaries of the system.

Elaboration: The term *domain* in the context of security has a broad meaning. Security domains may reflect one or any combination of the following: capability, functional, or service distinctions; data flow and control flow associated with capability, functional, or service distinctions; data and information sensitivity; data and information security; or administrative, management, operational, or jurisdictional authority. Security domains that are defined in the context of one or more of the above items, reflect a protection-focused partitioning of the system that translates to relationships driven by trust concerns.

SR-1.3 Define the security aspects of the system requirements definition strategy.

Elaboration: The security aspects of the system requirements definition strategy include considerations of specific methods or approaches to be used and considerations driven by the varying levels of assurance associated with development of system requirements.

SR-1.4 Identify, plan for, and obtain access to enabling systems or services to support the security aspects of the system requirements definition process.

Elaboration: Specific enabling systems and services may be required to support the security aspects of the system requirements definition process. These enabling systems and services are relied upon to provide the capability to realize and support the system-of-interest, and therefore impact the trustworthiness of the system. The system requirements definition-oriented security concerns for enabling systems and services used to support the system requirements definition process must be determined and captured as security requirements and as security-driven constraints for the interfaces and interactions with the system-of-interest. The *Validation* process is used to confirm that enabling systems and services achieve their intended use and do so with an appropriate level of trustworthiness.

References: ISO/IEC/IEEE 15288, Section 6.4.3.3 a); ISO/IEC 15026.

Related Publications: ISO/IEC 21827; ISO/IEC 27001; ISO/IEC 27002; FIPS Publication 199; FIPS Publication 200; NIST SP 800-37; NIST SP 800-53.

SR-2 DEFINE SYSTEM SECURITY REQUIREMENTS

SR-2.1 Define each security function that the system is required to perform.

Elaboration: Security functions are defined for all system states, modes, and conditions of system operation and use, to include the associated transitions between system states and modes. Security functions include those oriented to delivery of capability and the ability of the system to execute with preservation of its inherent security characteristics.

SR-2.2 Define system security requirements, security constraints on system requirements, and rationale.

Elaboration: The system security requirements express security functions provided by the system and security-driven constraints levied on the entire system. System security applies to the entire system (to include the security functions) in terms of susceptibility to disruption, hazard, and threat resulting in adverse consequences. The proper realization of the protection provided by the security functions of the system depend on adherence to security-driven constraints in all aspects of system architecture, design, and implementation. Security-driven constraints on the system are driven by disruption, hazards, threats, uncertainty, and risk, taking into account performance objectives and level of assurance. These constraints are informed by stakeholder requirements, architecture definition, and solution limitations across the life cycle.

Rationale for system security requirements and associated constraints is developed to support the analysis and inclusion of security concerns as part of the system requirements. System security requirements include security capability and functional requirements, security performance and effectiveness requirements, and security assurance requirements. The definition of system security requirements and security constraints on the system requirements interacts with the *Architecture Definition, Design Definition*, and *Implementation* processes. The *System Analysis* process provides data to inform trade decisions for the effective definition of security-driven constraints.

SR-2.3   Incorporate system security requirements and associated constraints into system requirements and define rationale.

Elaboration: The system security requirements are integrated into the system requirements so as to complement the specified capability, performance, and effectiveness of the system. Security-driven constraints inform performance and effectiveness aspects of the system requirements. The rationale for the security requirements and security-driven constraints is incorporated into the rationale for system requirements.

SR-2.4   Apply security metadata tagging to identify system security requirements and security-driven constraints.

Elaboration: Security metadata tagging is employed to identify system security requirements and system requirements that contain security constraints. Metadata tagging provides an accurate security view of all system requirements and supports preservation of the security view of the system as variances occur. Metadata tagging also supports the analysis of consistency and completeness across interrelated viewpoints and views of the system.

References: ISO/IEC/IEEE 15288, Section 6.4.3.3 b); ISO/IEC 15026; ISO/IEC 27036; ISO/IEC/IEEE 29148; ISO 25030.

Related Publications: ISO/IEC 12207, Section 6.4.2.3.1; ISO/IEC 15408; ISO/IEC 27034-1, (SDL) Section A.9.2; ISO/IEC 21827; ISO/IEC 27001; ISO/IEC 27002; FIPS Publication 200; NIST SP 800-37; NIST SP 800-53.

SR-3   ANALYZE SYSTEM SECURITY IN SYSTEM REQUIREMENTS

SR-3.1   Analyze the complete set of system requirements in consideration of security concerns.

Elaboration: System requirements are analyzed to ensure that individual requirements and any combination of requirements fully and properly capture security protection and security-constraint considerations. Rationale is captured to support analysis conclusions and provides a basis to conclude that the analysis has the proper perspective and is fully aware of assumptions made.

SR-3.2   Define security-driven performance and assurance measures that enable the assessment of technical achievement.

Elaboration: The assessment of system security may dictate specific types of performance and assurance measures conducted with a fidelity and rigor that correspond to desired assurance and trustworthiness objectives. The selection of performance and assurance measures can translate to cost, schedule, and performance risk, making it imperative that the proper measures are identified, defined, and used.

SR-3.3   Provide the analyzed system security requirements and security-driven constraints to applicable stakeholders for review.

Elaboration: This review includes explaining to stakeholders the definition and context for the security of the system and life cycle security concepts, how the system security requirements and associated constraints are necessary to meet the stakeholder security requirements and security concerns, and the risks associated with the security technical view of the system. A particularly important stakeholder class is the regulatory, certification, accreditation, and authorization stakeholders. These stakeholders are engaged to ensure that the security aspects captured in the system requirements are consistent with the objectives and criteria that inform their decision-making authority.

SR-3.4   Resolve system security requirements and security-driven constraints issues.

Elaboration: System security requirements and security-driven constraints issues mirror those of all system requirements. Additional security issues include level of assurance and trustworthiness objectives that are captured in the requirements. Additionally, any resolution to identified issues must ensure that assurance and trustworthiness objectives are not violated by the resolution actions taken.

References: ISO/IEC/IEEE 15288, Section 6.4.3.3 c); ISO/IEC 15026; ISO/IEC 15939; ISO/IEC/IEEE 29148; INCOSE TP-2003-020-01.

Related Publications: ISO/IEC 12207, Section 6.4.2.3.2; ISO/IEC 21827; ISO/IEC 27001; ISO/IEC 27002; FIPS Publication 200; NIST SP 800-37; NIST SP 800-53.

SR-4   MANAGE SYSTEM SECURITY REQUIREMENTS

SR-4.1   Obtain explicit agreement on the system security requirements and security-driven constraints.

Elaboration: Stakeholder concurrence with the system security requirements ensures a common basis for understanding the security aspects of the technical view of the solution. The *Validation* process is used to validate of security aspects of the solution.

SR-4.2   Maintain traceability of system security requirements and security-driven constraints.

Elaboration: Traceability of system security requirements and security-driven constraints is maintained to protection needs, stakeholder security requirements, architecture elements, interface definitions, analysis results, verification methods, and all allocated, decomposed, and *derived requirements* (in their system, system element, security protection, and security-driven constraint forms), risk and loss tolerance, and assurance and trustworthiness objectives. Security-driven metadata tagging can be employed to system requirements to identify those requirements that have security relevance. Security-driven metadata tagging of system requirements enables security views and viewpoints to be associated with all other views and viewpoints of the system requirements. Such security-driven metadata tagging also supports traceability and determining the security impacts that are driven by variances throughout the system life cycle.

SR-4.3   Provide security-relevant information items required for systems requirements definition to baselines.

Elaboration: Security aspects are captured in various artifacts that are maintained in an identified baseline for the life cycle of the system. The security-relevant configuration items from this process are identified and incorporated into engineering baselines so that they may be produced and made available as required throughout the system life cycle. The *Configuration Management* process manages the baseline and the artifacts identified by this process. The *Information Management* process determines the appropriate forms of information and protections for the information that is provided to stakeholders.

References: ISO/IEC/IEEE 15288, Section 6.4.3.3 d); ISO/IEC 15026.

Related Publications: ISO/IEC 21827; NIST SP 800-37.

3.4.4 Architecture Definition Process

Purpose

"The purpose of the Architecture Definition process is to generate system architecture alternatives, to select one or more alternative(s) that frame stakeholder concerns and meet system requirements, and to express this in a set of consistent views."

ISO/IEC/IEEE 15288-2015. Reprinted with permission from IEEE, Copyright IEEE 2015, All rights reserved.

Systems Security Engineering Purpose

Systems security engineering, as part of the *Architecture Definition* process, generates a set of representative security views of the system architecture alternatives to inform the selection of one or more alternatives. It also ascertains vulnerability and susceptibility to disruptions, hazards, and threats across all representative *architecture views*. System security architecture analyses inform risk assessments, risk treatment, and engineering decision making and trades. This process is synchronized with the *System Requirements Definition* and *Design Definition* processes. Further, this process iterates with the *Business and Mission Analysis* and *System Requirements Definition* processes to achieve a negotiated understanding of the particular security concerns and associated characteristics of the problem to be solved and the proposed solution to the problem. In particular, the security concerns associated with emergent system security properties and behavior begin to form as a result of system architecture definition. This process also employs the *System Analysis* process to conduct security analyses of the system and security architecture alternatives.

Systems Security Engineering Outcomes

- Stakeholder security concerns are addressed by the system architecture.

- The concept of secure function for the system at the architecture level is defined.

- Security viewpoints, views, and models of the system architecture are developed.

- Security context, domains, boundaries, and external interfaces of the system are defined.

- Security concepts, properties, characteristics, functions, behavior, or constraints are allocated to architectural elements.

- Security-relevant system elements and their interfaces are identified.

- The security aspects of candidate system architectures are analyzed and assessed.

- Alignment of the architecture with the system security requirements and security design characteristics is achieved.

- Any enabling systems or services needed for the security aspects of architecture definition are available.

- Traceability of architecture elements to stakeholder and system security requirements is established.

- Candidate security-related architecture metrics are identified.

Systems Security Engineering Activities and Tasks

AR-1   PREPARE FOR ARCHITECTURE DEFINITION FROM THE SECURITY VIEWPOINT

AR-1.1   Identify the key drivers that impact the security aspects of the system architecture.

Elaboration: Key drivers and security concerns include, for example: stakeholder protection needs, objectives, and concerns; life cycle security concepts; regulatory, legislative, and policy constraints; the types and nature of disruptions, hazards, and threats; system design requirements; cost and schedule; operational and technical performance objectives; system requirements and security requirements; risk and loss tolerance; level of assurance and trustworthiness, and any other security-related factors that can affect the suitability, viability, or acceptability of the system. The requirements elicitation and analysis techniques used in the *Business and Mission Analysis* and *Stakeholder Needs and Requirements Definition* processes identify and capture the data and information required by this task.

AR-1.2   Identify stakeholder security concerns.

Elaboration: Stakeholder architecture-related concerns represent the expectations and constraints associated with specific life cycle stages and concepts such as usability, availability, evolvability, scalability, agility, resilience, survivability, and security. In addition to the stakeholders identified during the *Business and Mission Analysis* and the *Stakeholder Needs and Requirements Definition* processes, additional stakeholders are identified to fully capture the security concerns related to architecture.

AR-1.3   Define the security aspects of the architecture definition roadmap, approach, and strategy.

Elaboration: The security aspects of the architecture definition roadmap, approach, and strategy can constrain or exclude specific methods or approaches that might otherwise be suitable for use. In particular, the *concept of secure function*, associated implementation technologies, and assurance and trustworthiness objectives may require specific types of reviews, evaluation approaches and criteria, and measurement methods.

AR-1.4   Define evaluation criteria based on stakeholder security concerns and security-relevant requirements.

Elaboration: Security-relevant requirements are the system security requirements and the system requirements with metadata tagging that indicate they contain a security constraint. The evaluation criteria are intended to produce the evidentiary data necessary to convince stakeholders that their security concerns are sufficiently addressed and demonstrate that security requirements have been satisfied.

AR-1.5   Identify, plan for, and obtain access to enabling systems or services to support the security aspects of the architecture definition process.

Elaboration: Specific enabling systems and services may be required to support the security aspects of the architecture definition process. These enabling systems and services are relied upon to provide the capability to realize and support the system-of-interest, and therefore impact the trustworthiness of the system. The architecture definition-oriented security concerns for enabling systems and services used to support the architecture definition process must be determined and captured as security requirements and as security-driven constraints for the interfaces and interactions with the system-of-interest. The *Validation* process is used to confirm that enabling systems and services achieve their intended use and do so with an appropriate level of trustworthiness.

References: ISO/IEC/IEEE 15288, Section 6.4.4.3 a); ISO/IEC 15026; ISO/IEC/IEEE 42010.

Related Publications: ISO/IEC 21827; ISO/IEC 27001; ISO/IEC 27002; FIPS Publication 200; NIST SP 800-37; NIST SP 800-53.

AR-2   DEVELOP SECURITY VIEWPOINTS OF THE ARCHITECTURE

AR-2.1   Define the concept of secure function for the system at the architecture level.

Elaboration: The concept of secure function is a strategy for system security and is an aspect captured in or that drives the aspects of a security viewpoint. The strategy must be comprehensive relative to all identified stakeholder security concerns. The concept of secure function provides a conceptual model of how the system is structured and behaves in order to deliver the specified protection capability and achieve the intended emergent security behavior. The concept of secure function encompasses the protection strategies, methods, and techniques employed in the application of security design principles and concepts to the system architecture. These security design principles and concepts include, but are not limited to: separation; isolation; encapsulation; non-bypassability; layering; modularity; hierarchical trust; hierarchical protection; and secure distributed composition. The principles and concepts must be properly applied with respect to their inherent capabilities and limitations relative to architectural security concerns. Appendix F provides a discussion of the fundamental security design and trust principles.

AR-2.2   Select, adapt, or develop the security viewpoints and model kinds based on stakeholder security concerns.

Elaboration: Architectural viewpoints facilitate a more complete understanding of complex systems and organize the elements of the problem and solution space so as to better capture and address separate stakeholder concerns. A security viewpoint addresses security concerns and requirements so as to describe the security protection capability within the system architecture and the security constraints that drive all aspects of the system architecture. In particular, a security viewpoint identifies and prescribes the security principles, concepts, model types, correspondence rules, methods, and analysis techniques that are provided by the security view. A security view is specified by one or more security viewpoints. A security viewpoint may be driven by desired levels of assurance.

AR-2.3   Identify the security architecture frameworks to be used in developing the security models and security views of the system architecture.

Elaboration: Security architecture frameworks are oriented to addressing security concerns, the security viewpoints that frame the security concerns, and any correspondence rules associated with elements in the architecture description (e.g., stakeholders, security concerns, security viewpoints, security views, security models, and security-related decisions and rationale).

AR-2.4   Record the rationale for the selection of architecture frameworks that address security concerns, security viewpoints, and security model types.

Elaboration: The rationale serves to frame the subjective aspects of analyses and decisions conducted relative to the viewpoints. These include viewpoint-driven security analyses and decisions about architecture capability, suitability, and effectiveness relative to operational and technical performance objectives in consideration of disruption, hazard, threat, and level of assurance.

AR-2.5   Select or develop supporting security modeling techniques and tools.

Elaboration: None.

References: ISO/IEC/IEEE 15288, Section 6.4.4.3 b); ISO/IEC 15026; ISO/IEC/IEEE 42010.

Related Publications: ISO/IEC 21827; ISO/IEC 27001; ISO/IEC 27002; FIPS Publication 200; NIST SP 800-37; NIST SP 800-53.

AR-3 DEVELOP SECURITY MODELS AND SECURITY VIEWS OF CANDIDATE ARCHITECTURES

AR-3.1 Define the security context and boundaries of the system in terms of interfaces, interconnections, and interactions with external entities.

Elaboration: The security context includes security domains, protection domains, trust domains, and the security-driven constraints associated with system boundaries, interfaces, interconnections, and interactions with external entities. The security context and boundaries may align to the physical and/or logical boundaries of the system. This means that the security perspective may produce interpretations of system boundaries that are defined in addition to those defined from a non-security perspective. The interaction across interconnections between the system-of-interest and external entities includes data, control, and information flow that cross security, protection, or trust domains.

AR-3.2 Identify architectural entities and relationships between entities that address key stakeholder security concerns and system security requirements.

Elaboration: Architectural entities can be physical, logical, or conceptual. These entities, either singularly or in combination, provide specified security functions that address stakeholder security concerns and system security requirements.

AR-3.3 Allocate security concepts, properties, characteristics, behavior, functions, or constraints to architectural entities.

Elaboration: The allocation of security concepts, properties, characteristics, behavior, functions, or constraints is to be consistent with decisions of whether technical, physical, or procedural measures, alone or in combination, are most appropriate to satisfy stakeholder security concerns, system security requirements, and level of assurance, to include consideration of any security, protection, and trust domains. The allocation takes into account the decision of whether acquiring an off-the-shelf product, accessing/subscribing/leasing a service, developing custom software, or fabricating hardware is most appropriate; and whether the decision to select a particular product or service is best made by the *Architectural Definition* process or by the *Design Definition* process.

AR-3.4 Select, adapt, or develop security models of the candidate architectures.

Elaboration: Security models include physical, logical, or information models. Security models should be selected that are best able to address the security concerns of stakeholders.

AR-3.5 Compose views in accordance with security viewpoints to express how the architecture addresses stakeholder security concerns and meets stakeholder and system security requirements.

Elaboration: The composed views include those that express the architecture in terms of security protection capability and those that express the architecture in terms of security-driven constraints and concerns on the architecture.

AR-3.6 Harmonize the security models and security views with each other and with the concept of secure function.

Elaboration: Harmonization serves to identify any gaps, inconsistencies, and conflicts that if unresolved, present possible security vulnerabilities in the architecture, or that constitute an inaccurate representation of the concept of secure function. Architecture vulnerabilities may also propagate to vulnerabilities in the system design.

References: ISO/IEC/IEEE 15288, Section 6.4.4.3 c); ISO/IEC 15026; ISO/IEC/IEEE 42010.

Related Publications: ISO/IEC 12207, Section 6.4.3.3.1, Section 7.1.3.3.1; ISO/IEC 21827; FIPS Publication 200; NIST SP 800-37; NIST SP 800-53.

AR-4   RELATE SECURITY VIEWS OF THE ARCHITECTURE TO DESIGN

AR-4.1   Identify the security-relevant system elements that relate to architectural entities and the nature of these relationships.

Elaboration: The security-relevant elements of the system either directly provide or support the provision of security functions. Security-relevant elements can include, for example: systems, subsystems, assemblies, infrastructures, components, or devices. The nature of the relationship between each security-relevant system element and architectural entity provides insight into the manner in which architectural decisions reflect the concept of secure function, and serve as security-driven constraints on design.

AR-4.2   Define the security interfaces, interconnections, and interactions between the system elements and with external entities.

Elaboration: The concepts used to define the security context and boundaries of the system in terms of interfaces, interconnections, and interactions with external entities, are also employed in this task. The specific focus is on system elements and how those elements interact and behave to provide protection capability, to include security considerations on system elements relative to their role in support of interaction with external entities (i.e., entities of other systems and enabling systems). Consideration is given to system internal security contexts, as in security domains, protection domains, trust domains, and security-driven constraints associated with the internal boundaries, interfaces, interconnections, and interactions. The security context and boundaries may align to the physical and/or logical boundaries of the system. This means that the security perspective may produce interpretations of internal boundaries that are defined in addition to those defined from a non-security perspective. The interaction across the internal interconnections includes data, control, and information flow that cross security, protection, or trust domains.

AR-4.3   Allocate system security requirements to architectural entities and system elements.

Elaboration: The allocation of system security requirements determines the specific security-relevant responsibility assigned to each system element. This assignment takes into account the concept of secure function and the partitioning and grouping of functions within the architecture in the form of subsystems and assemblies, in order to optimize across performance objectives and associated life cycle and assurance considerations.

AR-4.4   Map security-relevant system elements and architectural entities to security design characteristics.

Elaboration: Architecture decisions define and frame the security design characteristics and the security-driven constraints for design. The mapping captures security-driven characteristics and constraints and may be reflected in design patterns, reference designs, and/or models. Design characteristics can include, for example: security-driven thresholds and limitations; strength of function; technology-specific application of foundational security design principles and concepts; and levels of assurance. Security design principles and concepts are described in Appendix F. Mapping activities may identify new, derived, or decomposed requirements. Each requirement must be addressed in terms of security functions and constraints. The identification of new, derived, and decomposed requirements requires a revisit of stakeholder needs and concerns, stakeholder and system requirements, architecture viewpoints and views, and design decisions to ascertain the security impact, its extent, and resolution. This requires that the *Business or Mission Analysis, Stakeholder Requirements Definition, Requirements Analysis,* and *Design Definition* processes be performed in conjunction with the decisions made during this process.

AR-4.5   Define the security design principles for the system design and evolution that reflect the concept of secure function.

Elaboration: The concept of secure function at the architectural level is interpreted and applied to define the principles for security design and secure evolution of the design. A description of those security design principles and concepts is provided in Appendix F.

References: ISO/IEC/IEEE 15288, Section 6.4.4.3 d); ISO/IEC 15026; ISO/IEC/IEEE 42010.

Related Publications: ISO/IEC 27034-1, (SDL) Section A.9.3; ISO/IEC 15408; ISO/IEC 21827; ISO/IEC 27001; ISO/IEC 27002; FIPS Publication 200; NIST SP 800-37; NIST SP 800-53.

AR-5   SELECT CANDIDATE ARCHITECTURE

AR-5.1 Assess each candidate architecture against the security requirements and security-related constraints.

Elaboration: This assessment is oriented to determining technical suitability of the candidate architecture in terms of its coverage relative to the system security requirements and associated security-related constraints. The assessment is conducted using the established evaluation criteria. The assessment process is supported by the *System Analysis* and *Risk Management* processes.

AR-5.2 Assess each candidate architecture against stakeholder security concerns using evaluation criteria.

Elaboration: This assessment is oriented to determining the effectiveness and suitability of the candidate architecture in terms of how well it addresses the stakeholder security concerns. The assessment is based on evaluation criteria that is agreed to with stakeholders. The assessment is supported by the *System Analysis* and *Risk Management* processes.

AR-5.3 Select the preferred architecture(s) and capture key security decisions and rationale for those decisions.

Elaboration: The selection of preferred architecture(s) may be informed by security-related assumptions or decisions. The rationale for the architecture selection should capture the basis for any security assumptions and decisions. The selection of the preferred architecture is supported by the *Decision Management* process.

AR-5.4 Establish the security aspects of the architecture baseline of the selected architecture.

Elaboration: The architecture baseline is to include security models, security views, security viewpoints, and other relevant security architectural data/information items that are part of the architecture descriptions. The *Configuration Management* process is used to establish and maintain the architecture baselines.

References: ISO/IEC/IEEE 15288, Section 6.4.4.3 e); ISO/IEC/IEEE 42010.

Related Publications: ISO/IEC 12207, Section 6.4.3.3.2; ISO/IEC 21827; ISO/IEC 27001; ISO/IEC 27002; FIPS Publication 200; NIST SP 800-37; NIST SP 800-53.

AR-6   MANAGE THE SECURITY VIEW OF THE SELECTED ARCHITECTURE

AR-6.1 Formalize the security aspects of the architecture governance approach and specify security governance-related roles and responsibilities, accountabilities, and authorities.

Elaboration: The architecture may be subject to authorities with specific legal, regulatory, or other responsibility and accountability expectations such as certification that either includes security, or for which security is the primary focus of the responsibility and accountability expectations.

AR-6.2 Obtain explicit acceptance of the security aspects of the architecture by stakeholders.

Elaboration: Explicit stakeholder acceptance records the achievement of a common informed understanding of the selected architecture relative to and across all stakeholder expectations, needs, and constraints with respect to security. The *Verification* and *Validation* processes support the generation of evidence needed to obtain such stakeholder acceptance.

AR-6.3 Maintain concordance and completeness of the security architectural entities and their security-related architectural characteristics.

Elaboration: The architecture reflects a cross section of competing, conflicting, and coordinated decisions from the technical, organizational, operational, function, sustainment, evolvability, and other concerns. The security aspects appear throughout but are not always explicitly visible. It is necessary to ensure the concordance and completeness of the architecture, its description, and that the security views and viewpoints are maintained as the architecture matures and evolves.

AR-6.4 Organize, assess, and control the evolution of the security models and security views of the architecture.

Elaboration: The security aspects appear throughout the architecture but are not always explicitly visible. The evolution of the security models and security views is paramount to ensuring that stakeholder security concerns are continuously addressed as the system architecture evolves. This includes ensuring that regulatory and related certification views are accurately maintained to be reflected in and consistent with the system architecture as it evolves.

AR-6.5 Maintain the security aspects of the architecture definition and evaluation strategy.

Elaboration: The security aspects of the architecture definition and the evaluation strategy may change over time. This occurs as the architecture matures and evolves based on changes to the technology and implementation; based on experiences in utilization and support; and in response to new variances in operational needs. Another consideration for maintaining the security aspects is the variances in the level of assurance which drives architecture definition and the evaluation strategy.

AR-6.6 Maintain traceability of the security aspects of the architecture.

Elaboration: The *Architecture Definition* process outlines the broad scope of the architecture description and the data that is obtained to properly capture the security views, viewpoints, and constraints. Traceability across all relationships is necessary to ensure that the architecture is properly informing and informed by the results of all related technical processes, and the *Risk Management* and *Decision Management* processes.

AR-6.7 Provide security-relevant information items required for architecture definition to baselines.

Elaboration: Security aspects are captured in various artifacts that are maintained in an identified baseline for the life cycle of the system. The security-relevant configuration items from this process are identified and incorporated into engineering baselines so that they may be produced and made available as required throughout the system life cycle. The *Configuration Management* process manages the baseline and the artifacts identified by this process. The *Information Management* process determines the appropriate forms of information and protections for the information that is provided to stakeholders.

References: ISO/IEC/IEEE 15288, Section 6.4.4.3 f); ISO/IEC 15026; ISO/IEC/IEEE 42010.

Related Publications: ISO/IEC 21827; NIST SP 800-37.

3.4.5 Design Definition Process

> **Purpose**
>
> "The purpose of the Design Definition process is to provide sufficient detailed data and information about the system and its elements to enable the implementation consistent with architectural entities as defined in models and views of the system architecture."
>
> *ISO/IEC/IEEE 15288-2015. Reprinted with permission from IEEE, Copyright IEEE 2015, All rights reserved.*

Systems Security Engineering Purpose

Systems security engineering, as part of the *Design Definition* process, provides security-related data and information about the system and its elements to enable implementation consistent with security architectural entities and constraints as defined in the models and views of the system architecture.[40] In addition, the data and information constitute constraints on system design so as to eliminate, minimize, or contain design vulnerability and susceptibility to disruption, hazards, and threats. The process is driven by the requirements and concerns that have been thoroughly analyzed and vetted across varying viewpoints during the *Architecture Definition* process. To the extent possible, the system architecture is design-agnostic, allowing for maximum flexibility in the design trade space—recognizing, however, that there are potential architecture-level concerns that dictate constraints to be imposed on the design so as to realize the emergent properties of the system, which includes but is not limited to security. The process also provides security design-related constraints and feedback to the *Architecture Definition* process to confirm the allocation, partitioning, and alignment of architectural entities to system elements that compose the system.

The security design definition provides a level of security detail that is suitable to implement the design. It considers any applicable general and security technologies, and their contribution to the security aspects of the system solution. This process is fully synchronized with the *System Requirements Definition* and *Architecture Definition* processes. In addition, it employs the *System Analysis* process to provide the data required by engineering trades and risk-informed decision making. The *Design Definition* process is also informed by several other processes, including the *Implementation, Integration, Transition, Operation, Maintenance,* and *Disposal* processes.

Systems Security Engineering Outcomes

- Security design characteristics of each system element are defined.
- System security requirements are allocated to system elements.
- Design enablers necessary for the security aspects of design definition are selected or defined.
- Security interfaces and security aspects of interfaces between system elements composing the system are defined or refined.
- Security-driven design alternatives for system elements are assessed.
- Design artifacts that include security considerations and constraints are developed.

---

[40] The use of the term *design* includes all of its forms as related to the system concept, the physical and logical aspects of the system's makeup and composition, and the technologies employed to realize the system design.

- Any enabling systems or services needed for the security aspects of design definition are available.

- Traceability of security design characteristics to the architectural entities of the system architecture is established.

- Candidate security-related design metrics are identified.

Systems Security Engineering Activities and Tasks

DE-1   PREPARE FOR SECURITY DESIGN DEFINITION

> **DE-1.1**   Apply the concept of secure function for the system at the design level.
>
> **Elaboration:** The concept of secure function at the architectural level establishes the context for its natural decomposition to guide the security design of architectural entities. The concept of secure function is refined to reflect how it is applied to the design of the entire system and to each architectural entity. The design-level concept of secure function encompasses security design principles and concepts that include, for example: separation; isolation; encapsulation; least privilege; modularity; non-bypassability; layering; hierarchical trust; hierarchical protection; and secure distributed composition. The principles apply to subsystems, assemblies, components, or other design-oriented constructs. Appendix F provides a complete listing of security design principles and concepts.
>
> **DE-1.2**   Determine the security technologies required for each system element composing the system.
>
> **Elaboration:** Considerations include present and emerging technologies and the ability to satisfy functional, performance, and assurance objectives. Security technologies include, for example: cryptography; secure operating systems, virtual machines, and hypervisors; identity and strong authentication; domain perimeter, domain separation, and cross-domain technologies; security instrumentation and monitoring; physical and electronic tamper protection; and protection against reverse engineering.
>
> **DE-1.3**   Determine the types of security design characteristics.
>
> **Elaboration:** The security technologies employed may have design characteristics and constraints associated with their proper use that apply to all aspects of system design. These characteristics and constraints may be reflected in design patterns, reference designs, or models. The design characteristics and constraints are associated with strength of function; technology-specific application of foundational security design principles and concepts; and target levels of assurance. Security design principles and concepts are described in Appendix F.
>
> **DE-1.4**   Define the principles for secure evolution of the system design.
>
> **Elaboration:** The principles for secure evolution of the system design address changes driven by the natural evolution of the system as planned; by changes in stakeholder objectives and concerns; by technology obsolescence; or by changes in the nature of disruptions, hazards, and threats and the effectiveness of system protection. These types of changes require periodic assessment of the concept of secure function; architecture, viewpoints, and the validity of the prevailing viewpoints; and the assumptions, forecasts, inferences, correspondence, and constraints associated with all of the above.
>
> **DE-1.5**   Define the security aspects of the design definition strategy.
>
> **Elaboration:** The security aspects of the design definition strategy are a design-oriented parallel to the architecture definition strategy. These security aspects can either constrain or exclude specific methods or approaches that might otherwise be suitable for use. The concept of secure function,

associated implementation technologies, and assurance and trustworthiness objectives may require specific types of reviews, evaluation approaches/criteria, and measurement methods. The security aspects of the design definition strategy help eliminate, minimize, or contain design weaknesses, flaws, and errors that may lead to vulnerability.

DE-1.6 Identify, plan for, and obtain access to enabling systems or services to support the security aspects of the design definition process.

Elaboration: Specific enabling systems and services may be required to support the security aspects of the design definition process. These enabling systems and services are relied upon to provide the capability to realize and support the system-of-interest, and therefore impact the trustworthiness of the system. The design definition-oriented security concerns for enabling systems and services used to support the design definition process must be determined and captured as security requirements and as security-driven constraints for the interfaces and interactions with the system-of-interest. The *Validation* process is used to confirm that enabling systems and services achieve their intended use and do so with an appropriate level of trustworthiness.

References: ISO/IEC/IEEE 15288, Section 6.4.5.3 a); ISO/IEC 15026.

Related Publications: ISO/IEC 21827; ISO/IEC 27001; ISO/IEC 27002; FIPS Publication 200; NIST SP 800-37; NIST SP 800-53.

DE-2 ESTABLISH SECURITY DESIGN CHARACTERISTICS AND ENABLERS FOR EACH SYSTEM ELEMENT

DE-2.1 Allocate system security requirements to system elements.

Elaboration: System security requirements are allocated to those system elements that provide or support the provision of a specified protection capability and to all system elements in the form of security-driven constraints. The allocation of system security requirements defines what, if any, security-relevant responsibility and constraints are assigned to or levied on each system element.

DE-2.2 Transform security architectural characteristics into security design characteristics.

Elaboration: The transformation applies the architectural, trust, and security design principles in successively finer-grained contexts to express the security design characteristics for the constituent components of architectural entities. Security design characteristics apply to security functional capability and to the avoidance and minimization of vulnerability and performance impacts in all aspects of system design.

DE-2.3 Define the necessary security design enablers.

Elaboration: Security design enablers include, for example: security policy models; security protocol models; strength of mechanism models; security algorithms; and formal expressions of security functional behavior and interaction.

DE-2.4 Examine security design alternatives.

Elaboration: The objective is to determine the feasibility of each alternative design in achieving the specified security design characteristics and effectiveness within the constraints of cost, schedule, life cycle concepts, and level of assurance. Trades are made in the architecture or requirements space for those security design characteristics that cannot be implemented. The *System Analysis* process conducts the necessary security-oriented analyses to provide the data necessary to support the assessments of the security design alternatives. Security design trade decisions may result in new, changed, deleted, or derived requirements/constraints. These changes require that the *Architecture Definition* process be revisited in conjunction with the *Stakeholder Needs and Requirements Definition* and the *System Requirements Definition* processes. Cost-benefit analyses of the security design are also conducted. The benefit derived from the security design is determined by several factors: the effectiveness of a security function in providing the protection allocated to it; the trustworthiness that can be placed on the security function; the impact of security design on system capability performance and on performance relative to other system emergent properties; and the risk associated with the use of the security function.

DE-2.5 Refine or define the security interfaces between the system elements and with external entities.

Elaboration: The security interfaces and security aspects interfaces defined by the *Architecture Definition* process reflect the level of detail needed to make architecture decisions. The details of the defined interfaces are refined to capture additional details provided by the security design. In addition, security interfaces, interconnections, behavior, and interactions for components within the system of interest are identified, as are the security-driven design constraints applied on all interfaces, interactions, and behavior between components of the system-of-interest.

DE-2.6 Develop the security design artifacts.

Elaboration: Security design artifacts include, for example: specifications, data sheets, databases, and documents. These artifacts are developed specific to the nature of the system design element implementation strategy (e.g., machine, technology, method of implementation, human, physical, or combination thereof).

References: ISO/IEC/IEEE 15288, Section 6.4.5.3 b); ISO/IEC 15026.

Related Publications: ISO/IEC 12207, Section 6.4.3.3.1, Section 7.1.4.3.1; ISO/IEC 27034-1, (SDL) Section A.9.3; ISO/IEC 15408; ISO/IEC 21827; ISO/IEC 27001; ISO/IEC 27002; FIPS Publication 200; NIST SP 800-37; NIST SP 800-53.

DE-3 ASSESS THE ALTERNATIVES FOR OBTAINING SECURITY-RELEVANT SYSTEM ELEMENTS

DE-3.1 Identify security-relevant nondevelopmental items (NDI) that may be considered for use.

Elaboration: Security-relevant NDI are those items that provide or directly support a security protection capability.

DE-3.2 Assess each candidate NDI and new design alternative against the criteria developed from expected security design characteristics or system element security requirements to determine suitability for the intended application.

Elaboration: Security considerations for NDI include, for example: the level of assurance that can be obtained relative to assurance objectives; the functionality contained beyond that required to satisfy allocated requirements; the interoperability with other system elements; and the pedigree of the NDI and all associated development, fabrication, storage, handling, and distribution concerns associated with component logistics and supply chain. The security considerations for design alternatives include, for example: security performance, effectiveness, and strength of mechanism, and the capabilities and limitations of the design relative to the security design characteristics and system element security requirements. The *System Analysis* process is used to provide data in support of the NDI security-informed assessments and alternative design assessments.

DE-3.3 Determine the preferred alternative among candidate NDI solutions and new design alternatives for a system element.

Elaboration: The preferred candidate is identified with explicit consideration of key security considerations of assurance, trustworthiness, effectiveness, and risk. The *Decision Management* process, informed by the *System Analysis* process, is used to perform the selection.

References: ISO/IEC/IEEE 15288, Section 6.4.5.3 c); ISO/IEC 15026.

Related Publications: ISO/IEC 12207, Section 6.4.3.3.2; ISO/IEC 21827; NIST SP 800-37.

DE-4   MANAGE THE SECURITY DESIGN

DE-4.1   Map the security design characteristics to the system elements.

Elaboration: The security design characteristics are allocated as they apply to individual or combinations of machine/technical, physical, and human system elements. The relationships and dependencies between the design characteristics and the type of system elements to which they are mapped are determined and captured as part of the mapping. The mapping ensures that all security design characteristics are mapped to system elements and traced to architecture entities.

DE-4.2   Capture the security design and rationale.

Elaboration: The security design and rationale is captured in a form most effective for its life cycle. In many cases, the security design is reflected in constraints and considerations offered as notes, cautions, or warnings, relative to the overarching system design.

DE-4.3   Maintain traceability of the security aspects of the system design.

Elaboration: Traceability is maintained between the security design characteristics and the security architectural entities, system element requirements, interface definitions, analysis results, and verification/validation methods or techniques. A traceability analysis of the security design to the system architecture ensures that all system security requirements, concerns, and constraints are allocated to and/or reflected in the design of security elements.

DE-4.4   Provide security-relevant information items required for the system design definition to baselines.

Elaboration: Security aspects are captured in various artifacts that are maintained in an identified baseline for the life cycle of the system. The security-relevant configuration items from this process are identified and incorporated into engineering baselines so that they may be produced and made available as required throughout the system life cycle. The *Configuration Management* process manages the baseline and the artifacts identified by this process. The *Information Management* process determines the appropriate forms of information and protections for the information that is provided to stakeholders.

References: ISO/IEC/IEEE 15288, Section 6.4.5.3 d).

Related Publications: ISO/IEC 15408; ISO/IEC 21827; NIST SP 800-37.

3.4.6 System Analysis Process

> ## Purpose
>
> "The purpose of the System Analysis process is to provide a rigorous basis of data and information for technical understanding to aid decision making across the life cycle."
>
> *ISO/IEC/IEEE 15288-2015. Reprinted with permission from IEEE, Copyright IEEE 2015, All rights reserved.*

Systems Security Engineering Purpose

Systems security engineering, as part of the *System Analysis* process, provides a security view to system analyses and contributes specific system security analyses to provide essential data and information for the technical understanding of the security aspects of decision making. System security analyses support both the technical assessments and decision making that occur during the execution of the system life cycle processes. System security analyses leverage a common foundation of methods, processes, and techniques that are differentiated and applied within the context of the need for security-oriented engineering data. The analyses are conducted with a level of analytical fidelity and rigor that is commensurate with the level of assurance required by the decision to be made.

Systems Security Engineering Outcomes

- The security aspects of system analysis needs are identified.

- Assumptions and results related to the security aspects of system analysis are identified and validated.

- System security analysis results are provided for decisions.

- Any enabling systems or services needed for the security aspects of system analysis are available.

- Traceability of system security analysis results is established.

Systems Security Engineering Activities and Tasks

SA-1   PREPARE FOR THE SECURITY ASPECTS OF SYSTEM ANALYSIS

    SA-1.1   Identify the security aspects of the problem or question that requires system analysis.

    Elaboration: The problem or question that drives the need for system analysis may or may not have obvious security considerations and aspects. The relevant security aspects may impact the definition of the analysis objectives and the expectations and utility of the analysis results. The objectives of system analysis may be problems or questions oriented to technical, functional, and nonfunctional objectives.

    SA-1.2   Identify the stakeholders of the security aspects of system analysis.

    Elaboration: The stakeholders of the system analysis serve to properly frame and confirm the security aspects of the problem or question to be answered and to set the expectations for the sufficiency of results.

SA-1.3 Define the objectives, scope, level of fidelity, and level of assurance of the security aspects of system analysis.

Elaboration: The expectations and utility of the security aspects of the system analysis may dictate specific minimum levels of fidelity in terms of accuracy, precision, and rigor, and driven by the desired level of assurance. These are defined in terms of the objectives and scope of the problem or question, and are to be compatible with the non-security aspects of the analysis.

SA-1.4 Select the methods associated with the security aspects of system analysis.

Elaboration: The analysis methods selected and employed are the methods that best enable the achievement of expectations for the utility of the data and information produced by the analysis. The methods selected to address the security aspects are to be compatible with the methods selected for other aspects of the analysis.

SA-1.5 Define the security aspects of the system analysis strategy.

Elaboration: The security aspects of system analysis strategy include, for example, security-driven dependencies on methods; the sequencing and timing of the analysis techniques, methods, and processes; and the quality and validity checks and verification to ensure that the results meet expectations and provide the necessary utility.

SA-1.6 Identify, plan for, and obtain access to enabling systems or services to support the security aspects of the system analysis process.

Elaboration: Specific enabling systems and services may be required to support the security aspects of the system analysis process. These enabling systems and services are relied upon to provide the capability to realize and support the system-of-interest, and therefore impact the trustworthiness of the system. The system analysis-oriented security concerns for enabling systems and services used to support the system analysis process must be determined and captured as security requirements and as security-driven constraints for the interfaces and interactions with the system-of-interest. The *Validation* process is used to confirm that enabling systems and services achieve their intended use and do so with an appropriate level of trustworthiness.

SA-1.7 Collect the data and inputs needed for the security aspects of system analysis.

Elaboration: Any data and inputs collected to inform and support the security aspects of system analysis inputs are validated within the scope, fidelity, and level of assurance dictated by the objectives of the system analysis.

References: ISO/IEC/IEEE 15288, Section 6.4.6.3 a); ISO/IEC 15026.

Related Publications: ISO/IEC 21827.

SA-2 PERFORM THE SECURITY ASPECTS OF SYSTEM ANALYSIS

SA-2.1 Identify and validate the assumptions associated with the security aspects of system analysis.

Elaboration: Assumptions associated with the security aspects of system analysis cannot be implicit; they must be explicit and validated. Each analysis assumption is validated to capture the relevance of the assumption to aspects of the analysis and the analysis results. Assumptions that cannot be validated are identified and correlated to the analysis results that are dependent on that assumption. Assumptions that cannot be validated are revisited and reconsidered for validation to remove all uncertainty about the analysis results and the utility of those results.

SA-2.2 Apply the selected security analysis methods to perform the security aspects of required system analysis.

Elaboration: The security analysis methods are performed in accordance with the system analysis strategy so as to remain within the capabilities and limitations of the selected method. Security analysis may use data produced by other analyses, for example, a security analysis for protection needs might be based on data produced by varying forms of criticality analysis.

SA-2.3   Review the security aspects of the system analysis results for quality and validity.

Elaboration: The security aspects of system analysis results are reviewed to address quality and validity as outlined in the system analysis strategy.

SA-2.4   Establish conclusions, recommendations, and rationale based on the results of the security aspects of system analysis.

Elaboration: The conclusions and recommendations are established to be defensible based on relevant data and information and validated assumptions. Conclusions and recommendations that are impacted by non-validated assumptions are identified as such. In all cases, the conclusions and recommendations capture the limitations and constraints on the interpretation of results, to include supporting rationale. Stakeholders and other individuals with appropriate subject-matter expertise are consulted and participate in the formulation of conclusions and recommendations.

SA-2.5   Record the results of the security aspects of system analysis.

Elaboration: The results of security analysis for aspects of the system analysis are captured in a form suitable for communication and utilization of the results.

References: ISO/IEC/IEEE 15288, Section 6.4.6.3 b).

Related Publications: ISO/IEC 12207, Section 7.1.2.3.1; ISO/IEC 27034-1, (SDL) Section A.9.3; ISO/IEC 15408; ISO/IEC 21827.

SA-3   MANAGE THE SECURITY ASPECTS OF SYSTEM ANALYSIS

SA-3.1   Maintain traceability of the security aspects of the system analysis results.

Elaboration: Bidirectional traceability captures the relationship between the security aspects of the system analysis results, the security methods employed, the other analysis methods, and the context that defines the problem or question that the system analysis addresses.

SA-3.2   Provide security-relevant system analysis information items that have been selected for baselines.

Elaboration: Security-relevant system analysis results are captured in various artifacts that are maintained in an identified baseline for the life cycle of the system. The security-relevant configuration items from this process are identified and incorporated into engineering baselines so that they may be produced and made available as required throughout the system life cycle. The *Configuration Management* process manages the baseline and the artifacts identified by this process. The *Information Management* process determines the appropriate forms of information and protections for the information that is provided to stakeholders.

References: ISO/IEC/IEEE 15288, Section 6.4.6.3 c).

Related Publications: ISO/IEC 15408; ISO/IEC 21827.

3.4.7 Implementation Process

Purpose

"The purpose of the Implementation process is to realize a specified system element."

ISO/IEC/IEEE 15288-2015. Reprinted with permission from IEEE, Copyright IEEE 2015, All rights reserved.

Systems Security Engineering Purpose

Systems security engineering, as part of the *Implementation* process, realizes the security aspects of all system elements. The process transforms the security aspects of requirements, architecture, design, interfaces, interconnections, and specified behavior into actions that create a system element according to the security practices of the selected implementation technology. Security aspects include the active protection capability of a system element (e.g., security functions or mechanisms that provide a security capability, service, or that serve as a control, safeguard, or countermeasure) and as the passive protection capability realized through the implementation methods, processes, and tools associated with development and fabrication. This process results in a system element that satisfies specified system security requirements, architecture, and design.

Systems Security Engineering Outcomes

• The security aspects of the implementation strategy are developed.

• The security aspects of implementation that constrain the requirements, architecture, or design are identified.

• A security-relevant or security-informed system element is realized.

• System elements are securely packaged and stored.

• Any enabling systems or services needed for the security aspects of implementation are available.

• Traceability of the security aspects of the implemented system elements is established.

Systems Security Engineering Activities and Tasks

IP-1   PREPARE FOR THE SECURITY ASPECTS OF IMPLEMENTATION

IP-1.1   Develop the security aspects of the implementation strategy.

Elaboration: The security aspects of the implementation strategy apply to all system elements regardless of their role in the system. They serve to guide and inform the implementation activities to realize the specified protection capability of security-relevant system elements, while informing the implementation activities of all system elements with the intent of avoiding the introduction of weaknesses and flaws that lead to vulnerability. The security aspects are oriented to the choice of the implementation technology; the manner in which the system element is to be realized (e.g., development, fabrication, adaptation, reuse, repurpose, purchase, subscription or lease); the targeted level of assurance; and security verification uncertainties. The strategy also applies to enabling systems and services that enable or support implementation; specialized needs for personnel performing high-assurance or trusted development; and security concerns associated with implementation-related logistics, supply, and distribution of components. The *Agreement* and *Infrastructure Management* processes are leveraged to support this process.

IP-1.2 Identify constraints from the security aspects of the implementation strategy and technology on the system requirements, architecture, design, or implementation techniques.

Elaboration: Security aspects, considerations, and characteristics associated with implementation (including choice of implementation technology, implementation method, enabling systems, and target level of assurance) may translate to explicit needs, constraints, and limitations captured in the system requirements, architecture, and design. Such considerations, aspects, and characteristics are identified and provided as input to needs analyses, requirements analyses, and architecture and design definition processes.

IP-1.3 Identify, plan for, and obtain access to enabling systems or services to support the security aspects of implementation.

Elaboration: Specific enabling systems and services may be required to support the security aspects of the implementation process. These enabling systems and services are relied upon to provide the capability to realize and support the system-of-interest, and therefore impact the trustworthiness of the system. The implementation-oriented security concerns for enabling systems and services used to support the implementation process must be determined and captured as security requirements and as security-driven constraints for the interfaces and interactions with the system-of-interest. The *Validation* process is used to confirm that enabling systems and services achieve their intended use and do so with an appropriate level of trustworthiness.

References: ISO/IEC/IEEE 15288, Section 6.4.7.3 a): ISO/IEC 15026; ISO/IEC 27036.

Related Publications: NIST SP 800-37.

IP-2 PERFORM THE SECURITY ASPECTS OF IMPLEMENTATION

IP-2.1 Realize or adapt system elements in accordance with the security aspects of the implementation strategy, defined implementation procedures, and security-driven constraints.

Elaboration: Implementation is accomplished by hardware fabrication; software development; adaptation and reuse of existing capabilities; the acquisition or leasing of components and services; and the development of life cycle concept policies and procedures to govern the actions of individuals in their use of and interaction with the technology/machine and physical elements of the system.

Hardware:

Hardware elements are either acquired or fabricated. The key security consideration is the trade space of cost, capability, and assurance. Custom hardware fabrication provides the opportunity to acquire insight into the details of design and implementation to include all associated processes, methods, and tools utilized. These insights translate to increased assurance (positive and negative). Having this insight offers the opportunity to influence decisions to avoid the introduction of vulnerabilities; to identify and remove vulnerabilities that are introduced; and to manage or contain those vulnerabilities that must remain.

Acquired hardware elements may not provide the opportunity to achieve the same insight into the details of design and implementation as is the case for hardware fabrication. In addition, acquired hardware elements may offer more functionality and capability than required. The limits of what can be known about the internals of the hardware elements translate to a level of uncertainty about vulnerability and to the maximum assurance that can be achieved.

Software:

Software elements are either acquired or developed. The key security consideration is the trade space of cost, capability, and assurance. Custom software development provides the opportunity to acquire insight into the details of design and implementation to include all associated processes, methods, and tools utilized. These insights translate to increased assurance (positive and negative). Having this insight offers the opportunity to influence decisions to avoid the introduction of vulnerabilities; to identify and remove vulnerabilities that are introduced; and to manage or contain those vulnerabilities that must remain.

Acquired software elements may not provide the opportunity to achieve the same insight into the details of design and implementation as is the case for hardware fabrication. In addition, acquired software elements may offer more functionality and capability than required. The limits of what can be known about the internals of the software elements translate to a level of uncertainty about vulnerability and to the maximum assurance that can be achieved.

Firmware:

Firmware exhibits properties of hardware and software. Firmware elements are either acquired, or developed to realize the software aspects of the element and then fabricated to realize the physical form of the hardware aspects of the element. Firmware elements therefore adhere to the security implementation considerations of both hardware and software elements.

Services:

System elements implemented by obtaining or leasing services include machine/technology, human, and physical system element considerations. These elements are subject to the same criteria used to acquire hardware, firmware, and software, but must also address security considerations associated with utilization and support resources.

Utilization and Support Resources:

The security considerations of services acquired or leased must account for the specific roles and responsibilities of individuals of the service/lease provider and their ability to account for all of the security requirements and constraints associated with delivery, utilization, and sustainment of the service or capability being leased.

IP-2.2   Develop initial training materials for users for operation, sustainment, and support.

Elaboration: Initial training capability and draft training documentation is used to provide the user community with the ability to securely operate the system, conduct failure detection and isolation, conduct contingency scenarios, and maintain system elements, either as stand-alone end items or as part of a larger system, as appropriate. Identify or define security training and qualification requirements, and train personnel needed for system operation.

IP-2.3   Securely package and store system elements.

Elaboration: The secure packaging and storing of system elements preserves the security characteristics of those elements until such time that they are needed. Security considerations include protection from unauthorized knowledge of existence of the system element and its storage location; details about the handling and movement of the element; protection from unauthorized access, use, or removal (e.g., theft); protection to detect an attempt to modify the system element or to detect actual modification of the system element; and protection from damage or destruction.

IP-2.4   Record evidence that system elements meet the system security requirements.

Elaboration: The evidence recorded is used to substantiate claims that the security requirements have been satisfied in accordance with the security architecture, security design, and all associated security concerns. Evidence is provided in accordance with the verification methods identified by the requirements allocated to the individual system element, and in accordance with the response to nonconformances found during the *Verification* and *Validation* processes.

References: ISO/IEC/IEEE 15288, Section 6.4.7.3 b); ISO/IEC 15026; ISO/IEC 27036.

Related Publications: ISO/IEC 12207, Section 7.1.5.3.1; ISO/IEC 27034-1, (SDL) Section A.9.4; NIST SP 800-37.

IP-3   MANAGE RESULTS OF THE SECURITY ASPECTS OF IMPLEMENTATION

IP-3.1   Record the security aspects of implementation results and any security-related anomalies encountered.

Elaboration: The recorded implementation results include security-related nonconformance issues, anomalies, or problems. These results inform analyses to determine required corrective actions. Corrective actions can affect the security aspects of the architecture definition, design definition, system security requirements and associated constraints, level of assurance that can be obtained, and/or the implementation strategy to include its security aspects. The *System Analysis, Decision Management, Risk Management,* and *Project Assessment and Control* processes all interact to address the identified nonconformance issues, anomalies, and problems.

IP-3.2   Maintain traceability of the security aspects of implemented system elements.

Elaboration: Bidirectional traceability of the security aspects of the implemented system elements to the system security requirements, the security views of the architecture, the security design, and the security interface requirements is maintained throughout the stages of the system life cycle. Traceability demonstrates completeness of the implementation process activities and provides evidence that supports assurance and trustworthiness claims.

IP-3.3   Provide security-relevant information items required for implementation to baselines.

Elaboration: Security aspects are captured in various artifacts that are maintained in an identified baseline for the life cycle of the system. The security-relevant configuration items are identified and incorporated into engineering baselines so that they may be produced and made available as required throughout the system life cycle. The *Configuration Management* process manages the baseline and the associated artifacts identified by this process. The *Information Management* process determines the appropriate forms of information and protections for the information that is provided to stakeholders.

References: ISO/IEC/IEEE 15288, Section 6.4.7.3 c); ISO/IEC 15026.

Related Publications: NIST SP 800-37.

3.4.8 Integration Process

Purpose

"The purpose of the Integration process is to synthesize a set of system elements into a realized system (product or service) that satisfies system requirements, architecture, and design."

ISO/IEC/IEEE 15288-2015. Reprinted with permission from IEEE, Copyright IEEE 2015, All rights reserved.

Systems Security Engineering Purpose

Systems security engineering, as part of the *Integration* process, addresses the security aspects in the assembly of a set of system elements such that the realized system achieves the protection capability in a trustworthy manner, as specified by the system security requirements, and in accordance with the system architecture and system design. The process iteratively combines the implemented system elements to form a complete or partially secure system configuration, which in turn is combined to build the secure product or service. Achieving a trustworthy secure system requires the iterative application of this process to identify the security-driven constraints for interfaces, interconnections, and interactions to achieve the desired emergent security behavior. This process requires close coordination with the *Architecture Definition* and *Design Definition* processes to make sure the interface definitions take into account security-driven constraints as part of the integration needs.

Systems Security Engineering Outcomes

- The security aspects of the integration strategy are developed.

- The security-driven integration constraints that influence requirements, architecture, design, or interfaces and interactions are identified.

- An approach and checkpoints for the correct secure operation of the assembled interfaces, interactions, behavior, and system functions are developed.

- Any enabling systems or services needed to achieve the security aspects of integration are available.

- A trustworthy secure system composed of implemented system elements is integrated.

- The security behavior and interactions between interfaces of implemented system elements are checked.

- The security behavior and interactions between the system and the external environment are checked.

- The security aspects of integration results and security anomalies are identified.

- Traceability of the security aspects of the integrated system elements is established.

Systems Security Engineering Activities and Tasks

IN-1   PREPARE FOR THE SECURITY ASPECTS OF INTEGRATION

> **IN-1.1**   Identify and define checkpoints for the trustworthy secure operation of the assembled interfaces and selected system functions.

Elaboration: Checkpoints for trustworthy secure operation at the system level support progressive in-process determination that the intended security characteristics at and between interfaces of interacting system elements (i.e., the interconnection or channel that allows for element interaction or communication) are achieved. The checkpoints also make it possible to identify any unspecified emergent behavior that occurs, regardless if that behavior is desirable or undesirable. Attention is also given to the trustworthy secure operation of the system-of-interest at its interfaces to enabling and other systems. The detailed verification of the security characteristics associated with those interfaces is performed by the *Verification* Process. The identification of checkpoints for trustworthy secure operation is accomplished in combination with the *Architecture Definition* process.

IN-1.2   Develop the security aspects of the integration strategy.

Elaboration: The security aspects of the integration strategy address the approach to bring together increasingly larger system elements of the system-of-interest hierarchy (e.g., component, assemblies, subsystem, systems) until the entire system is realized. The strategy encompasses secure assembly sequences and checkpoints for the system elements based on the system security requirements, security architecture, security design, and security interfaces. The strategy has objectives to optimize secure integration activities so as to minimize integration time, cost, and risk, while maximizing assurance and trustworthiness. The strategy also addresses integration issues for those interactions between the system-of-interest and other systems where the other systems are not likely to be available during integration, and therefore such interactions require simulation or other equivalent methods to successfully conduct security integration. The security aspects of the integration strategy are comprehensive in scope and address the role of the human as a contributing element to system integration and realization of trustworthy secure operation. The security aspects of the integration strategy also include the secure transport and acceptance of system elements from their storage or supply source to the location where integration activities are performed. These security aspects may be captured in agreements.

IN-1.3   Identify, plan for, and obtain access to enabling systems or services to support the security aspects of integration.

Elaboration: Specific enabling systems and services may be required to support the security aspects of the integration process. Enabling systems and services are relied upon to provide the capability to realize and support the system-of-interest, and therefore impact the trustworthiness of the system. The integration-oriented security concerns for enabling systems and services used to support the integration process must be determined and captured as security requirements and as security-driven constraints for the interfaces and interactions with the system-of-interest. The *Validation* process is used to confirm that enabling systems and services achieve their intended use and do so with an appropriate level of trustworthiness.

IN-1.4   Identify the constraints resulting from the security aspects of integration to be incorporated into the system requirements, architecture, or design.

Elaboration: Security-driven constraints are necessary to achieve trusted end-to-end security protections in terms of the behavior of the system at its interfaces and across the interconnection with other system elements, enabling systems, and other systems in the intended operational environment. These constraints serve to ensure correct secure operation and eliminate, minimize, or contain vulnerabilities so as to minimize, if not eliminate, unspecified emergent behavior and erroneous behavior due to adversity and uncertainty. Constraints resulting from the security aspects of integration take into account the system-of-interest, its enabling systems, and other systems. These constraints inform the system requirements, architecture, design, and all associated security viewpoints.

References: ISO/IEC/IEEE 15288, Section 6.4.8.3 a); ISO/IEC 15026; ISO/IEC 27036.

Related Publications: ISO/IEC 21827; NIST SP 800-37.

IN-2   PERFORM THE SECURITY ASPECTS OF INTEGRATION

IN-2.1   Obtain implemented system elements in accordance with security criteria and requirements established in agreements and schedules.

Elaboration: Security criteria address the handling, distribution, delivery, and acceptance of all forms of system elements as they are obtained from suppliers or withdrawn from storage. The criteria attempt to prevent and/or detect unauthorized knowledge of/about, access to/control over, use of, and modification to system elements as they are delivered to the integration location.

IN-2.2   Assemble the implemented systems elements to achieve secure configurations.

Elaboration: The assembly is performed as outlined by the security aspects of the integration strategy to bring together increasingly larger system elements of the system-of-interest hierarchy (e.g., component, assemblies, subsystem, systems) until the entire system-of-interest is realized.

IN-2.3   Perform checks of the security characteristics of interfaces, functional behavior, and behavior across interconnections.

Elaboration: Security integration checks verify the correct security operation in terms of behavior, interaction, performance, and effectiveness between system elements; between the system-of-interest and its enabling systems; and between the system-of-interest and other systems. These checks include specified behavior, strength of function, unspecified emergent behavior, forced behavior (i.e., type of behavior resulting from intentional malicious activity), and uncertainty. The security integration checks are conducted to address all system normal and degraded modes of operation and configurations. Security interfaces and functions are checked using the *Verification* process.

References: ISO/IEC/IEEE 15288, Section 6.4.8.3 b); ISO/IEC 27036.

Related Publications: ISO/IEC 12207, Section 6.4.5.3.2, Section 7.1.6.3.1; ISO/IEC 27034-1, (SDL) Section A.9.4; ISO/IEC 21827; NIST SP 800-37.

IN-3   MANAGE RESULTS OF THE SECURITY ASPECTS OF INTEGRATION

IN-3.1   Record the security aspects of integration results and any security anomalies encountered.

Elaboration: The recorded integration results include security-related nonconformance issues, anomalies, or problems. These results inform analyses to determine corrective actions. Corrective actions can affect the security aspects of architecture definition, design definition, the system security requirements and associated constraints, the level of assurance that can be obtained, and/or the integration strategy to include its security aspects. The *System Analysis, Decision Management, Risk Management,* and *Project Assessment and Control* processes all interact to address the identified nonconformance issues, anomalies, and problems.

IN-3.2   Maintain traceability of the security aspects of integrated system elements.

Elaboration: Bidirectional traceability of the security aspects of the integrated system elements to the system security requirements, security views of the architecture, security design, and security interface requirements is maintained throughout the stages of the system life cycle. Traceability demonstrates completeness of the integration process activities and provides evidence that supports assurance and trustworthiness claims.

IN-3.3   Provide security-relevant information items required for integration to baselines.

Elaboration: Security aspects of integration are captured in various artifacts that are maintained in an identified baseline for the life cycle of the system. The security-relevant configuration items from this process are identified and incorporated into engineering baselines so that they may be produced and made available as required throughout the system life cycle. The *Configuration*

Management process manages the baseline and the artifacts identified by this process. The *Information Management* process determines the appropriate forms of information and protections for the information that is provided to stakeholders.

References: ISO/IEC/IEEE 15288, Section 6.4.8.3 c); ISO/IEC 15026.

Related Publications: ISO/IEC 21827; NIST SP 800-37.

3.4.9 *Verification Process*

Purpose

"The purpose of the Verification process is to provide objective evidence that a system or system element fulfils its specified requirements and characteristics."

ISO/IEC/IEEE 15288-2015. Reprinted with permission from IEEE, Copyright IEEE 2015, All rights reserved.

Systems Security Engineering Purpose

Systems security engineering, as part of the *Verification* process, produces evidence sufficient to demonstrate that the system satisfies its security requirements and security characteristics with the level of assurance that applies to the system. A fundamental security characteristic is that the system exhibits only specified behaviors, interactions, and outcomes. This security characteristic establishes a burden to demonstrate the absence of specific behaviors, interactions, and outcomes. Another key characteristic of system assurance is that it applies to all methods, processes, and techniques, the fidelity and rigor in how they are employed, and the results that are achieved. Security verification therefore, requires interpretation, analysis, and reasoning about subjective evidence in addition to the objective evidence that is obtained through demonstration, inspection, evaluation, and testing. Security verification also identifies and produces evidence that describes anomalies (i.e., defects, errors, defects, faults, flaws, or weaknesses) that are assessed by the *System Analysis* process. This assessment determines if those anomalies constitute vulnerability relative to system requirements and characteristics.

Systems Security Engineering Outcomes

- The security aspects of the verification strategy are developed.

- The security aspects of verification that constrain system requirements, architecture, or design are identified.

- Any enabling systems or services needed to achieve the security aspects of verification are available.

- The security requirements and security characteristics of the system or system element are verified.

- Security-driven data providing information for corrective actions is reported.

- Evidence that the realized system satisfies the system security requirements, security views of the architecture, and security design is provided.

- The security aspects of verification results and security anomalies are identified.

- Traceability of the security aspects of the verified system elements is established.

Systems Security Engineering Activities and Tasks

VE-1   PREPARE FOR THE SECURITY ASPECTS OF VERIFICATION

        VE-1.1   Identify the security aspects within the verification scope and corresponding security-focused verification actions.

Elaboration: The security aspects and security-focused verification activities are identified for each scope of verification. The scope includes requirements, architecture, design characteristics, or other properties to be verified relative to a target system element or artifact (e.g., system, model, prototype, mock-up, procedure, plan, or document). The security-focused verification actions include those oriented to strength of function/mechanism, resistance to tamper, misuse or abuse, penetration resistance, level of assurance, absence of flaws, weaknesses, and the absence of unspecified emergent behavior and outcomes.

VE-1.2 Identify the constraints that can potentially limit the feasibility of the security-focused verification actions.

Elaboration: Constraints that can potentially affect security-focused verification include, for example: level of assurance and the availability of human and material resource enablers; the availability of relevant and credible vulnerability, hazard, and threat data; access to details about the system element or artifact to be verified; technology employed; size and complexity of the system element or artifact and cost and time allotted for the verification.

VE-1.3 Select the appropriate methods or techniques for the security aspects of verification and the associated security criteria for each security-focused verification action.

Elaboration: The methods and techniques appropriate for security verification are largely driven by the evidence required to accomplish the verification action so as to achieve the desired level of assurance. Selection of appropriate methods includes, for example, the depth and breadth of the scope of verification and the rigor of the methods employed. It may be the case that a method or technique is unsuitable to produce the necessary evidence with the required level of assurance to support verification conclusions, or alternatively, to inform system analyses that provide data to inform verification conclusions.

VE-1.4 Define the security aspects of the verification strategy.

Elaboration: The security aspects of the verification strategy address the approach used to incorporate security considerations into all verification actions, to include the incorporation of security-specific verification actions. The security aspects of the verification strategy apply to the entire system and all associated artifacts. The security aspects of the verification strategy achieve an acceptable trade-off between the scope, depth, and rigor of verification, given the constraints and feasibility considerations, to accomplish verification actions at the desired level of assurance while recognizing the risk in not conducting adequate security-focused verification.

VE-1.5 Identify the system constraints resulting from the security aspects of the verification strategy to be incorporated into the system requirements, architecture, or design.

Elaboration: The security aspects of the verification strategy will result in system constraints associated with the clarity, accuracy, and precision in the expression of requirements, architecture definition, and design definition, in order to achieve the desired level of assurance and to do so with certainty and repeatability. Additionally, security-driven verification constraints will be associated with choice of security and other technologies.

VE-1.6 Identify, plan for, and obtain access to enabling systems or services to support the security aspects of verification.

Elaboration: Specific enabling systems and services may be required to support the security aspects of the verification process. Enabling systems and services are relied upon to provide the capability to realize and support the system-of-interest, and therefore impact the trustworthiness of the system. The verification-oriented security concerns for enabling systems and services used to support the verification process must be determined and captured as security requirements and as security-driven constraints for the interfaces and interactions with the system-of-interest. The

Validation process is used to confirm that enabling systems and services achieve their intended use and do so with an appropriate level of trustworthiness.

References: ISO/IEC/IEEE 15288, Section 6.4.9.3 a); ISO/IEC 15026; ISO/IEC 29119; ISO/IEC/IEEE 29148.

Related Publications: ISO/IEC 12207, Section 7.2.4.3.1; ISO/IEC 21827; NIST SP 800-37; NIST SP 800-53A.

VE-2   PERFORM SECURITY-FOCUSED VERIFICATION

VE-2.1   Define the security aspects of the verification procedures, each supporting one or a set of security-focused verification actions.

Elaboration: The security-focused verification procedures include the verification methods or techniques to be employed, the skills and expertise required of individuals conducting the verification actions, and any specialized equipment that may be needed. These procedures focus on the security aspects of correctness, vulnerability susceptibility, penetration susceptibility, and misuse and abuse susceptibility. The procedures also define the security objectives and the criteria for success. The security aspects of the verification procedures address security considerations in standard systems engineering verification methods and additional security-focused verification actions that include search for vulnerabilities; penetration testing; misuse and abuse case testing; and tamper resistance testing. Each security-focused verification procedure is targeted to the particular system element undergoing verification and includes the use, sequencing, and ordering of all enabling systems; methods, tools, and techniques employed; system states, configuration, and modes of operation; environmental conditions; and personnel resources.

VE-2.2   Perform security verification procedures.

Elaboration: Security verification, in accordance with the verification strategy, occurs at the appropriate times in the system life cycle for the artifact identified by the verification procedure.

Correctness:

Security correctness procedures address capability, behavior, outcomes, properties, characteristics, performance, effectiveness, strength of mechanism/function, precision, accuracy, in consideration of identified constraints.

Vulnerability:

Security vulnerability procedures address flaws, deficiencies, and weaknesses that can be intentionally or unintentionally leveraged, exploited, triggered, or that may combine in some manner to produce an adverse consequence.

Penetration:

Security penetration procedures address strategically and/or tactically planned and controlled methods with intent to defeat, overwhelm, overcome, or bypass the protection capability, technologies, materials, or methods. Penetration procedures may simulate the actions of a given class of adversary within the context of specific rules of engagement, using the knowledge, methods, techniques, and tools the adversary is expected to employ to achieve an objective.

Abuse and misuse:

Security abuse and misuse procedures address the manner in which the system can be utilized to produce unspecified behavior and outcomes. These procedures may target the security guidance, policies, procedures, and any other available information directed at users, operators, maintainers, administrators, and trainers. Abuse and misuse verification is able to identify overly complex, erroneous, or ambiguous information that leads users, administrators, operators, or maintainers to inadvertently place the system into a nonsecure state.

VE-2.3   Analyze security-focused verification results against any established expectations and success criteria.

Elaboration: The analysis of security verification results helps to determine whether the system or system element being verified indicates conformance.

References: ISO/IEC/IEEE 15288, Section 6.4.9.3 b).

Related Publications: ISO/IEC 12207, Section 6.4.6.3.1, Section 7.1.7.3.1, Section 7.2.4.3.2; ISO/IEC 27034-1, (SDL) Section A.9.5; ISO/IEC 21827; NIST SP 800-37; NIST SP 800-53A.

VE-3   MANAGE RESULTS OF SECURITY-FOCUSED VERIFICATION

VE-3.1   Record the security aspects of verification results and any security anomalies encountered.

Elaboration: The recorded verification results include security-related nonconformance issues, anomalies, or problems. These results inform analyses to determine causes and enable corrective or improvement actions. Corrective actions can affect the security aspects of the architecture definition, design definition, system security requirements and associated constraints, the level of assurance that can be obtained, and the implementation strategy to include its security aspects. The *System Analysis, Decision Management, Risk Management,* and *Project Assessment and Control* processes all interact to address and respond to nonconformance issues, anomalies, and problems.

VE-3.2   Record the security characteristics of operational incidents and problems and track their resolution.

Elaboration: Security incidents that occur in the operational environment of the system are recorded and subsequently correlated to verification activities and results. This is an important feedback loop for continuous improvement in the engineering of trustworthy secure systems. This data is critical in determining the limits of performance, effectiveness, and certainty with respect to threats, vulnerabilities, and associated loss consequences. The data provided from operational incidents is to have comprehensive coverage of all involved technology/machine, human, and physical system elements. The *Quality Assurance* and *Project Assessment and Control* processes are directly involved in addressing the management and handling of incident reports from the operational system.

VE-3.3   Obtain stakeholder agreement that the system or system element meets the specified system security requirements and characteristics.

Elaboration: Stakeholder agreement of the sufficiency of security-focused verification results is associated with key checkpoints in the engineering process. Stakeholder approval contributes to the overall determination that the system is justifiably able to proceed to the next phase of the engineering process with explicit consideration of security capabilities, limitations, assumptions, and open/unresolved items.

VE-3.4   Maintain traceability of the security aspects of verified system elements.

Elaboration: Bidirectional traceability of the security aspects of verified system elements to the system security requirements, security views of the architecture, security design, and security interface requirements is maintained throughout the stages of the system life cycle. Traceability demonstrates completeness of the verification process and provides evidence that supports the assurance and trustworthiness claims.

VE-3.5   Provide security-relevant information items required for verification to baselines.

Elaboration: The security aspects of verification are captured in the various artifacts that are maintained in an identified baseline for the life cycle of the system. The security-relevant configuration items from this process are identified and incorporated into engineering baselines so that they may be produced and made available as required throughout the system life cycle. The *Configuration Management* process manages the baseline and the artifacts identified by this process. The *Information Management* process determines the appropriate forms of information and protections for the information that is provided to stakeholders.

References: ISO/IEC/IEEE 15288, Section 6.4.9.3 c); ISO/IEC 15026; ISO/IEC 27034-1, (SDL) Section A.9.6.

Related Publications: ISO/IEC 21827; NIST SP 800-37; NIST SP 800-53A.

3.4.10 Transition Process

Purpose

"The purpose of the Transition process is to establish a capability for a system to provide services specified by stakeholder requirements in the operational environment."

ISO/IEC/IEEE 15288-2015. Reprinted with permission from IEEE, Copyright IEEE 2015, All rights reserved.

Systems Security Engineering Purpose

Systems security engineering, as part of the *Transition* process, establishes a capability to preserve the system security characteristics during all aspects of an orderly and planned transition of the system into operational status. Security characteristics of transition apply to the verified system-of-interest and its relevant enabling systems, and include storage, handling, delivery, installation, configuration, start-up, and commissioning of the verified system.

Systems Security Engineering Outcomes

- The security aspects of the transition strategy are developed.

- The security aspects of transition that constrain system requirements, architecture, or design are identified.

- Any enabling systems or services needed to achieve the security aspects of transition are available.

- The preparation of the operational site includes its security aspects.

- The system and its enabling systems are securely installed in their operational environment and are capable of delivering the specified security functions and exhibiting secure behavior and characteristics.

- Individuals involved with the operation, sustainment, and support of the system are trained in the systems security capabilities and limitations.

- Security-relevant results and anomalies are identified.

- The installed system is activated and ready for operation in consideration of security-relevant capability, constraints, limitations, and identified anomalies.

- Traceability of the security aspects of the transitioned elements is established.

Systems Security Engineering Activities and Tasks

TR-1   PREPARE FOR THE SECURITY ASPECTS OF TRANSITION

> **TR-1.1**   Develop the security aspects of the transition strategy.

> **Elaboration:** The security aspects of the transition strategy address the approach used to preserve the system security characteristics to maintain the target level of assurance and trustworthiness throughout all transition activities. The security aspects of transition focus on the confidentiality, integrity, and availability concerns of system elements and all associated data and information from their transition points of origin to site delivery, installation and assembly, checkout, and commissioning of the system. The confidentiality concerns include knowledge of and about the

activities, methods, means, materiel, and personnel involved in all aspects of system transition. The security aspects account for interim secure storage, accountability of system elements throughout the transition process, and the security qualifications and authorizations of individuals associated with the transition of the system. The security aspects address system integrity to ensure that the delivered system corresponds precisely to the system verified; any actual and attempted tampering of the system elements; substitution or replacement of system elements; and attempts to masquerade as authorized personnel associated with the system transition process. The security aspects also address system availability in terms of timely movement and accountability of system elements and account for enabling systems and all interconnections of the system-of-interest with other systems in the operational environment so as to achieve protection and security objectives in consideration of constraints imposed by the other systems.

TR-1.2   Identify the facility or site changes needed for security purposes.

Elaboration: Facility or site changes may be driven by assumptions and constraints associated with the specified security capability so as to achieve specified assurance and trustworthiness objectives. These assumptions must be realized by the facility or site so as to properly match the security aspects of the transition strategy. Changes to the site or facility potentially affecting the secure operation of the system include, for example, physical access and movement control mechanisms; surveillance mechanisms; security policies, procedures, and plans; ingress or egress points including access roads; fire protection and suppression systems; emergency power and lighting capability; and electromagnetic signals emanation protection mechanisms.

TR-1.3   Identify the constraints resulting from the security aspects of transition to be incorporated into the system requirements, architecture, and design.

Elaboration: Security aspects, considerations, and characteristics associated with system transition may translate to explicit needs, constraints, and limitations captured in the system requirements, architecture, and design. Such considerations, aspects, and characteristics are identified and provided as input to needs analyses, requirements analyses, and architecture and design definition processes.

TR-1.4   Identify and arrange the training necessary for secure system utilization, sustainment, and support.

Elaboration: Security considerations are necessarily part of all human element behavior and interactions. The development and provision of security training for all recipients of the system undergoing transition is necessary to successfully complete the transition with assurance that the system can be utilized and sustained as intended within its specified capabilities and limitations. The training should include general security awareness training and specific role-based, function-based, and objective-based security training. The *Implementation* process is used to develop the initial training capability that is provided during the *Transition* process.

TR-1.5   Identify, plan for, and obtain access to enabling systems or services to support the security aspects of transition.

Elaboration: Specific enabling systems and services may be required to support the security aspects of the transition process. Enabling systems and services are relied upon to provide the capability to realize and support the system-of-interest, and therefore impact the trustworthiness of the system. The transition-oriented security concerns for enabling systems and services used to support the transition process must be determined and captured as security requirements and as security-driven constraints for the interfaces and interactions with the system-of-interest. The *Validation* process is used to confirm that enabling systems and services achieve their intended use and do so with an appropriate level of trustworthiness.

References: ISO/IEC/IEEE 15288, Section 6.4.10.3 a); ISO/IEC 15026.

Related Publications: NIST SP 800-37; NIST SP 800-53A.

TR-2   PERFORM THE SECURITY ASPECTS OF TRANSITION

TR-2.1   Prepare the facility or site in accordance with the secure installation requirements.

Elaboration: Preparation is carried out in accordance with agreements, requirements, directives, policies, procedures, regulations, and ordinances.

TR-2.2   Securely deliver the system for installation.

Elaboration: The secure delivery of the system to the correct location is a necessary step in establishing the intended security posture of the system in its operational environment. Secure delivery takes into account the various forms, means, and methods that accomplish end-to-end transport of system elements. This includes all intermediate stops, storage, and transitions from carrier-to-carrier or system-to-system (for electronic delivery forms). Ensuring delivery to the correct location is particularly important where a specific system element is preconfigured for site-specific capability, function, and use.

TR-2.3   Install the system at its specified location and establish secure interconnections to its environment.

Elaboration: Procedures that conform to the transition strategy are used to guide the installation, generation, data and information population, secure configuration, and start-up of the system so as to achieve the intended secure configuration and proper integration with enabling systems and other systems. These procedures also account for the interconnection of the system with its physical environment, other systems, and any enabling systems to which it interacts so as to achieve specified trust relationships. These procedures are to be properly verified so as to provide confidence that the intended system configuration across all system modes and states is achieved.

TR-2.4   Demonstrate proper achievement of the security aspects of system installation.

Elaboration: Security acceptance tests defined in agreements serve as the basis to determine proper installation of the system. The demonstration includes security aspects associated with physical connections between the system and the environment.

TR-2.5   Provide security training for stakeholders that interact with the system.

Elaboration: Stakeholder security training accounts for the security behavior, characteristics, and concerns, including risk, for life cycle utilization, sustainment, and support. Security training is oriented to the details of the system as it is installed in its operational environment. These criteria may vary across instances of the system as it is employed for use.

TR-2.6   Perform activation and checkout of the security aspects of the system.

Elaboration: Security activation checkout demonstrates that the system is able to initialize to its initial secure operational state for all defined modes of operation and takes into account all of the interconnections to other systems across physical, virtual, and wireless interfaces, where such interfaces impact the demonstration of secure checkout. The activation checkout also takes into account all operational procedures, policies, and regulations. The *Validation* process is used to confirm that the system, as installed and configured, fulfills the stakeholder security requirements.

TR-2.7   Demonstrate that the installed system is capable of delivering the required protection capability.

Elaboration: Acceptance tests and associated acceptance criteria as specified in agreements, establish the basis to determine the operational readiness of the system. The ability to deliver the required protection capability is determined by the use of trained staff. The acceptance criteria may include acceptance based on demonstration of security behavior and interactions using simulated or other means should aspects of the physical environment or other systems not be available at the time of demonstration. The capability to deliver the required protections is demonstrated across all defined system modes and states, and includes penetration testing based on vulnerability and threat assessments. The *Validation* process is used to demonstrate the effectiveness of the system when used as intended to achieve stakeholder business or mission objectives.

TR-2.8   Demonstrate that the security functions provided by the system are sustainable by the enabling systems.

Elaboration: Acceptance tests and associated acceptance criteria as specified in agreements, establish the basis to determine the operational readiness of any enabling systems. The ability to deliver the required protection capability is determined by the use of trained staff. The capability to deliver the required protections is demonstrated across all defined system modes and states, and includes penetration testing based on vulnerability and threat assessments. The *Validation* process is used to demonstrate the effectiveness of the enabling systems that provide services upon which the system-of-interest depends.

TR-2.9   Review the security aspects of the system for operational readiness.

Elaboration: The results of installation, operational, and enabling system checkouts are reviewed to determine if the security performance and effectiveness are sufficient to justify operational use. This determination includes the results of penetration tests, threat and vulnerability assessments, and the determination of residual risk in terms of risk tolerance and loss tolerance. The *Decision Management* and *Risk Management* processes support decision making for operational readiness.

TR-2.10   Commission the system for secure operation.

Elaboration: The commissioning of the system completes the transition of the system from the development/production engineering context to the operations and sustainment context. Security support to system stakeholders starts at the time of the commissioning of the system.

References: ISO/IEC/IEEE 15288, Section 6.4.10.3 b).

Related Publications: ISO/IEC 12207, Section 6.4.7.3.1, Section 6.4.8.3.1, Section 6.4.9.3.2; NIST SP 800-37; NIST SP 800-53A.

TR-3   MANAGE RESULTS OF THE SECURITY APECTS OF TRANSITION

TR-3.1   Record the security aspects of transition results and any security anomalies encountered.

Elaboration: The security aspects and anomalies are recorded based on the scope of the transition strategy, the system, the enabling systems, the checkout methods and findings, and the findings of susceptibility to threat. Security findings that involve interactions with other systems require that those findings be provided to the appropriate stakeholders of those systems. The results of these findings are utilized by the *System Analysis* and *Decision Management* processes to establish root and contributing causes so as to decide on corrective actions. The *Project Assessment and Control* process is used to support these efforts.

TR-3.2   Record the security aspects of operational incidents and problems and track their resolution.

Elaboration: The *Operation* process is used to collect security incident data. Tracking the resolution of security incidents is important to ensuring the continued secure operation of the system.

TR-3.3   Maintain traceability of the security aspects of transitioned system elements.

Elaboration: Bidirectional traceability is maintained between all identified security aspects and supporting data associated with the transition strategy and the system requirements, system architecture, and system design. Traceability demonstrates completeness of the verification process and provides evidence that supports assurance and trustworthiness claims.

TR-3.4   Provide security-relevant information items required for transition to baselines.

Elaboration: The security aspects of system transition are captured in various artifacts that are maintained in an identified baseline for the life cycle of the system. The security-relevant configuration items from this process are identified and incorporated into engineering baselines so that they may be produced and made available as required throughout the system life cycle. The *Configuration Management* process manages the baseline and the artifacts identified by this process. The *Information Management* process determines the appropriate forms of information and protections for the information that is provided to stakeholders.

References: ISO/IEC/IEEE 15288, Section 6.4.10.3 c); ISO/IEC 15026.

Related Publications: NIST SP 800-37; NIST SP 800-53A.

3.4.11 Validation Process

Purpose

"The purpose of the Validation process is to provide objective evidence that the system, when in use, fulfills its business or mission objectives and stakeholder requirements, achieving its intended use in its intended operational environment."

ISO/IEC/IEEE 15288-2015. Reprinted with permission from IEEE, Copyright IEEE 2015, All rights reserved.

Systems Security Engineering Purpose

Systems security engineering, as part of the *Validation* process, provides evidence sufficient to demonstrate that the system, while in use, fulfills its business or mission objectives while being able to provide adequate protection of stakeholder and business or mission assets; minimize or contain asset loss and associated consequences; and achieve its intended use in its intended operational environment with the desired level of trustworthiness. A key trustworthiness characteristic is that the system exhibits only specified behaviors, interactions, and outcomes. This establishes the burden to demonstrate the absence of specific behaviors, interactions, and outcomes, to include those that can be forced or manipulated by an adversary. Security validation is, therefore, able to demonstrate the trustworthy capability of the system to achieve established security objectives relative to disruptions, hazards, and threats anticipated in the operational environment.

Systems Security Engineering Outcomes

- The security aspects of the validation strategy are developed.

- Validation criteria for stakeholder security requirements are defined.

- The availability of security services required by stakeholders is confirmed.

- The security aspects of validation that constrain requirements, architecture, or design are identified.

- The security aspects of the system or system element are validated.

- Any enabling systems or services needed to achieve the security aspects of validation are available.

- Security-focused validation results and security anomalies are identified.

- Evidence that the realized system or system element satisfies stakeholder protection needs is provided.

- Traceability of the validated security-relevant system elements is established.

Systems Security Engineering Activities and Tasks

VA-1   PREPARE FOR THE SECURITY ASPECTS OF VALIDATION

  VA-1.1   Identify the security aspects of the validation scope and corresponding security-focused validation actions.

Elaboration: The security aspects of validation focus on stakeholder's protection needs, concerns, and associated stakeholder security requirements. Security-focused validation can occur at any stage in the system life cycle or during any of the engineering process activities. The scope of security validation includes system elements, the entire system, or any artifact that impacts the stakeholder's confidence in the system and the decision to accept the system as being trustworthy for its intended use.

VA-1.2   Identify the constraints that can potentially limit the feasibility of the security-focused validation actions.

Elaboration: Constraints that can potentially affect security-focused validation actions include, for example: the level of assurance and the availability of business or mission stakeholders to support validation activities; the availability of relevant and credible vulnerability, hazard, and threat data; the limits on conducting validation activities in actual operational conditions across all business and mission modes and all associated system states and modes; technology employed; size and complexity of the system element or artifact; and the cost and time allotted for validation activities.

VA-1.3   Select the appropriate methods or techniques for the security aspects of validation and the associated security criteria for each security-focused validation action.

Elaboration: The methods and techniques appropriate for security validation are largely driven by the evidence required to accomplish the validation action so as to achieve the desired level of trustworthiness. Selection of appropriate methods includes the depth and breadth of the scope of validation and the rigor of methods employed. It may be the case that a method or technique is unsuitable to produce evidence with the required level of trustworthiness to support validation conclusions.

VA-1.4   Develop the security aspects of the validation strategy.

Elaboration: The security aspects of the validation strategy address the approach to incorporate security considerations into all validation actions, to include the incorporation of security-specific validation actions. The security aspects of the validation strategy apply to the entire system and all associated artifacts. The security aspects of the validation strategy achieve an acceptable trade-off between the scope, depth, and rigor of validation, given constraints and feasibility considerations, to accomplish validation actions at the desired level of assurance while recognizing the risk in not conducting adequate security-focused validation. The security-specific validation actions in the strategy include adequacy of protections, strength of protection functions/mechanisms, compliance with security concepts of operation, performance, interoperability, and identification of residual vulnerability and the resultant susceptibility to disruption, hazards, and threats. The validation strategy may include business or mission use case-directed vulnerability assessment which scopes penetration and misuse testing to identify means and methods used to exploit vulnerabilities via intentional attacks or to trigger vulnerabilities via incidental and accidental actions.

VA-1.5   Identify system constraints resulting from the security aspects of validation to be incorporated into the stakeholder security requirements.

Elaboration: The security aspects of the validation strategy will result in constraints associated with the clarity, accuracy, and precision in the expression of stakeholder security requirements, so as to ascertain the targeted level of assurance and to do so with certainty and repeatability.

VA-1.6   Identify, plan for, and obtain access to enabling systems or services to support the security aspects of validation.

Elaboration: Specific enabling systems and services may be required to support the security aspects of the validation process. Enabling systems and services are relied upon to provide the capability to realize and support the system-of-interest, and therefore impact the trustworthiness of the system. The validation-oriented security concerns for enabling systems and services used to support the transition process must be determined and captured as security requirements and as security-driven constraints for the interfaces and interactions with the system-of-interest.

References: ISO/IEC/IEEE 15288, Section 6.4.11.3 a); ISO/IEC 15026.

Related Publications: ISO/IEC 12207, Section 7.2.5.3.1; ISO/IEC 21827; NIST SP 800-37; NIST SP 800-53A.

VA-2   PERFORM SECURITY-FOCUSED VALIDATION

VA-2.1   Define the security aspects of the validation procedures, each supporting one or a set of security-focused validation actions.

Elaboration: Security-focused validation procedures include the validation methods or techniques to be employed, the skills and expertise required of individuals conducing the validation, and any specialized equipment that may be needed. These procedures focus on the security aspects of correctness, vulnerability susceptibility, penetration susceptibility, and misuse and abuse susceptibility. The procedures also define the security objectives and the criteria for success. The security aspects of the validation procedures address security considerations in generalized validation methods and additional security-focused validation actions that include search for vulnerabilities; penetration testing; misuse and abuse case testing; and tamper resistance testing. Each security-focused validation procedure is targeted to the particular system element undergoing validation and includes the use, sequencing, and ordering of all enabling systems; methods, tools, and techniques employed; system states, mode, and configuration; environmental conditions; and personnel resources.

VA-2.2   Perform security validation procedures in the defined environment.

Elaboration: Security-focused validation procedures demonstrate that the right system was built; that the system is sufficiently trustworthy; and that the system satisfies the defined stakeholder security objectives, protection needs, and security requirements. Security validation, in accordance with the validation strategy, occurs at the appropriate time in the system life cycle for the artifact identified by the validation procedure.

Correctness:

Security correctness procedures address capability, behavior, outcomes, properties, characteristics, performance, effectiveness, strength of mechanism/function, precision, and accuracy, in consideration of identified constraints.

Vulnerability:

Security vulnerability procedures address flaws, deficiencies, and weaknesses that can be intentionally or unintentionally leveraged, exploited, triggered, or that may combine in some manner to produce an adverse consequence.

Penetration:

Security penetration procedures addresses strategically and/or tactically planned and controlled methods with intent to defeat, overwhelm, overcome, or bypass the protection capability, technologies, material, or methods. Penetration procedures may simulate the actions of a given class of adversary within the context of specific rules of engagement, using the knowledge, methods, techniques, and tools that the adversary is expected to employ to achieve an objective.

Abuse and misuse:

Security abuse and misuse procedures address the manner in which the system can be utilized to produce unspecified behavior and outcomes. These procedures may target the security guidance, policies, procedures, and any other available information directed at users, operators, maintainers, administrators, and trainers. Abuse and misuse verification is able to identify overly complex, erroneous, or ambiguous information that leads users, administrators, operators, or maintainers to inadvertently place the system in a nonsecure state.

VA-2.3 Review security-focused validation results to confirm that the protection services of the system that are required by stakeholders are available.

Elaboration: The confirmation of the availability of security protection services is ascertained in the same manner as the confirmation of all other system services. The certification of the system, or the certification of combinations, collections, or individual system elements can contribute to the overall base of evidence generated to support the *Validation* process.

References: ISO/IEC/IEEE 15288, Section 6.4.11.3 b).

Related Publications: ISO/IEC 12207, Section 6.4.8.3.1, Section 7.2.5.3.2; ISO/IEC 21827; NIST SP 800-37; NIST SP 800-53A.

VA-3 MANAGE RESULTS OF SECURITY-FOCUSED VALIDATION

VA-3.1 Record the security aspects of validation results and any security anomalies encountered.

Elaboration: The recorded validation results include security-related nonconformance issues, anomalies, or problems. These results inform analyses to determine causes and enable corrective or improvement actions. Corrective actions can affect the security aspects of the architecture definition, design definition, system security requirements and associated constraints, the level of assurance that can be obtained, and/or the implementation strategy to include its security aspects. The *System Analysis, Decision Management, Risk Management,* and *Project Assessment and Control* processes all interact to address the identified and respond to nonconformance issues, anomalies, and problems.

VA-3.2 Record the security characteristics of operational incidents and problems and track their resolution.

Elaboration: Security incidents that occur in the operational environment of the system are recorded and subsequently correlated to validation activities and results. This is an important feedback loop for continuous improvement in the engineering of trustworthy secure systems. This data is critical in determining the limits of performance, effectiveness, and certainty with respect to threats, vulnerabilities, and associated loss consequences. The data provided from operational incidents is to have comprehensive coverage of all involved technology/machine, human, and physical system elements. The *Quality Assurance* and *Project Assessment and Control* processes are directly involved in addressing the management and handling of incident reports from the operational system.

VA-3.3 Obtain stakeholder agreement that the system or system element meets the stakeholder protection needs.

Elaboration: Stakeholder agreement of the sufficiency of security-focused validation results is associated with key checkpoints in the engineering process. Stakeholder approval contributes to the overall determination that the system is justifiably able to proceed to the next phase of the engineering process with explicit consideration of security capabilities, limitations, assumptions, and open/unresolved items. Ultimately, stakeholder agreement confirms that the system is sufficiently trustworthy and fit for purpose.

VA-3.4 Maintain traceability of the security aspects of validated system elements.

Elaboration: Bidirectional traceability of the security aspects of validated system elements to stakeholder protection needs and security concerns, and to stakeholder security requirements is maintained throughout the stages of the system life cycle. Traceability demonstrates completeness of the validation process and provides evidence that supports assurance and trustworthiness claims.

VA-3.5 Provide security-relevant information items required for validation to baselines.

Elaboration: The security aspects of validation are captured in various artifacts that are maintained in an identified baseline for the life cycle of the system. The security-relevant configuration items from this process are identified and incorporated into engineering baselines so that they may be produced and made available as required throughout the system life cycle. The *Configuration Management* process manages the baseline and the artifacts identified by this process. The *Information Management* process determines the appropriate forms of information and protections for the information that is provided to stakeholders.

References: ISO/IEC/IEEE 15288, Section 6.4.11.3 c); ISO/IEC 15026.

Related Publications: ISO/IEC 21827; NIST SP 800-37; NIST SP 800-53A.

3.4.12 Operation Process

Purpose

"The purpose of the Operation process is to use the system to deliver its services."

ISO/IEC/IEEE 15288-2015. Reprinted with permission from IEEE, Copyright IEEE 2015, All rights reserved.

Systems Security Engineering Purpose

Systems security engineering, as part of the *Operation* process, establishes the requirements and constraints to enable the secure operation of the system in a manner consistent with its intended uses, in its intended operational environment, and for all system modes of operation. This process identifies the security-relevant capabilities, knowledge, and skills for those individuals assigned responsibility to operate and to interact with the system; identifies and analyzes the operational anomalies to determine the security-relevant issues associated with those anomalies; and provides security-related support to operations elements.

Systems Security Engineering Outcomes

- The security aspects of the operation strategy are developed.

- The security aspects of operation that constrain system requirements, architecture, or design are identified.

- Any enabling systems or services needed to support the secure operation of the system are available.

- Trained and qualified personnel capable of securely operating the system are available.

- System services that meet stakeholder security requirements are delivered.

- The security aspects of system performance during operation are monitored.

- Traceability of the security aspects of operations elements is established.

- Security support to the customer is provided.

Systems Security Engineering Activities and Tasks

OP-1 PREPARE FOR SECURE OPERATION

OP-1.1 Develop the security aspects of the operation strategy.

Elaboration: The security aspects of the operation strategy address the approach to enable the continuous secure operation and use of the system and its security services in a manner that conforms to the design intent and intended use of the system, and the provision of support to operations elements to address anomalies identified during operation and use of the system. The strategy considers approaches, schedules, resources, and specific considerations of continuous secure operation.

Service availability:

The security aspects of service availability include the incorporation of new or modified services, the removal or termination of services, and all coordination to ensure continuity in the security posture of the system while addressing service availability issues. The security aspects apply to all services and are not limited to security protection-oriented services of the system.

Staffing strategy for operators:

The security aspects of staffing include the number, qualifications, and scheduling of operators, contingency operations, and all associated training, competency, regulatory, and compliance needs.

Release and reacceptance criteria:

The security aspects of release and reacceptance criteria preserve the security posture of the system and address the timing and methods to securely incorporate services, revisions, patches, and enhancements in accordance with strategic plans and in response to on-demand needs.

Operational and contingency, degraded, alternative, and other modes of operation:

The security aspects of the operation strategy address the security posture of the system, inclusive of its security functions, across the defined modes of operation. The defined modes of operation, to include the shutdown/halted, standby, normal, degraded, reduced capacity, training, simulation, test, and other operations or sustainment modes specific to the system and its intended uses. Each mode of operation is defined by a security configuration and behavior that includes all defined transitions within and between modes. The aspects of the security strategy also include security-driven constraints and risks associated with operations actions in response to disruptions, hazards, and threats that may be warranted, but that may obviate the defined system security capabilities, limitations, constraints, and assumptions.

Measures for operation that provide insight into performance levels:

System operators need to be made aware of the security aspects of performance and be trained to detect and determine when security performance levels are not being met or when other system performance issues impact security performance.

Safety considerations:

Security and safety share the common characteristic of addressing what the system is not to do in terms of how the system is not to behave, the interactions that are not to occur, and the outcomes that the system should not produce. The system aspects of secure operation may intersect, complement, or be in direct conflict or contradiction with those of safe operation of the system. System operators and other personnel that interact with the system in its operational modes are to be made aware of these issues and be trained accordingly.

Monitoring for changes in hazards and threats and the results of operational monitoring activities:

The security aspects of the operations strategy include data and information collection for security situational awareness assessment. The data collection provides insight into variances in the knowledge of disruption, hazard, and threat events in the environment and how they combine with operations to provide vulnerability with potential security-relevant consequences. The security aspects also include determination of the limits of certainty about the data and information collected; the inherent uncertainty of conclusions and decisions made as a result of the monitoring activities; and the effectiveness, limitations, and constraints of monitoring activities.

OP-1.2   Identify the constraints resulting from the security aspects of operation to be incorporated into the system requirements, architecture, and design.

Elaboration: The security aspects, considerations, and characteristics associated with achieving continuous secure operation across all system modes, the training of individuals to be able to operate the system in a secure manner, and the provision of security support to operations elements, may translate to explicit needs, constraints, and limitations captured in the system requirements, architecture, and design. Such considerations, aspects, and characteristics are identified and provided as input to needs analyses, requirements analyses, and architecture and design definition processes.

OP-1.3   Identify, plan for, and obtain access to enabling systems or services to support the security aspects of operation.

Elaboration: Specific enabling systems and services may be required to support the security aspects of the operation process. Enabling systems and services are relied upon to provide the capability to realize and support the system-of-interest, and therefore impact the trustworthiness of the system. The operation-oriented security concerns for enabling systems and services used to support the operation process must be determined and captured as security requirements and as security-driven constraints for the interfaces and interactions with the system-of-interest. The *Validation* process is used to confirm that enabling systems and services achieve their intended use and do so with an appropriate level of trustworthiness.

OP-1.4 Identify or define security training and qualification requirements; train, and assign personnel needed for system operation.

Elaboration: Secure system operation requires properly qualified and trained personnel. Security qualification and training is based on identified requirements, and may include, for example, competency, proficiency, certification, and other criteria (perhaps recurring) to ensure that personnel are reasonably able to operate and use the system in all of its defined modes or states relative to operational element needs and constraints. The training and qualification address specialized role- and function-oriented objectives and also include generalized security awareness training.

References: ISO/IEC/IEEE 15288, Section 6.4.12.3 a); ISO/IEC 27036.

Related Publications: ISO/IEC 12207, Section 6.4.9.3.1; ISO/IEC 21827; NIST SP 800-37; NIST SP 800-53A; NIST SP 800-137.

OP-2   PERFORM SECURE OPERATION

OP-2.1 Securely use the system in its intended operational environment.

Elaboration: The operation strategy contains the security aspects of operation and is used to guide all aspects of secure use of the system within the capabilities and limitations of its intended use; in its intended operational environments; and in all specified system modes and contingency modes.

OP-2.2 Apply materials and other resources, as required, to operate the system in a secure manner and sustain its security services.

Elaboration: Sustained secure operation of the system may require specific materials and resources. These include security-oriented human infrastructure and material resources needs.

OP-2.3 Monitor the security aspects of system operation.

Elaboration: The security aspects of the operation strategy and security concept of operations serve to guide the monitoring of the system. Monitoring the security aspects of system operations focuses on adherence to the operation strategy; assurance that the system is operated in a secure manner and compliant with governing legislation and operations guidelines; and confirming that expected performance and effectiveness objectives are being met.

Adherence to the operation strategy:

The operation strategy drives all security-relevant behavior and outcomes. Security concerns related to the operation strategy include nonconformance in execution and insufficiency of the operation strategy. A nonconformance in execution of the operation strategy may invalidate the assumptions and expectations for intended use within stated capabilities and limitations, and with resultant security-relevant consequences. Nonconformance includes activities of misuse, abuse, and actions of adversaries, as they may achieve their objectives by intentionally violating the operation strategy. Insufficiency of the operation strategy includes weaknesses, flaws, and errors whereby the strategy lacks coverage, completeness, or effectiveness in addressing the security consequences of disruption, hazards, and threats.

Assurance the system is operated in a secure manner and compliant with governing legislative and operations policies, directives, and regulations:

System security analysis leads to an assurance and trustworthiness determination, and residual risk acceptance that is predicated on operating the system only as specified within its stated capabilities and limitations, and for its intended use. Security concerns associated with operations monitoring focuses on capturing data that demonstrates that all governing legislative and operations policies, directives, Executive Orders, regulations, instructions, and procedures are followed and satisfy compliance requirements.

Confirmation that service performance is within acceptable parameters:

The secure operation of the system is achieved based on an expectation that the system is capable of performing as specified (i.e., correctness and effectiveness in its ability to provide for its self-protection and the protection of all stakeholder assets), and that it is able to continuously do so despite failure (forced or unforced) associated with disruptions, hazards, and threats. Security concerns associated with performance monitoring involve the collection of data that supports the analysis and determination that the required protection capability is effective and continues to be effective despite disruptions, hazards, and threats. Security operations monitoring has two forms: it is designed into the system and is part of the inherent system security capability; and it serves to confirm realization of "as specified" behavior and performance.

OP-2.4 Identify and record when system security performance is not within acceptable parameters.

Elaboration: Focus for system security performance is placed on the results of system behavior and the outcomes associated with the entire system: machine/technology (e.g., hardware, software, and firmware); personnel (e.g., policies, procedures, and practices); and physical/environment (e.g., facilities, structures). These results may be identified and recorded by a combination of manual, automated, and autonomous means. Unacceptable system performance may have clear security relevance (e.g., a security incident tied to nonconformance with operational concepts, policies, or procedures; protection-related failures associated with disruption, hazards, or threats), while other incidents might require forensics, operations, and other types of analyses to identify and substantiate security relevance.

OP-2.5 Perform system security contingency operations, if necessary.

Elaboration: The system must be able to continue to operate in a secure manner, as necessary, in accordance with defined system capabilities and limitations across all identified contingency situations. Contingency operations may include degraded, diminished capacity, and other modes and states with the goal to provide for security operation throughout the contingency mode of operation. Contingency operations also include those operations that securely recover the system to a fully functional operational mode. There may be certain modes of operation for which security functions and services are reduced or eliminated to achieve higher-criticality system functions and services. The balance between security performance and other system performance objectives during contingency operations is captured in operational concepts and procedures.

References: ISO/IEC/IEEE 15288, Section 6.4.12.3 b); ISO/IEC 15026.

Related Publications: ISO/IEC 12207, Section 6.4.9.3.3; ISO/IEC 21827; NIST SP 800-37; NIST SP 800-53A; NIST SP 800-137.

OP-3 MANAGE RESULTS OF SECURE OPERATION

OP-3.1 Record results of secure operation and any security anomalies encountered.

Elaboration: Focus is placed on the correctness, effectiveness, and practicality of the operation strategy; the operation of enabling systems; the execution of the operation; and system definition.

The *Project Assessment and Control* process is used to analyze the data to identify causes; to enable corrective or improvement actions; and to record lessons learned.

OP-3.2   Record the security aspects of operational incidents and problems and track their resolution.

Elaboration: Focus for the security-related operational incidents and problem is placed on results of system behavior and the outcomes associated with the entire system: machine/technology (e.g., hardware, software, and firmware); personnel (e.g., policies, procedures, and practices); and physical/environment (e.g., facilities, structures). These results may be recorded by a combination of manual, automated, and autonomous means. Resolution may require forensics, operations, and other analyses to identity and substantiate security relevance. Tracking the resolution ensures that any perceived or actual security relevance is explicitly addressed. The *System Analysis*, *Quality Assurance*, and *Project Assessment and Control* processes are used to support the recording and tracking of security-related incidents and problems. The other technical processes are used in coordination with the *Risk Management* and *Decision Management* processes to address changes to the requirements, architecture, design, or system elements.

OP-3.3   Maintain traceability of the security aspects of the operations elements.

Elaboration: Traceability of operational system elements to the system security requirements, security architecture, and security design is maintained throughout the stages of the system life cycle. Traceability demonstrates that the system is capable of being operated and used in a secure manner and provides the evidence that supports assurance and trustworthiness claims.

OP-3.4   Provide security-relevant information items required for operation to baselines.

Elaboration: The security aspects of operation are captured in various artifacts that are maintained in an identified baseline for the life cycle of the system. The security-relevant configuration items are identified and incorporated into engineering baselines so that they may be produced and made available as required throughout the system life cycle. The *Configuration Management* process manages the baseline and the artifacts identified by this process. The *Information Management* process determines the appropriate forms of information and protections for the information that is provided to stakeholders.

References: ISO/IEC/IEEE 15288, Section 6.4.12.3 c); ISO/IEC 15026.

Related Publications: ISO/IEC 21827; NIST SP 800-37; NIST SP 800-53A; NIST SP 800-137.

OP-4   SUPPORT SECURITY NEEDS OF CUSTOMERS

OP-4.1   Provide security assistance and consultation to customers as requested.

Elaboration: Security assistance and consultation is provided as specified in agreements and may include direct-support services or the identification of recommended sources for security support assistance and services.

OP-4.2   Record and monitor requests and subsequent actions for security support.

Elaboration: Requests for support may not explicitly identify a security-related support need and the resultant action may fail to address a legitimate security concern or may cause a security-related issue. Monitoring requests and subsequent actions may identify trends or enable the correlation of specific security issues across varying types of requests for support.

OP-4.3   Determine the degree to which the delivered system security services satisfy the needs of the customers.

Elaboration: The ongoing results of provided system security support services are analyzed and required action is identified to provide continued customer satisfaction. Customer security support service satisfaction data is input to the *Quality Management* process to support continuous quality improvement objectives.

References: ISO/IEC/IEEE 15288, Section 6.4.12.3 d).

Related Publications: ISO/IEC 12207, Section 6.4.9.3.4, Section 6.4.9.3.5; ISO/IEC 21827; NIST SP 800-37; NIST SP 800-137.

3.4.13 Maintenance Process

Purpose

"The purpose of the Maintenance process is to sustain the capability of the system to provide a service."

ISO/IEC/IEEE 15288-2015. Reprinted with permission from IEEE, Copyright IEEE 2015, All rights reserved.

Systems Security Engineering Purpose

Systems security engineering, as part of the *Maintenance* process, establishes the requirements and constraints to enable maintenance elements to sustain delivery of the specified system security services and provides engineering support to maintenance elements. This process identifies the security-relevant capabilities, knowledge, and skills for those individuals assigned responsibility to maintain the system-of-interest; monitors the system's capability to deliver security functions and services; records incidents for security analysis; takes corrective, adaptive, perfective, and preventive actions; and confirms restored system security posture and associated capability to deliver security functions and services. This process also addresses the requirements and constraints to securely sustain logistics support and capacity and to ensure asset protection capability is properly extended to system element parts, components, and supplies, and to the logistics methods, enabling systems, supply chains, and tools utilized by maintenance elements.

Systems Security Engineering Outcomes

- The security aspects of the maintenance strategy are developed.

- The security aspects of maintenance and logistics that constrain system requirements, architecture, or design are identified.

- Any enabling systems or services needed to support the security aspects of system maintenance and logistics are available.

- Replacement, repaired, or modified system elements are available in consideration of their security aspects.

- The need for changes to address security-relevant corrective, perfective, or adaptive maintenance is reported.

- Security-relevant aspects, failure, and lifetime data, including associated costs, are determined.

- Traceability of the security aspects of the maintained elements is established.

Systems Security Engineering Activities and Tasks

MA-1 PREPARE FOR THE SECURITY ASPECTS OF MAINTENANCE

    MA-1.1 Define the security aspects of the maintenance strategy.

    Elaboration: The security aspects of the maintenance strategy or maintenance concept, address the approaches, schedules, resources, and specific security considerations required to perform maintenance of the system and systems elements in conformance with operational availability requirements. The strategy spans corrective and preventive maintenance, scheduled preventive actions, the logistics strategy, number and types of replacements, counterfeit protection, personnel levels and skills, and maintenance performance measures. The maintenance strategy applies regardless of the security-relevant role of the system element. It provides assurance for all maintenance actions; the individuals that perform those actions; how the actions are performed; the resources used to perform the actions; and the criteria for acceptance of the results of the maintenance actions.

Corrective and preventive maintenance:

These security aspects include the secure transition of the system or system element from an operational mode or state into a suitable maintenance mode or state (and back again), to include the need to perform corrective or preventive maintenance actions while the system or system element remains in operational mode or state. Additional security aspects include performance of corrective and preventive maintenance actions in conformance with all applicable laws, directives, regulations, policies, or instructions; in conformance with approved maintenance-enabling systems and tools; and to accomplish the maintenance actions securely regardless of the physical location or maintenance element that performs the actions.

Scheduled preventive actions:

The security aspects reduce the likelihood of security incidents; unaccounted for exposure and therefore vulnerability; or the degradation or failure of system security function or service performance or effectiveness. The security aspects contribute to a reduced likelihood of the undue loss of services or impact on normal operations due to system security concerns. The scheduled preventive actions may be required by law or regulation.

Logistics strategy:

The security aspects address acquisition and operations logistics. The aspects provide for secure identification and marking, sourcing, packaging, distribution, handling, storage, provisioning, and acceptance of necessary material, data, information, and other resources to ensure their availability in the right quantity and quality, at the right place and time throughout the system life cycle.

Number and type of replacements:

The security aspects address the criteria and means to provide for the security of system element replacements at their storage locations; their secure storage conditions and needs; and their storage life and renewal frequency.

Counterfeit and modification prevention:

The security aspects focus on achieving authenticity and integrity of system elements with respect to unauthorized alteration, adaptation, modification, substitution, or replacement. The objective is to prevent counterfeit or modified system elements from being introduced into the system by the application of prevention and detection measures throughout logistics and maintenance activities. The measures address misuse, abuse, and malicious activities that result in counterfeit or modified system elements. These security considerations are incorporated into acceptance methods and procedures, and are also related to maintenance performance measures.

Personnel levels and skills:

The security aspects address security-specific qualifications, skills, and competencies associated with security technologies used in system elements, and general security awareness understanding, levels, and skills for all maintenance and logistics personnel.

Maintenance and logistics performance measures:

The security aspects provide data used to acquire security insight into performance levels, effectiveness, efficiency of, and assurance in maintenance and logistics strategies, methods, technique, and tools. The security insight gained applies to explicit security maintenance and logistics activities, and to the security constraints levied on maintenance and logistics activities.

MA-1.2 Identify the system constraints resulting from the security aspects of maintenance and logistics to be incorporated into the system requirements, architecture, and design.

Elaboration: Security aspects, considerations, and characteristics associated with maintaining the system and with system logistics may translate to explicit needs, constraints, and limitations captured in the system requirements, architecture, and design. Such considerations, aspects, and characteristics are identified and provided as input to needs analyses, requirements analyses, and architecture and design definition processes.

MA-1.3 Identify trades such that the security aspects of system maintenance and logistics result in a solution that is trustworthy, secure, affordable, operable, supportable, and sustainable.

Elaboration: The ability to sustain the delivered security functions and services of the system at a defined level of trustworthiness is dependent on life cycle considerations driven by maintenance and logistics. All system trades must be informed by security considerations of maintenance and logistics to balance security objectives against system life cycle affordability, supportability, and sustainability relative to operational performance objectives and acceptance of loss and risk. The *System Analysis* and *Decision Management* processes are used to support trade space activities regarding the conduct of secure maintenance and logistics actions.

MA-1.4 Identify, plan for, and obtain enabling systems or services to support the security aspects of system maintenance and logistics.

Elaboration: Specific enabling systems and services may be required to support the security aspects of the maintenance process including the logistics aspects of the process. Enabling systems and services are relied upon to provide the capability to sustain and support the system-of-interest, and therefore impact the trustworthiness of the system. The maintenance- and logistics-oriented security concerns for enabling systems and services used to support the maintenance process must be determined and captured as security requirements and as security-driven constraints for the interfaces and interactions with the system-of-interest. The *Validation* process is used to confirm that enabling systems and services achieve their intended use and do so with an appropriate level of trustworthiness.

The vastness and complexity of the system maintenance and logistics hierarchies, geographical distribution, and shear number of personnel and systems involved presents a challenging security problem in the potential for abuse, misuse, and attacks that result in direct or indirect harm to the system-of-interest, its security functions and services, and its protection of stakeholder assets. Maintenance systems and services include support equipment, tools, facilities, and specialized methods and techniques provided by maintenance elements. Logistics systems and services include parts storage, selection, and handling systems and services; transportation, distribution, and delivery systems and services; and all associated specialized methods and techniques provided by logistics elements.

References: ISO/IEC/IEEE 15288, Section 6.4.13.3 a); ISO/IEC 15026; ISO/IEC 27036.

Related Publications: ISO/IEC 12207, Section 6.4.10.3.1; ISO/IEC 21827; NIST SP 800-37.

MA-2 PERFORM THE SECURITY ASPECTS OF MAINTENANCE

MA-2.1 Review incident and problem reports to identify security relevance and associated maintenance needs.

Elaboration: Maintenance needs are addressed by a combination of corrective, adaptive, perfective, and preventive maintenance. Incident and problem reports include security and non-security incident reports. However, there may be security relevance to incidents and reports that are absent of security specifics or that appear to have no security connection or basis. The review of incident and problem reports for security relevance and applicability informs the identification of maintenance need and provides the security consideration for the conduct of the maintenance actions.

MA-2.2 Record the security aspects of maintenance incidents and problems and track their resolution.

Elaboration: A reported maintenance incident may constitute a security incident or may have security-relevant ramifications. These security aspects are recorded and tracked to support continuous improvement in validated maintenance procedures. The information recorded is provided to the *Quality Assurance* and *Project Assessment and Control* processes for tracking and corrective action resolution.

MA-2.3 Implement the procedures for the correction of random faults or scheduled replacement of system elements to ensure the ability to deliver system security functions and services.

Elaboration: Maintenance actions must be completed, with a level of assurance achieved through performance verification, that the system is able to deliver its security functions and services. This requires procedures for addressing random system faults and the replacement of system elements. The random faults may or may not be attributed to security-relevant elements. However, these random faults may impact the delivery of security functions and services. Similarly, system element replacement may not involve an element that provides or supports a security function or service, but may impact the ability of the system to deliver security functions and services.

MA-2.4 Implement action to restore the system to secure operational status when a random fault causes a system failure.

Elaboration: System requirements include those requirements that address secure operational status, the ability to maintain secure operational status, and the ability to restore the system to a contingency operational mode. The results of the action taken are verified. The particular action taken is decided with consideration of verification success and stakeholder needs relative to the operational objectives and constraints levied by the environment. The action taken may be based on whether security performance dominates operational capability and other system properties, or if operational capability and other system properties dominate security function and service.

MA-2.5 Perform preventive maintenance by replacing or servicing system elements prior to failure with security-related impact.

Elaboration: Timely and effective preventive maintenance can reduce the number of failures that result in asset loss and associated consequences. Preventive maintenance in response to knowledge gained from misuse, abuse, attacks, disruptions, hazards, and threats may be affected through periodic revisions, upgrades, patches, and other means. The timing of preventive maintenance activities is to be coordinated with operations elements to minimize overall impact. Preventive maintenance activity may alter system configuration, performance, and effectiveness, to include established assurance and trustworthiness and any related assumptions, constraints, or limitations that support assurance and trustworthiness conclusions. Preventive maintenance activities require verification prior to incorporating those activities into the system-of-interest, and/or prior to utilization of the system elements that received preventive maintenance action.

MA-2.6 Perform failure identification actions when security noncompliance has occurred in the system.

Elaboration: Security noncompliance is determined relative to stakeholder requirements and associated concerns. These are informed by the expectations, scope, and limits established by laws, regulations, directives, policies, regulatory bodies, and Executive Orders. An identified security noncompliance is reviewed to identify the cause or causes of the failure in order to take appropriate and effective corrective action to make the system security compliant. Security noncompliance may be identified outside the scope of the maintenance element and therefore is closely associated with the operations element, logistics element, and other elements.

MA-2.7 Identify when security-relevant adaptive or perfective maintenance is required.

Elaboration: Security analyses are conducted to determine the nature of any required adaptive or perfective maintenance driven by security concerns. The resultant maintenance action may apply to system elements that provide security functions and service or to any system element. The identified security-relevant adaptive and perfective maintenance action may result in changes to system requirements, architecture, and design. Such actions may also result in new or changed protection needs, which require analyses to determine how those needs are captured in the system requirements, architecture, and design. Any maintenance action taken requires verification and validation prior to making the system available for use.

References: ISO/IEC/IEEE 15288, Section 6.4.13.3 b); ISO/IEC 15026.

Related Publications: ISO/IEC 12207, Section 6.4.10.3.2, Section 6.4.10.3.3, Section 6.4.10.3.4, Section 6.4.10.3.5; ISO/IEC 21827; NIST SP 800-37.

MA-3 PERFORM THE SECURITY ASPECTS OF LOGISTICS SUPPORT

MA-3.1 Perform the security aspects of acquisition logistics.

Elaboration: The logistics strategy contains the security aspects of acquisition logistics and is used to guide all logistics actions in conjunction with agreements resulting from the agreement processes. The security aspects of acquisition logistics ensure that security protection capability, performance, effectiveness, and trustworthiness are factored into trades where those objectives impact, and are impacted by, logistics actions and implications across the life cycle.

MA-3.2 Perform the security aspects of operational logistics.

Elaboration: The logistics strategy contains the security aspects of operational logistics and is used to guide and inform all logistics actions in conjunction with agreements resulting from the agreement processes and the system resulting from the technical processes. The security aspects of operational logistics ensure that security protection capability, performance, effectiveness, and trustworthiness are factored into trades where those objectives impact, and are impacted by, logistics actions and implications across the life cycle.

MA-3.3 Implement any secure packaging, handling, storage, and transportation needed during the life cycle of the system.

Elaboration: This includes security identification and marking; secure sourcing, packaging and handling; trusted distribution; secure handling, storage, provisioning; and acceptance of material, data and information, and other resources to ensure their availability in the right quantity and quality, at the right place and time, throughout the system life cycle. Security considerations apply to logistics support systems, facilities and structures, transport vehicles, and to personnel and associated methods and processes.

MA-3.4 Confirm that security aspects incorporated into logistics actions satisfy the required protection levels so that system elements are securely stored and able to meet repair rates and planned schedules.

Elaboration: Data is collected to confirm that instituted storage protections and procedures are being properly used and are adequate and effective in order to enable secure storage of system elements with no adverse impact on repair rates and planned schedules.

MA-3.5 Confirm that the security aspects of logistics actions include security supportability requirements that are planned, resourced, and implemented.

Elaboration: Security supportability requirements for logistics include, for example, properly trained, qualified, and staffed personnel; the availability of validated security-informed methods, manuals, equipment, and tools utilized by logistics personnel; and secured facilities. The logistics supportability requirements must address security concerns at a level of assurance commensurate with the target level of assurance for the system-of-interest. Data is collected to confirm that these requirements are identified and satisfied in the planning, resourcing, and implementation of the logistics actions performed by logistics elements.

References: ISO/IEC/IEEE 15288, Section 6.4.13.3 c); ISO/IEC 15026; ISO/IEC 27036.

Related Publications: ISO/IEC 21827; NIST SP 800-37.

MA-4 MANAGE RESULTS OF THE SECURITY ASPECTS OF MAINTENANCE AND LOGISTICS

MA-4.1 Record the security aspects of maintenance and logistics results and any security anomalies encountered.

Elaboration: The security aspects and anomalies focus on the correctness, effectiveness, execution, and feasibility of the maintenance and logistics strategy; the maintenance and logistics of enabling systems; and the system definition. The *Project Assessment and Control* process is used to analyze the data to identify causes, to enable corrective or improvement actions, and to record lessons learned.

MA-4.2 Record operational security incidents and security problems and track their resolution.

Elaboration: Focus is placed on results of system behavior and outcomes associated with the entire system including machine/technology (e.g., hardware, software, and firmware); personnel (e.g., policies, procedures, and practices); and physical/environment (e.g., facilities, structures). The results may be recorded by a combination of manual, automated, and autonomous means. Resolution may require forensics, operations, and other analyses to identify and substantiate security relevance. Tracking the resolution ensures that any perceived or actual security relevance is explicitly addressed. The *System Analysis*, *Quality Assurance*, and *Project Assessment and Control* processes interact with this task. The other technical processes interact with the *Risk Management* and *Decision Management* processes to address any changes to the requirements, architecture, design, or system elements. The task relies on the same data and information as the equivalent task in the *Operation* process.

MA-4.3 Identify and record the security-related trends of incidents, problems, and maintenance and logistics actions.

Elaboration: Security-related trends of incidents, problems, and maintenance actions may be indicative of technology issues; personnel issues associated with processes, procedures, skills, competency, training, or related issues; awareness of previously unknown or undetected vulnerabilities; or variances in the hazard and threat environment. Focus is placed on results of behavior/outcomes for the entire system including machine/technology (e.g., hardware, software, and firmware); personnel (e.g., policies, procedures, and practices); and physical/environment (e.g., facilities, structures). The results may be identified and recorded by a combination of manual, automated, and autonomous means. Trends may have clear security relevance (e.g., a security incident tied to nonconformance with operational, maintenance, or logistics concepts, policy, and procedure; protection-related failures associated with disruption, hazards, and threats), while other trends might require forensics, operations, procedural, or other analyses to identify and substantiate any security relevance. The *System Analysis* process is informed by data collected by this task.

MA-4.4 Maintain traceability of system elements and the security aspects of maintenance actions and logistics actions performed.

Elaboration: Traceability of system elements to the system security requirements, security architecture, and security design is maintained throughout the stages of the system life cycle. Traceability of the security aspects of maintenance and logistics actions demonstrates that the system is capable of being operated and used in a sustained, secure manner as system elements undergo maintenance actions, and provides the evidence that supports the associated assurance and trustworthiness claims.

MA-4.5 Provide security-relevant configuration items from system maintenance to baselines.

Elaboration: The security aspects of maintenance and logistics are captured in various artifacts that are maintained in an identified baseline for the life cycle of the system. The security-relevant maintenance and logistics configuration items are identified and incorporated into engineering baselines so that they may be produced and made available as required throughout the system life cycle. The *Configuration Management* process manages the baseline and the artifacts identified by this process. The *Information Management* process determines the appropriate forms of information and protections for the information that is provided to stakeholders.

MA-4.6 Monitor customer satisfaction with the security aspects of system performance and maintenance support.

Elaboration: Data is collected, analyzed, and response actions are identified to ensure customer satisfaction in the security aspects of system performance, and maintenance and logistics support. The data is provided as input to the *Quality Management* process to support continuous quality improvement objectives.

References: ISO/IEC/IEEE 15288, Section 6.4.13.3 d); ISO/IEC 15026; ISO 10004.

Related Publications: ISO/IEC 21827; NIST SP 800-37.

3.4.14 Disposal Process

Purpose

"The purpose of the Disposal process is to end the existence of a system element or system for a specified intended use, appropriately handle replaced or retired elements, and to properly attend to identified critical disposal needs (e.g., per an agreement, per organizational policy, or for environmental, legal, safety, security aspects)."

ISO/IEC/IEEE 15288-2015. Reprinted with permission from IEEE, Copyright IEEE 2015, All rights reserved.

Systems Security Engineering Purpose

Systems security engineering, as part of the *Disposal* process, provides for the security aspects of ending the existence of a system element or system for a specified intended use. It accounts for the methods and techniques used to securely handle, transport, package, store, or destroy retired elements, to include the data and information associated with the system or contained in system elements. It also accounts for the protection and/or sanitization methods employed in the handling of sensitive system components, data, and information during the disposal process to achieve stakeholder security objectives and to comply with regulatory guidelines. The termination of a system element also applies to human resources and addresses all concerns to ensure they are securely removed from their role as a system element that contributes to the security posture of the system.

Systems Security Engineering Outcomes

- The security aspects of the disposal strategy are developed.

- The security aspects of disposal that constrain system requirements, architecture, or design are identified.

- Any enabling systems or services needed to support the security aspects of disposal are available.

- System elements are securely removed from service, destroyed, stored, reclaimed, or recycled.

- The environment is returned to its original secure or agreed-upon secure state.

- Records of secure disposal actions and analysis are available.

Systems Security Engineering Activities and Tasks

DS-1   PREPARE FOR THE SECURITY ASPECTS OF DISPOSAL

   DS-1.1   Develop the security aspects of the disposal strategy.

   Elaboration: The security aspects of the disposal strategy address the approach used to securely terminate system functions and services; transform the system and environment into an acceptable secure state; address security concerns; and transition the system and system elements for future use. The strategy determines approaches, schedules, resources, specific considerations of secure disposal, and the effectiveness and completeness of secure disposal and disposition actions.

Permanent termination of system functions and delivery of services:

The security aspects address the removal, decommissioning, or destruction of the system elements associated with the terminated functions and services, while preserving the security posture of any remaining system functions and services.

Permanent termination of personnel:

The security aspects address the removal of system personnel with specific security-relevant roles, responsibilities, privileges, authorizations, or authorities. These aspects include required collection of access/authorization badges, keys, and tokens; collection of data and information; and revoking authorizations, passwords, tokens, and other means by which machine/technology and physical system elements can be utilized by the terminated personnel.

Transform the system and environment into an acceptable state:

The security aspects address any alterations made to the system, its operation, and the environment to ensure that stakeholder protection needs and concerns are addressed by the remaining portions of the system and the functions and services it provides. For the case where the entire system is removed, the security aspects address alterations to the environment to return it to its original or agreed-upon secure state.

Address security concerns for material, data, and information:

The security aspects address protections for sensitive components, technology, information, and data when they are removed from service, dismantled, stored, prepared for reuse, or destroyed. The security aspects may include the duration of protection level/state, downgrades, releasability, and criteria that defines authorized access and use during the storage period. The protection needs for disposal are defined by stakeholders, by agreements, and may also be subject to regulatory requirements, expectations, and constraints.

Transition the system and system elements for future use:

The security aspects address the transition of the system or system elements for future use in a modified or adapted form, to include legacy migration and return to service. The security aspects may include constraints, limitations, or other criteria to enable recovery of the systems' functions and services within a specified time period, or to ensure security-oriented interoperability with future enabling systems and other systems. These aspects may also include periodic inspections to account for the security posture and return-to-service readiness of stored system elements and associated data and information, and all supporting operations and sustainment support materials. The security aspects apply to all system functions and services and are not limited to only security protection-oriented functions and services of the system.

DS-1.2 Identify the system constraints resulting from the security aspects of disposal to be incorporated into the system requirements, architecture, and design.

Elaboration: Security aspects, considerations, and characteristics associated with system disposal may translate to explicit needs, constraints, and limitations captured in the system requirements, architecture, and design. Such considerations, aspects, and characteristics are identified and provided as input to needs analyses, requirements analyses, and architecture and design definition processes. The security-driven response to the termination of personnel may require specific constraints that are captured in the system requirements, architecture, and design.

DS-1.3 Identify, plan for, and obtain the enabling systems or services to support the secure disposal of the system.

Elaboration: Specific enabling systems and services may be required to support the security aspects of the disposal process. Enabling systems and services are relied upon to provide the capability to realize and support the system-of-interest, and therefore impact the trustworthiness of the system. The disposal-oriented security concerns for enabling systems and services used to support the disposal process must be determined and captured as security requirements and as security-driven constraints for the interfaces and interactions with the system-of-interest. The

Validation process is used to confirm that enabling systems and services achieve their intended use and do so with an appropriate level of trustworthiness.

DS-1.4 Specify secure storage criteria for the system if it is to be stored.

Elaboration: The criteria for secure storage address containment facilities, storage locations, inspection criteria, and storage periods/duration. The security criteria include, for example, physical access protections for storage facilities; the length of storage; the access authorizations for individuals; the storage verification checks, audits, and inspections; and the period after which the secure storage criteria is no longer applicable.

DS-1.5 Identify and preclude terminated personnel or disposed system elements and materials from being returned to service.

Elaboration: Terminated personnel and known or circumspect system elements are identified so as to prevent their subsequent use in a recovered system or use as an element of some other system. Terminated personnel may be subjected to permanent disbandment or other criteria that may allow their return to service. Material resources that are not to be repurposed, reclaimed, or reused are identified and dismantled, destroyed, or provided for analyses.

References: ISO/IEC/IEEE 15288, Section 6.4.14.3 a).

Related Publications: ISO/IEC 12207, Section 6.4.11.3.1; ISO/IEC 21827; NIST SP 800-37.

DS-2 PERFORM THE SECURITY ASPECTS OF DISPOSAL

DS-2.1 Deactivate the system or system element to prepare it for secure removal from operation.

Elaboration: Deactivation procedures and activities are to be accomplished such that there is no further use or reliance on the deactivated system or any system elements, and no further use or dependence on functions or services whose security characteristics are provided in full or in part by the deactivated system or system elements. This may require alternative security functions and services to be put into effect.

DS-2.2 Securely remove the system or system element from use for appropriate secure disposition and action.

Elaboration: Secure removal of the system or system element is performed to preserve secure function and service of those elements not removed. The removed system or system elements are then prepared for designated secure disposition including for reuse, recycling, overhaul, storage, or destruction. The secure disposition includes marking, packaging, and handling during transport from the operational environment to the destination at which the secure disposition takes place. The secure disposition of system elements not destroyed must account for those elements that are to undergo analysis or further action to determine their suitability for reuse and eventual return to service via the supply chain or other means. The security aspects for any disassembly that is required when a system or system element is removed from service must be addressed.

DS-2.3 Securely withdraw impacted operating staff from the system and record relevant secure operation knowledge.

Elaboration: Staff that are no longer needed as a result of the termination of system functions or system services or staff that are terminated for any other reason may constitute a security concern. Security-oriented closeout actions prevent such staff from constituting a threat to ongoing system functions or services or to data, information, and material associated with the system or terminated system elements. Methods to withdraw staff include revoking access authorizations; reclaiming access credentials, keys, and tokens; and collecting all sensitive data, information, and material assets.

DS-2.4 Disassemble the system or system element into manageable components and ensure that appropriate protections are in place for those components during removal for reuse, recycling, reconditioning, overhaul, archiving, or destruction.

Elaboration: Secure disassembly of the system or system element preserves the security characteristics of the disassembled system or system element until it is ready for the intended disposition action. The secure disassembly also preserves the security characteristics of those system elements not removed. The disposition actions for the system or system elements once removed from service must be addressed.

DS-2.5 Sanitize system elements and life cycle artifacts in a manner appropriate to the disposition action.

Elaboration: Disposition actions include reuse, recycling, reconditioning, overhaul, and destruction. System elements and life cycle artifacts such as technical manuals, operations procedures, system performance, incident, and trend data and reports are sanitized to remove sensitive proprietary intellectual property, and personnel data and information. Specialized sanitization or redaction techniques and methods may be required for a specific disposal action, technology, or artifact type. Documentation, tools, or equipment necessary for sanitization should be identified and acquired as part of the *Design* and *Implementation* processes. Additionally, there may be compliance requirements for governing laws and regulations to include those that prohibit destruction or that dictate retention time periods before destruction. Sanitization techniques include clearing, purging, cryptographic erase, physical modification, and physical destruction.

DS-2.6 Manage system elements and their parts that are not intended for reuse to prevent them from reentering the supply chain.

Elaboration: Security methods are put in place to confirm that any removed system element and associated parts are confirmed to be destroyed if there is no intent for them to be reused, recycled, refurbished, overhauled, or in any other matter utilized in a future system or system element.

References: ISO/IEC/IEEE 15288, Section 6.4.14.3 b).

Related Publications: ISO/IEC 12207, Section 6.4.11.3.2; ISO/IEC 21827; NIST SP 800-37.

DS-3   FINALIZE THE SECURITY ASPECTS OF DISPOSAL

DS-3.1 Confirm that no unresolved security factors exist following disposal of the system.

Elaboration: The completed disposal actions and the disposition of removed system elements are to result in no outstanding security issues or concerns. The effectiveness and completeness of these actions are confirmed based on criteria derived from the security aspects of the disposal strategy.

DS-3.2 Return the environment to its original state or to a secure state specified by agreement.

Elaboration: The disposed system or system elements may have required security-oriented modifications to the environment to satisfy the security assumptions levied on the environment. Removal of the system or system elements may obviate the continued need for some or all of these security-oriented modifications and the environment is returned to its original state (which may or may not be secure) or some agreed-upon secure state.

DS-3.3 Archive and protect information generated during the life cycle of the system.

Elaboration: The disposed system or system elements may have required security-oriented modifications to the environment to satisfy the security assumptions levied on the environment. Removal of the system or system elements may obviate the continued need for some or all of these security-oriented modifications and the environment is returned to its original state (which may or may not be secure) or some agreed-upon secure state.

References: ISO/IEC/IEEE 15288, Section 6.4.14.3 c).

Related Publications: ISO/IEC 21827; NIST SP 800-37.

APPENDIX A

REFERENCES

KEY REFERENCES RELATED TO SYSTEMS SECURITY ENGINEERING

LEGISLATION, POLICIES, DIRECTIVES, INSTRUCTIONS	
[EGovAct]	E-Government Act of 2002 (P.L. 107-347), December 17, 2002.
[FISMA]	Federal Information Security Modernization Act of 2014, (P.L. 113-283, Title II), December 18, 2014.
[OMB A-130]	Office of Management and Budget (OMB) Circular A-130, Appendix III, Transmittal Memorandum #4, *Management of Federal Information Resources*, November 2000.
[CNSSI 4009]	Committee on National Security Systems Instruction (CNSSI) No. 4009, *Committee on National Security Systems (CNSS) Glossary*, April 2015.
[DODD 8140.01]	Department of Defense (DoD) Directive 8140.01, *Cyberspace Workforce Management*, August 2015.

STANDARDS AND GUIDELINES	
[ANSI/EIA 649B]	American National Standards Institute/Electronic Industries Alliance (ANSI/EIA) 649B, *Configuration Management Standard*, June 2011.
[FIPS 199]	National Institute of Standards and Technology, Federal Information Processing Standards (FIPS) Publication 199, *Standards for Security Categorization of Federal Information and Information Systems*, February 2004. http://csrc.nist.gov/publications/fips/fips199/FIPS-PUB-199-final.pdf (accessed 10/28/16).
[FIPS 200]	National Institute of Standards and Technology, Federal Information Processing Standards (FIPS) Publication 200, *Minimum Security Requirements for Federal Information and Information Systems*, March 2006. http://csrc.nist.gov/publications/fips/fips200/FIPS-200-final-march.pdf (accessed 10/28/16).
[IEEE 610.12]	Institute of Electrical and Electronics Engineers (IEEE) Std. 610.12-1990, *IEEE Standard Glossary of Software Engineering Terminology*, December 1990.
[IEEE 828]	Institute of Electrical and Electronics Engineers (IEEE) Std. 828-2012, *IEEE Standard for Configuration Management in Systems and Software Engineering*, IEEE Computer Society, March 2012.
[IEEE 1471]	Institute of Electrical and Electronic Engineers (IEEE) Std. 1471:2000, *IEEE Recommended Practice for Architectural Description of Software-Intensive Systems*, September 2000.

[ISO 73]	International Organization for Standardization (ISO) Guide 73:2009, *Risk management – Vocabulary*, November 2009.
[ISO 9000]	International Organization for Standardization (ISO) 9000:2015, *Quality management systems – Fundamentals and vocabulary*, September 2015.
[ISO 9001]	International Organization for Standardization (ISO) 9001:2015, *Quality management systems – Requirements*, September 2015.
[ISO 9241]	International Organization for Standardization (ISO) 9241-210:2010, *Ergonomics of human-system interaction — Part 210: Human-centered design for interactive systems*, March 2010.
[ISO 10007]	International Organization for Standardization (ISO) 10007:2003, *Quality management systems – Guidelines for configuration management*, July 2003.
[ISO/TS 18152]	International Organization for Standardization/Technical Specification (ISO/TS) 18152:2010, *Ergonomics of human-system interaction — Specification for the process assessment of human-system issues*, June 2010.
[ISO 31000]	International Organization for Standardization (ISO) 31000:2009, *Risk management – Principles and guidelines*, November 2009.
[ISO/IEC 12207]	International Organization for Standardization/International Electrotechnical Commission/Institute of Electrical and Electronics Engineers (ISO/IEC/IEEE) 12207:2008, *Systems and software engineering – Software life cycle processes*, February 2008.
[ISO/IEC 15026-1]	International Organization for Standardization/International Electrotechnical Commission (ISO/IEC) 15026-1:2013, *Systems and software engineering -- Systems and software assurance -- Part 1: Concepts and vocabulary*, November 2013.
[ISO/IEC 15026-2]	International Organization for Standardization/International Electrotechnical Commission (ISO/IEC) 15026-2:2011, *Systems and software engineering -- Systems and software assurance -- Part 2: Assurance case*, February 2011.
[ISO/IEC 15026-3]	International Organization for Standardization/International Electrotechnical Commission (ISO/IEC) 15026-3:2015, *Systems and software engineering -- Systems and software assurance -- Part 3: System integrity levels*, November 2015.
[ISO/IEC 15026-4]	International Organization for Standardization/International Electrotechnical Commission (ISO/IEC) 15026-4:2012, *Systems and software engineering -- Systems and software assurance -- Part 4: Assurance in the life cycle*, October 2012.
[ISO/IEC/IEEE 15288]	International Organization for Standardization/International Electrotechnical Commission/Institute of Electrical and Electronics Engineers (ISO/IEC/IEEE) 15288:2015, *Systems and software engineering — Systems life cycle processes*, May 2015.

[ISO/IEC 16085]   International Organization for Standardization/International Electrotechnical Commission (ISO/IEC) 16085:2006, *Systems and software engineering — Life cycle processes — Risk management*, December 2006.

[ISO/IEC/IEEE 16326]   International Organization for Standardization/International Electrotechnical Commission/Institute of Electrical and Electronics Engineers (ISO/IEC/IEEE) 16326:2009, *Systems and software engineering — Life cycle processes — Project management*, February 2009.

[ISO/IEC 15408-1]   International Organization for Standardization/International Electrotechnical Commission (ISO/IEC) 15408-1:2009, *Information technology — Security techniques — Evaluation criteria for IT security — Part 1: Introduction and general model*.

[ISO/IEC 15408-2]   International Organization for Standardization/International Electrotechnical Commission (ISO/IEC) 15408-2:2008, *Information technology — Security techniques — Evaluation criteria for IT security — Part 2: Security functional requirements*.

[ISO/IEC 15408-3]   International Organization for Standardization/International Electrotechnical Commission (ISO/IEC) 15408-3:2008, *Information technology — Security techniques — Evaluation criteria for IT security — Part 3: Security assurance requirements*.

[ISO/IEC 15939]   International Organization for Standardization/International Electrotechnical Commission (ISO/IEC) 15939:2007, *Systems and software engineering – Measurement process*, August 2007.

[ISO/IEC 21827]   International Organization for Standardization/International Electrotechnical Commission (ISO/IEC) 21827:2008, *Information technology — Security techniques — Systems Security Engineering — Capability Maturity Model® (SSE-CMM®)*, October 2008.

[ISO/IEC 25010]   International Organization for Standardization/International Electrotechnical Commission (ISO/IEC) 25010:2011, *Systems and software engineering – Systems and software Quality Requirements and Evaluation (SQuaRE) – System and software quality models*, March 2011.

[ISO/IEC 25030]   International Organization for Standardization/International Electrotechnical Commission (ISO/IEC) 25030:2007, *Software Engineering — Software product Quality Requirements and Evaluation (SQuaRE) — Quality Requirements*, March 2007.

[ISO/IEC TR 25060]   International Organization for Standardization/International Electrotechnical Commission (ISO/IEC) TR 25060:2010, *Systems and software engineering — Systems and software product Quality Requirements and Evaluation (SQuaRE) — Common Industry Format (CIF) for usability: General framework for usability-related information*, July 2010.

[ISO/IEC 25063]   International Organization for Standardization/International
                      Electrotechnical Commission (ISO/IEC) 25063:2014, *Systems and
                      software engineering – Systems and software product Quality
                      Requirements and Evaluation (SQuaRE) – Common Industry Format
                      (CIF) for usability: Context of use description*, March 2014.

[ISO/IEC TR 24748-   International Organization for Standardization/International
1]   Electrotechnical Commission (ISO/IEC) TR 24748-1:2010, *Systems
                      and software engineering — Life cycle management — Part 1: Guide
                      for life cycle management*, October 2010.

[ISO/IEC/IEEE   International Organization for Standardization/International
24765]   Electrotechnical Commission/Institute of Electrical and Electronics
                      Engineers (ISO/IEC/IEEE) 24765:2010, *Systems and software
                      engineering — Vocabulary*, December 2010.

[ISO/IEC 27001]   International Organization for Standardization/International
                      Electrotechnical Commission (ISO/IEC) 27001:2013, *Information
                      technology -- Security techniques -- Information security management
                      systems -- Requirements*, September 2013.

[ISO/IEC 27002]   International Organization for Standardization/International
                      Electrotechnical Commission (ISO/IEC) 27002:2013, *Information
                      technology -- Security techniques -- Code of practice for information
                      security controls*, September 2013.

[ISO/IEC 27034-1]   International Organization for Standardization/International
                      Electrotechnical Commission (ISO/IEC) 27034-1:2011, *Information
                      technology — Security techniques — Application security — Part 1:
                      Overview and concepts*, November 2011.

[ISO/IEC 27036-1]   International Organization for Standardization/International
                      Electrotechnical Commission (ISO/IEC) 27036-1:2014, *Information
                      technology — Security techniques — Information security for supplier
                      relationships — Part 1: Overview and concepts*, April 2014.

[ISO/IEC 27036-2]   International Organization for Standardization/International
                      Electrotechnical Commission (ISO/IEC) 27036-2:2014, *Information
                      technology — Security techniques — Information security for supplier
                      relationships — Part 2: Requirements*, August 2014.

[ISO/IEC 27036-3]   International Organization for Standardization/International
                      Electrotechnical Commission (ISO/IEC) 27036-3:2013, *Information
                      technology — Security techniques — Information security for supplier
                      relationships — Part 3: Guidelines for information and
                      communication technology supply chain security*, November 2013.

[ISO/IEC 29119-1]   International Organization for Standardization/International
                      Electrotechnical Commission (ISO/IEC) 29119-1:2013, *Software
                      Testing: Concepts and Definitions*, September 2013.

[ISO/IEC 29119-2]   International Organization for Standardization/International
                      Electrotechnical Commission (ISO/IEC) 29119-2:2013, *Software
                      Testing: Test Processes*, September 2013.

[ISO/IEC 29119-3]   International Organization for Standardization/International
Electrotechnical Commission (ISO/IEC) 29119-3:2013, *Software
Testing: Test Documentation*, September 2013.

[ISO/IEC 29119-4]   International Organization for Standardization/International
Electrotechnical Commission (ISO/IEC) 29119-4:2014, *Software
Testing: Test Techniques*, December 2014.

[ISO/IEC/IEEE   International Organization for Standardization /International
29148]   Electrotechnical Commission/Institute of Electrical and Electronics
Engineers (ISO/IEC/IEEE) 29148:2011, *Systems and software
engineering — Life cycle processes – Requirements engineering*,
December 2011.

[ISO/IEC/IEEE   International Organization for Standardization (ISO)/International
42010]   Electrotechnical Commission (IEC)/Institute of Electrical and
Electronics Engineers (IEEE), ISO/IEC/IEEE 42010, *Systems and
Software Engineering — Architecture description*, December 2011.

[SP 800-30]   National Institute of Standards and Technology Special Publication
(SP) 800-30 Revision 1, *Guide for Conducting Risk Assessments*,
September 2012.
https://doi.org/10.6028/NIST.SP.800-30r1.

[SP 800-37]   National Institute of Standards and Technology Special Publication
(SP) 800-37 Revision 1, *Guide for Applying the Risk Management
Framework to Federal Information Systems: A Security Life Cycle
Approach*, February 2010 (updated June 5, 2014).
https://doi.org/10.6028/NIST.SP.800-37r1.

[SP 800-53]   National Institute of Standards and Technology Special Publication
(SP) 800-53 Revision 4, *Security and Privacy Controls for Federal
Information Systems and Organizations*, April 2013 (updated January
22, 2015).
https://doi.org/10.6028/NIST.SP.800-53r4.

[SP 800-53A]   National Institute of Standards and Technology Special Publication
(SP) 800-53A Revision 4, *Assessing Security and Privacy Controls in
Federal Information Systems and Organizations: Building Effective
Assessment Plans*, December 2014 (updated December 18, 2014).
https://doi.org/10.6028/NIST.SP.800-53Ar4.

[SP 800-137]   National Institute of Standards and Technology Special Publication
(SP) 800-137, *Information Security Continuous Monitoring for
Federal Information Systems and Organizations*, September 2011.
https://doi.org/10.6028/NIST.SP.800-137.

[SP 800-181]   National Institute of Standards and Technology Special Publication
(SP) 800-181 (Draft) *NICE Cybersecurity Workforce Framework
(NCWF): National Initiative for Cybersecurity Education (NICE)*,
November 2016.
http://csrc.nist.gov/publications/PubsSPs.html#SP-800-181.

	OTHER PUBLICATIONS
[Anderson72]	J. Anderson, *Computer Security Technology Planning Study*, Technical Report ESD-TR-73- 51, Air Force Electronic Systems Division, Hanscom AFB, October 1972.
[Bass12]	L. Bass, P. Clements, and R. Kazman, *Software Architecture in Practice*, 3rd ed., Upper Saddle River, New Jersey: Addison-Wesley, 2012.
[Bishop05]	M. Bishop, *Introduction to Computer Security*, Addison-Wesley, 2005.
[Bodeau11]	D. Bodeau and R. Graubart, *Cyber Resiliency Engineering Framework*, The MITRE Corporation, September 2011.
[DHS Risk]	Department of Homeland Security, *DHS Risk Lexicon*, September 2010.
[Herley2016]	C. Herley, *Unfalsifiability of Security Claims*, Microsoft Research, Proceedings of the National Academy of Sciences, April 2016.
[INCOSE14]	System Engineering Handbook—A Guide for System Engineering Life Cycle Processes and Activities, International Council On Systems Engineering TP-2003-002-04, 4th Edition, July 2015.
[Levin07]	T. Levin, C. Irvine, T. Benzel, G. Bhaskara, P. Clark, and T. Nguyen, *Design Principles and Guidelines for Security*, Technical Report NPS-CS-07-014, Naval Postgraduate School, November 2007.
[Madni09]	A. Madni and S. Jackson, *Towards a Conceptual Framework for Resilience Engineering*, IEEE Systems Journal, Vol. 3, No. 2, June 2009.
[Maier98]	M. Maier, *Architecting Principles for Systems-of-Systems*, The Aerospace Corporation, 1998.
[Mead10]	N. Mead, J. Allen, M. Ardis, T. Hilburn, A. Kornecki, R. Linger, and J. McDonald, *Software Assurance Curriculum Project Volume I: Master of Software Assurance Reference Curriculum*, (CMU/SEI-2010-TR-005) Software Engineering Institute, Carnegie Mellon University, August 2010.
[McEvilley15]	M. McEvilley, *Towards a Notional Framework for Systems Security Engineering*, The MITRE Corporation, NDIA 18th Annual Systems Engineering Conference, October 2015.
[MIL-HDBK]	Department of Defense Handbook, *System Security Engineering Program Management Requirements*, MIL-HDBK-1785, August 1995.
[Moore10]	J. Moore, *ISO/IEC/IEEE 15288 and ISO/IEC/IEEE 12207: The Entry-Level Process Standards*, The MITRE Corporation, April 2010.
[Myers80]	P. Myers, *Subversion: The Neglected Aspect of Computer Security*, Master's thesis, Naval Postgraduate School, June 1980.
[NASA11]	*National Aeronautics and Space Administration System Safety Handbook*, November 2011.

[Neumann04]   P. Neumann, *Principled Assuredly Trustworthy Composable Architectures*, CDRL A001 Final Report, SRI International, Menlo Park, CA, December 28, 2004.

[NIAC]   National Infrastructure Advisory Council, *A Framework for Establishing Critical Infrastructure Resilience Goals: Final Report and Recommendations by the Council*, October 2010.

[OPF]   *OPEN Process Framework (OPF)* [Web page], OPEN Process Framework Repository Organization (OPFRO), 2009.

[Roedler05]   G. Roedler and C. Jones, *Technical Measurement*, International Council on Systems Engineering, INCOSE TP-2003-020-01, December 2005.

[Saltzer75]   J. Saltzer and M. Schroeder, "The Protection of Information in Computer Systems," in *Proceedings of the IEEE 63(9)*, September 1975, pp. 1278-1308.

[SEI-Glossary]   *SEI Software Architecture Glossary* [Web page], Software Engineering Institute (SEI), Carnegie Mellon University, Pittsburgh, Pennsylvania.

[SEI-Over]   *SEI Software Architecture Overview* [Web page], Software Engineering Institute (SEI), Carnegie Mellon University, Pittsburgh, Pennsylvania.

[SEI-CERT]   Software Engineering Institute, *CERT Resilience Management Model, Version 1.0: Improving Operational Resilience Processes*, May 2010.

[Sterbenz06]   J. Sterbenz and D. Hutchinson, *ResilieNets: Multilevel Resilient and Survivable Networking Initiative*, August 2006.

[Sterne91]   D. Sterne, "On the Buzzword Security Policy," in *Proceedings of the 1991 IEEE Computer Society Symposium on Research in Security and Privacy*, May 20-22, 1991, pp. 219-230.
                  https://doi.org/10.1109/RISP.1991.130789.

[TOGAF]   *The Open Group Architecture Framework (TOGAF)* [Web page], Version 9.1, The Open Group, 2011.

[Ware70]   W. Ware, *Security Controls for Computer Systems*, Report of the Defense Science Board Task Force on Computer Security, February 1970.

[Weissman69]   C. Weissman, "Security Controls in the ADEPT-50 Time-Sharing System," in *AFIPS Conference Proceedings, Volume 35, 1969 Fall Joint Computer Conference*, November 18-20, 1969, pp. 119-133.

APPENDIX B

GLOSSARY

COMMON TERMS AND DEFINITIONS

Appendix B provides definitions for engineering and security terminology used within Special Publication 800-160.

acquirer [ISO/IEC/IEEE 15288]	Stakeholder that acquires or procures a product or service from a supplier.
acquisition [ISO/IEC/IEEE 15288]	Process of obtaining a system, product, or service.
activity [ISO/IEC/IEEE 15288]	Set of cohesive tasks of a process.
adverse consequence [ISO/IEC 15026]	An undesirable consequence associated with a loss.
agreement [ISO/IEC/IEEE 15288]	Mutual acknowledgement of terms and conditions under which a working relationship is conducted.
analysis of alternatives	An analytical comparison or evaluation of proposed approaches to meet an objective. An analysis of alternatives can be applied to anything—from a large military acquisition decision to a decision between two products. The formal or informal process involves identifying key decision factors, such as life cycle operations, support, training, and sustainment costs, risk, effectiveness, and assessing each alternative with respect to these factors.
	An analysis of alternatives is an analytical comparison of the operational effectiveness, cost, and risks of proposed materiel solutions to gaps and shortfalls in operational capability. Such analyses document the rationale for identifying/recommending a preferred solution or solutions to the identified shortfall. Threat changes, deficiencies, obsolescence of existing systems, or advances in technology can trigger an analysis of alternatives.
architecture	A set of related physical and logical representations (i.e., views) of a system or a solution. The architecture conveys information about system/solution elements, interconnections, relationships, and behavior at different levels of abstractions and with different scopes.
	Refer to *security architecture.*
architecture (system) [ISO/IEC/IEEE 42010]	Fundamental concepts or properties of a system in its environment embodied in its elements, relationships, and in the principles of its design and evolution.
architecture description [ISO/IEC/IEEE 42010]	A work product used to express an architecture.

architecture framework [ISO/IEC/IEEE 42010]	Conventions, principles, and practices for the description of architectures established within a specific domain of application and/or community of stakeholders.
architecture trade-off analysis	A method for evaluating architecture-level designs that considers multiple attributes including, for example, modifiability, security, performance, and reliability to gain insight as to whether the fully described architecture will meet its requirements. The method identifies trade-off points among these attributes, facilitates communication among stakeholders (e.g., customer, developer, maintainer) from the perspective of each attribute, clarifies and refines requirements, and provides a framework for an ongoing, concurrent process of system design and analysis.
architecture view [ISO/IEC/IEEE 42010]	A work product expressing the architecture of a system from the perspective of specific system concerns.
architecture viewpoint [ISO/IEC/IEEE 42010]	A work product establishing the conventions for the construction, interpretation, and use of architecture views to frame specific system concerns.
asset	An item of value to achievement of organizational mission/business objectives. *Note 1:* Assets have interrelated characteristics that include value, criticality, and the degree to which they are relied upon to achieve organizational mission/business objectives. From these characteristics, appropriate protections are to be engineered into solutions employed by the organization. *Note 2:* An asset may be tangible (e.g., physical item such as hardware, software, firmware, computing platform, network device, or other technology components) or intangible (e.g., information, data, trademark, copyright, patent, intellectual property, image, or reputation).
assurance [ISO/IEC 15026]	Grounds for justified confidence that a claim has been or will be achieved. *Note 1:* Assurance is typically obtained relative to a set of specific claims. The scope and focus of such claims may vary (e.g., security claims, safety claims) and the claims themselves may be interrelated. *Note 2:* Assurance is obtained through techniques and methods that generate credible evidence to substantiate claims.
assurance case [ISO/IEC 15026]	A reasoned, auditable artifact created that supports the contention that its top-level claim (or set of claims), is satisfied, including systematic argumentation and its underlying evidence and explicit assumptions that support the claim(s).
assurance evidence	The information upon which decisions regarding assurance, trustworthiness, and risk of the solution are substantiated. *Note:* Assurance evidence is specific to an agreed-to set of claims. The security perspective focuses on assurance evidence for security-relevant claims whereas other engineering disciplines may have their own focus (e.g., safety).

availability [EGovAct]	Ensuring timely and reliable access to and use of information.
	Note: Mission/business resiliency objectives extend the concept of availability to refer to a point-in-time availability (i.e., the system, component, or device is usable when needed) and the continuity of availability (i.e., the system, component, or device remains usable for the duration of the time it is needed).
baseline [IEEE 828]	Formally approved version of a configuration item, regardless of media, formally designated and fixed at a specific time during the configuration item's life cycle.
	Note: The engineering process generates many artifacts that are maintained as a baseline over the course of the engineering effort and after its completion. The configuration control processes of the engineering effort manage baselined artifacts. Examples include stakeholder requirements baseline, system requirements baseline, architecture/design baseline, and configuration baseline.
body of evidence	The totality of evidence used to substantiate trust, trustworthiness, and risk relative to the system.
claim [ISO/IEC 15026]	A true-false statement about the limitations on the values of an unambiguously defined property called the claim's property; and limitations on the uncertainty of the property's values falling within these limitations during the claim's duration of applicability under stated conditions.
component	See *system element*.
concept of secure function	A strategy for achievement of secure system function that embodies proactive and reactive protection capability of the system.
	Note 1: This strategy strives to prevent, minimize, or detect the events and conditions that can lead to the loss of an asset and the resultant adverse impact; prevent, minimize, or detect the loss of an asset or adverse asset impact; continuously deliver system capability at some acceptable level despite the impact of threats or uncertainty; and recover from an adverse asset impact to restore full system capability or to recover to some acceptable level of system capability.
	Note 2: The concept of secure function is adapted from historical and other secure system concepts such as *Philosophy of Protection*, *Theory of Design and Operation*, and *Theory of Compliance*.
concern (system) [ISO/IEC/IEEE 42010]	Interest in a system relevant to one or more of its stakeholders.
confidentiality [EGovAct]	Preserving authorized restrictions on information access and disclosure, including means for protecting personal privacy and proprietary information.
configuration item [ISO/IEC/IEEE 15288]	Item or aggregation of hardware, software, or both, that is designated for configuration management and treated as a single entity in the configuration management process.

consequence
[ISO/IEC 15026]

Effect (change or non-change), usually associated with an event or condition or with the system and usually allowed, facilitated, caused, prevented, changed, or contributed to by the event, condition, or system.

constraints

Factors that impose restrictions and limitations on the system or actual limitations associated with the use of the system.

criticality

An attribute assigned to an asset that reflects its relative importance or necessity in achieving or contributing to the achievement of stated goals.

customer
[ISO 9000]

Organization or person that receives a product or service.

cyber-physical system

A system that includes engineered, interacting networks of physical and computational components.

derived requirement

A requirement that is implied or transformed from a higher-level requirement.

Note 1: Implied requirements cannot be assessed since they are not contained in any requirements baseline. The decomposition of requirements throughout the engineering process makes implicit requirements explicit, allowing them to be stated and captured in appropriate baselines and allowing associated assessment criteria to be stated.

Note 2: A derived requirement must trace back to at least one higher-level requirement.

design
[ISO/IEC/IEEE 15288]

Process of defining the system elements, interfaces, and other characteristics of a system of interest in accordance with the requirements and architecture.

design trade-off analysis

Analysis that is focused on determining the design approach that is best suited for implementing the elements, physical safeguards, and procedural measures of the system.

Note: A design trade-off analysis includes the following considerations: whether technical elements, physical safeguards, or procedural measures are appropriate to implement the system security requirements; and whether acquiring an off-the-shelf product, accessing or developing a service or custom development is appropriate to implement the system security requirements.

element

Organizations, departments, facilities, or personnel responsible for a particular systems security engineering activity conducted within an engineering process (e.g., operations elements, logistics elements, maintenance elements, and training elements).

enabling system
[ISO/IEC/IEEE 15288]

System that supports a system-of-interest during its life cycle stages but does not necessarily contribute directly to its function during operation.

engineering team

The individuals on the systems engineering team with security responsibilities, systems security engineers that are part of the systems engineering team, or a combination thereof.

environment (system) [ISO/IEC/IEEE 42010]	Context determining the setting and circumstances of all influences upon a system.
event [ISO 73]	Occurrence or change of a particular set of circumstances.
evidence	Grounds for belief or disbelief; data on which to base proof or to establish truth or falsehood. *Note 1:* Evidence can be objective or subjective. Evidence is obtained through measurement, the results of analyses, experience, and the observation of behavior over time. *Note 2:* The security perspective places focus on credible evidence used to obtain assurance, substantiate trustworthiness, and assess risk.
facility [ISO/IEC/IEEE 15288]	Physical means or equipment for facilitating the performance of an action, e.g., buildings, instruments, tools.
incident [ISO/IEC/IEEE 15288]	Anomalous or unexpected event, set of events, condition, or situation at any time during the life cycle of a project, product, service, or system.
independent verification and validation [IEEE 610.12]	Verification and validation (V&V) performed by an organization that is technically, managerially, and financially independent of the development organization.
information system [EGovAct]	A discrete set of information resources organized for the collection, processing, maintenance, use, sharing, dissemination, or disposition of information. Refer to *system.*
integrity (information) [EGovAct]	Guarding against improper information modification or destruction, and includes ensuring information non-repudiation and authenticity.
level of risk [ISO 73]	Magnitude of a risk or combination of risks, expressed in terms of the combination of consequences and their likelihood.
life cycle [ISO/IEC/IEEE 15288]	Evolution of a system, product, service, project or other human-made entity from conception through retirement.
life cycle model [ISO/IEC/IEEE 15288]	Framework of processes and activities concerned with the life cycle that may be organized into stages, which also acts as a common reference for communication and understanding.
life cycle security concepts	The processes, methods, and procedures associated with the system throughout its life cycle and provides distinct contexts for the interpretation of system security. Life cycle security concepts apply during program management, development, engineering, acquisition, manufacturing, fabrication, production, operations, sustainment, training, and retirement.
likelihood [ISO 73]	Chance of something happening.

mechanism	A process or system that is used to produce a particular result.
	The fundamental processes involved in or responsible for an action, reaction, or other natural phenomenon.
	A natural or established process by which something takes place or is brought about.
	Refer to *security mechanism*.
	Note: A mechanism can be technology- or nontechnology-based (e.g., apparatus, device, instrument, procedure, process, system, operation, method, technique, means, or medium).
model kind [ISO/IEC/IEEE 42010]	Conventions for a type of modeling.
monitoring [ISO 73]	Continual checking, supervising, critically observing or determining the status in order to identify change from the performance level required or expected.
operator [ISO/IEC/IEEE 15288]	Individual or organization that performs the operations of a system.
organization [ISO 9000]	Group of people and facilities with an arrangement of responsibilities, authorities, and relationships.
party [ISO/IEC/IEEE 15288]	Organization entering into an agreement.
penetration testing	A test methodology intended to circumvent the security function of a system.
	Note: Penetration testing may leverage system documentation (e.g., system design, source code, manuals) and is conducted within specific constraints. Some penetration test methods use brute force techniques.
process [ISO 9000]	Set of interrelated or interacting activities which transforms inputs into outputs.
	A program in execution.
process purpose [ISO/IEC/IEEE 15288]	High-level objective of performing the process and the likely outcomes of effective implementation of the process.
process outcome [ISO/IEC/IEEE 12207]	Observable result of the successful achievement of the process purpose.
product [ISO 9000]	Result of a process.
	Note: A system as a "product" is what is delivered by systems engineering.
project [ISO/IEC/IEEE 15288]	Endeavour with defined start and finish criteria undertaken to create a product or service in accordance with specified resources and requirements.
project portfolio [ISO/IEC/IEEE 15288]	Collection of projects that addresses the strategic objectives of the organization.

protection needs	Informal statement or expression of the stakeholder security requirements focused on protecting information, systems, and services associated with mission/business functions throughout the system life cycle. *Note:* Requirements elicitation and security analyses transform the protection needs into a formalized statement of stakeholder security requirements that are managed as part of the validated stakeholder requirements baseline.
qualification [ISO/IEC/IEEE 12207]	Process of demonstrating whether an entity is capable of fulfilling specified requirements.
quality assurance [ISO 9000]	Part of quality management focused on providing confidence that quality requirements will be fulfilled.
quality management [ISO 9000]	Coordinated activities to direct and control an organization with regard to quality.
requirement [ISO/IEC/IEEE 29148] [IEEE 610.12, adapted]	Statement that translates or expresses a need and its associated constraints and conditions. A condition or capability that must be met or possessed by a system or system element to satisfy a contract, standard, specification, or other formally imposed documents.
requirements engineering	A series of successive decomposition and derivation actions beginning with stakeholder requirements and moving through high-level design requirements to low-level design requirements to the implementation of the design. During requirements engineering, several requirements baselines are defined. These baselines include: a functional baseline that provides the basis for contracting and controlling the system design; an allocated baseline that provides performance requirements for each configuration item of the system; and a product baseline that provides a detailed design specification for system elements.
retirement [ISO/IEC/IEEE 12207]	Withdrawal of active support by the operation and maintenance organization, partial or total replacement by a new system, or installation of an upgraded system.
residual risk [ISO 73]	Risk remaining after risk treatment.
risk [ISO 73]	Effect of uncertainty on objectives. *Note:* Risk can be positive or negative, where positive risk may also be referred to as an opportunity.
risk analysis [ISO 73]	Process to comprehend the nature of risk and to determine the level of risk.
risk assessment [ISO 73]	Overall process of risk identification, risk analysis, and risk evaluation.
risk criteria [ISO 73]	Terms of reference against which the significance of a risk is evaluated.

risk evaluation
[ISO 73]

Process of comparing the results of risk analysis with risk criteria to determine whether the risk and/or its magnitude is acceptable or tolerable.

risk identification
[ISO 73]

Process of finding, recognizing, and describing risks.

risk management
[ISO 73]

Coordinated activities to direct and control an organization with regard to risk.

risk tolerance
[ISO 73]

The organization's or stakeholder's readiness to bear the risk after risk treatment in order to achieve its objectives.

Note: Risk tolerance can be influenced by legal or regulatory requirements.

risk treatment
[ISO 73]

Process to modify risk.

security

Freedom from those conditions that can cause loss of assets with unacceptable consequences.

security architecture

A set of physical and logical security-relevant representations (i.e., views) of system architecture that conveys information about how the system is partitioned into security domains and makes use of security-relevant elements to enforce security policies within and between security domains based on how data and information must be protected.

Note: The security architecture reflects security domains, the placement of security-relevant elements within the security domains, the interconnections and trust relationships between the security-relevant elements, and the behavior and interactions between the security-relevant elements. The security architecture, similar to the system architecture, may be expressed at different levels of abstraction and with different scopes.

security concept of operations
[CNSSI 4009, adapted]

A security-focused description of a system, its operational policies, classes of users, interactions between the system and its users, and the system's contribution to the operational mission.

Note 1: The security concept of operations may address security for other life cycle concepts associated with the deployed system. These include, for example, concepts for sustainment, logistics, maintenance, and training.

Note 2: Security concept of operations is not the same as *concept for secure function*. Concept for secure function addresses the design philosophy for the system and is intended to achieve a system that is able to be used in a trustworthy secure manner. The security concept of operations must be consistent with the concept for secure function.

security control

A mechanism designed to address needs as specified by a set of security requirements.

security domain

A domain within which behaviors, interactions, and outcomes occur and that is defined by a governing security policy.

Note: A security domain is defined by rules for users, processes, systems, and services that apply to activity within the domain and activity with similar entities in other domains.

security function	The capability provided by the system or a system element. The capability may be expressed generally as a concept or specified precisely in requirements.
security mechanism	A method, tool, or procedure that is the realization of security requirements. *Note 1:* A security mechanism exists in machine, technology, human, and physical forms. *Note 2:* A security mechanism reflects security and trust principles. *Note 3:* A security mechanism may enforce security policy and therefore must have capabilities consistent with the intent of the security policy.
security policy	A set of rules that governs all aspects of security-relevant system and system element behavior. *Note 1:* System elements include technology, machine, and human, elements. *Note 2:* Rules can be stated at very high levels (e.g., an organizational policy defines acceptable behavior of employees in performing their mission/business functions) or at very low levels (e.g., an operating system policy that defines acceptable behavior of executing processes and use of resources by those processes).
security relevance	The term used to describe those functions or mechanisms that are relied upon, directly or indirectly, to enforce a security policy that governs confidentiality, integrity, and availability protections.
security requirement	A requirement that specifies the functional, assurance, and strength characteristics for a mechanism, system, or system element.
security service	A security capability of function provided by an entity.
security specification	The requirements for the security-relevant portion of the system. *Note:* The security specification may be provided as a separate document or may be captured with a broader specification.
service [ISO/IEC/IEEE 12207]	A capability or function provided by an entity. Performance of activities, work, or duties.
specification [IEEE 610.12]	A document that specifies, in a complete, precise, verifiable manner, the requirements, design, behavior, or other characteristics of a system or component and often the procedures for determining whether these provisions have been satisfied. Refer to *security specification*.
stage [ISO/IEC/IEEE 15288]	Period within the life cycle of an entity that relates to the state of its description or realization.
stakeholder [ISO/IEC/IEEE 15288]	Individual or organization having a right, share, claim, or interest in a system or in its possession of characteristics that meet their needs and expectations.
stakeholder (system) [ISO/IEC/IEEE 42010]	Individual, team, organization, or classes thereof, having an interest in a system.

strength of function

Criterion expressing the minimum efforts assumed necessary to defeat the specified security behavior of an implemented security function by directly attacking its underlying security mechanisms.

Note 1: Strength of function has as a prerequisite that assumes that the underlying security mechanisms are correctly implemented. The concept of strength of functions may be equally applied to services or other capability-based abstraction provided by security mechanisms.

Note 2: The term robustness combines the concepts of assurance of correct implementation with strength of function to provide finer granularity in determining the trustworthiness of a system.

supplier
[ISO/IEC/IEEE 15288]

Organization or an individual that enters into an agreement with the acquirer for the supply of a product or service.

system
[ISO/IEC/IEEE 15288]

Combination of interacting elements organized to achieve one or more stated purposes.

Note 1: There are many types of systems. Examples include: general and special-purpose information systems; command, control, and communication systems; crypto modules; central processing unit and graphics processor boards; industrial/process control systems; flight control systems; weapons, targeting, and fire control systems; medical devices and treatment systems; financial, banking, and merchandising transaction systems; and social networking systems.

Note 2: The interacting elements in the definition of system include hardware, software, data, humans, processes, facilities, materials, and naturally occurring physical entities.

Note 3: System of systems is included in the definition of system.

system-of-interest
[ISO/IEC/IEEE 15288]

System whose life cycle is under consideration in the context of International Standard ISO/IEC/IEEE 15288.

Note 1: The system-of-interest is the system that is the focus of the systems engineering effort. The system-of-interest contains system elements, system element interconnections, and the environment in which they are placed.

Note 2: The boundary of the system-of-interest is typically determined relative to the authorization boundary. However, it can also be determined by other "boundaries" established by programmatic, operational, or jurisdictional control.

system-of-systems
[INCOSE14]

System-of-interest whose system elements are themselves systems; typically, these entail large-scale interdisciplinary problems with multiple, heterogeneous, distributed systems.

system context

The specific system elements, boundaries, interconnections, interactions, and environment of operation that define a system.

system element
[ISO/IEC/IEEE 15288]

Member of a set of elements that constitute a system.

Note 1: A system element can be a discrete component, product, service, subsystem, system, infrastructure, or enterprise.

Note 2: Each element of the system is implemented to fulfill specified requirements.

Note 3: The recursive nature of the term allows the term *system* to apply equally when referring to a discrete component or to a large, complex, geographically distributed system-of-systems.

Note 4: System elements are implemented by: hardware, software, and firmware that perform operations on data/information; physical structures, devices, and components in the environment of operation; and the people, processes, and procedures for operating, sustaining, and supporting the system elements.

system life cycle
[IEEE 610.12]

The period of time that begins when a system is conceived and ends when the system is no longer available for use.

Refer to *life cycle stages*.

system security requirements

System requirements that have security relevance. System security requirements define the protection capabilities provided by the system, the performance and behavioral characteristics exhibited by the system, and the evidence used to determine that the system security requirements have been satisfied.

Note: Each system security requirement is expressed in a manner that makes verification possible via analysis, observation, test, inspection, measurement, or other defined and achievable means.

systems engineering
[ISO/IEC/IEEE 24765]

Interdisciplinary approach governing the total technical and managerial effort required to transform a set of stakeholder needs, expectations, and constraints into a solution and to support that solution throughout its life.

[INCOSE]

An engineering discipline whose responsibility is creating and executing an interdisciplinary process to ensure that the customer and all other stakeholder needs are satisfied in a high-quality, trustworthy, cost-efficient, and schedule-compliant manner throughout a system's entire life cycle.

systems security engineer

Individual that performs any or all of the activities defined by the systems security engineering process, regardless of their formal title. Additionally, the term *systems security engineer* refers to multiple individuals operating on the same team or cooperating teams.

systems security engineering

Systems security engineering is a specialty engineering discipline of systems engineering that applies scientific, mathematical, engineering, and measurement principles, concepts, and methods to coordinate, orchestrate, and direct the activities of various security engineering specialties and other contributing engineering specialties to provide a fully integrated, system-level perspective of system security.

task
[ISO/IEC/IEEE 15288]

Required, recommended, or permissible action, intended to contribute to the achievement of one or more outcomes of a process.

threat

An event or condition that has the potential for causing asset loss and the undesirable consequences or impact from such loss.

Note: The specific causes of asset loss, and for which the consequences of asset loss are assessed, can arise from a variety of conditions and events related to adversity, typically referred to as disruptions, hazards, or threats. Regardless of the specific term used, the basis of asset loss constitutes all forms of intentional, unintentional, accidental, incidental, misuse, abuse, error, weakness, defect, fault, and/or failure events and associated conditions.

threat assessment

Assessment to evaluate the actual or potential effect of a threat to a system.

Note: The threat assessment may include identifying and describing the nature of the threat.

traceability analysis

The analysis of the relationships between two or more products of the development process conducted to determine that objectives have been met or that the effort represented by the products is completed.

Note: A requirements traceability analysis demonstrates that all system security requirements have been traced to and are justified by at least one stakeholder security requirement, and that each stakeholder security requirement is satisfied by at least one system security requirement.

traceability matrix
[IEEE 610.12]

A matrix that records the relationship between two or more products of the development process (e.g., a matrix that records the relationship between the requirements and the design of a given software component).

Note 1: A traceability matrix can record the relationship between a set of requirements and one or more products of the development process and can be used to demonstrate completeness and coverage of an activity or analysis based upon the requirements contained in the matrix.

Note 2: A traceability matrix may be conveyed as a set of matrices representing requirements at different levels of decomposition. Such a traceability matrix enables the tracing of requirements stated in their most abstract form (e.g., statement of stakeholder requirements) through decomposition steps that result in the implementation that satisfies the requirements.

trade-off
[ISO/IEC/IEEE 15288]

Decision-making actions that select from various requirements and alternative solutions on the basis of net benefit to the stakeholders.

trade-off analysis

Determining the effect of decreasing one or more key factors and simultaneously increasing one or more other key factors in a decision, design, or project.

trust relationship	An agreed upon relationship between two or more system elements that is governed by criteria for secure interaction, behavior, and outcomes relative to the protection of assets.
	Note: This refers to trust relationships between system elements implemented by hardware, firmware, and software.
trustworthiness [Neumann04]	Worthy of being trusted to fulfill whatever critical requirements may be needed for a particular component, subsystem, system, network, application, mission, enterprise, or other entity.
	Note: From a security perspective, a trustworthy system is a system that meets specific security requirements in addition to meeting other critical requirements.
trustworthy	The degree to which the security behavior of a component is demonstrably compliant with its stated functionality.
user [ISO/IEC 25010]	Individual or group that interacts with a system or benefits from a system during its utilization.
validation [ISO 9000]	Confirmation, through the provision of objective evidence, that the requirements for a specific intended use or application have been fulfilled.
verification [ISO 9000]	Confirmation, through the provision of objective evidence, that specified requirements have been fulfilled.
verification and validation [IEEE 610.12]	The process of determining whether the requirements for a system or component are complete and correct, the products of each development phase fulfill the requirements or conditions imposed by the previous phase, and the final system or component complies with specified requirements.
vulnerability [CNSSI 4009, adapted]	Weakness in a system, system security procedures, internal controls, or implementation that could be exploited or triggered by a threat.
vulnerability assessment [CNSSI 4009]	Systematic examination of an information system or product to determine the adequacy of security measures, identify security deficiencies, provide data from which to predict the effectiveness of proposed security measures, and confirm the adequacy of such measures after implementation.

APPENDIX C

ACRONYMS

COMMON ABBREVIATIONS

CNSS	Committee on National Security Systems
DoD	Department of Defense
IEC	International Electrotechnical Commission
IEEE	Institute of Electrical and Electronics Engineers
INCOSE	International Council on Systems Engineering
INFOSEC	Information Security
ISO	International Organization for Standardization
IT	Information Technology
NIST	National Institute of Standards and Technology
NDI	Non-Developmental Item
OASIS	Organization for the Advancement of Structured Information Standards
RFI	Request for Information
RFP	Request for Proposal
SDL	Security Development Lifecycle
SOW	Statement of Work
SSE	Systems Security Engineering

SUMMARY OF SYSTEMS SECURITY ACTIVITIES AND TASKS
SYSTEMS SECURITY ACTIVITIES AND TASKS FOR EACH SYSTEMS ENGINEERING PROCESS

The following tables provide a summary of the systems security engineering activities and tasks that are associated with the system life cycle processes in ISO/IEC/IEEE 15288:

- Table D-1 summarizes the activities and tasks from the *Agreement* processes;

- Table D-2 summarizes the activities and tasks from the *Organization Project-Enabling* processes;

- Table D-3 summarizes the activities and tasks from the *Technical Management* processes; and

- Table D-4 summarizes the activities and tasks from the *Technical* processes.

TABLE D-1: SSE ACTIVITIES AND TASKS IN THE AGREEMENT PROCESSES

	AGREEMENT PROCESSES
AQ	**Acquisition**
AQ-1	PREPARE FOR SECURITY ASPECTS OF THE AQUISITION
AQ-1.1	Define the security aspects for how the acquisition will be conducted.
AQ-1.2	Prepare a request for a product or service that includes the security requirements.
AQ-2	ADVERTISE THE ACQUISITION AND SELECT THE SUPPLIER TO CONFORM WITH THE SECURITY ASPECTS OF THE ACQUISITION
AQ-2.1	Communicate the request for a product or service to potential suppliers consistent with security requirements.
AQ-2.2	Select one or more suppliers that meet the security criteria.
AQ-3	ESTABLISH AND MAINTAIN THE SECURITY ASPECTS OF AGREEMENTS
AQ-3.1	Develop an agreement with the supplier to satisfy the security aspects of acquiring the product or service and supplier acceptance criteria.
AQ-3.2	Identify and evaluate the security impact of necessary changes to the agreement.
AQ-3.3	Negotiate and institute changes to the agreement with the supplier to address identified security impacts.
AQ-4	MONITOR THE SECURITY ASPECTS OF AGREEMENTS
AQ-4.1	Assess the execution of the security aspects of the agreement.
AQ-4.2	Provide data needed by the supplier in a secure manner in order to achieve timely resolution of issues.
AQ-5	ACCEPT THE PRODUCT OR SERVICE
AQ-5.1	Confirm that the delivered product or service complies with the security aspects of the agreement.
AQ-5.2	Accept the product or service from the supplier or other party, as directed by the security criteria in the agreement.
SP	**Supply**
SP-1	PREPARE FOR THE SECURITY ASPECTS OF THE SUPPLY
SP-1.1	Identify the security aspects of the acquirer's need for a product or service.
SP-1.2	Define the security aspects of the supply strategy.
SP-2	RESPOND TO A SOLICITATION
SP-2.1	Evaluate a request for a product or service with respect to the feasibility of satisfying the security criteria.
SP-2.2	Prepare a response that satisfies the security criteria expressed in the solicitation.
SP-3	ESTABLISH AND MAINTAIN THE SECURITY ASPECTS OF AGREEMENTS
SP-3.1	Develop an agreement with the acquirer to satisfy the security aspects of the product or service and security acceptance criteria.
SP-3.2	Identify and evaluate the security impact of necessary changes to the agreement.
SP-3.3	Negotiate and institute changes to the agreement with the acquirer to address identified security impacts.

AGREEMENT PROCESSES	
SP-4	EXECUTE THE SECURITY ASPECTS OF AGREEMENTS
SP-4.1	Execute the security aspects of the agreement according to the engineering project plans.
SP-4.2	Assess the execution of the security aspects of the agreement.
SP-5	DELIVER AND SUPPORT THE SECURITY ASPECTS OF THE PRODUCT OR SERVICE
SP-5.1	Deliver the product or service in accordance with the security aspects and considerations in the agreement with the acquirer.
SP-5.2	Provide security assistance to the acquirer as stated in the agreement.
SP-5.3	Transfer the responsibility for the product or service to the acquirer or other party, as directed by the security aspects and considerations in the agreement.

TABLE D-2: SSE ACTIVITIES AND TASKS IN THE ORGANIZATION PROJECT-ENABLING PROCESSES

	ORGANIZATION PROJECT-ENABLING PROCESSES
LM	**Life Cycle Model Management**
LM-1	ESTABLISH THE SECURITY ASPECTS OF THE PROCESS
LM-1.1	Establish policies and procedures for process management and deployment that are consistent with the security aspects of organizational strategies.
LM-1.2	Define the security roles, responsibilities, and authorities to facilitate implementation of the security aspects of processes and the strategic management of life cycles.
LM-1.3	Define the security aspects of the business criteria that control progression through the life cycle.
LM-1.4	Establish the security criteria of standard life cycle models for the organization.
LM-2	ASSESS THE SECURITY ASPECTS OF THE PROCESS
LM-2.1	Monitor and analyze the security aspects of process execution across the organization.
LM-2.2	Conduct periodic reviews of the security aspects of the life cycle models used by the projects.
LM-2.3	Identify security improvement opportunities from assessment results.
LM-3	IMPROVE THE SECURITY ASPECTS OF THE PROCESS
LM-3.1	Prioritize and plan for security improvement opportunities.
LM-3.2	Implement security improvement opportunities and inform appropriate stakeholders.
IF	**Infrastructure Management**
IF-1	ESTABLISH THE SECURE INFRASTRUCTURE
IF-1.1	Define the infrastructure security requirements.
IF-1.2	Identify, obtain, and provide the infrastructure resources and services that provide security functions and services that are adequate to securely implement and support projects.
IF-2	MAINTAIN THE SECURE INFRASTRUCTURE
IF-2.1	Evaluate the degree to which delivered infrastructure resources satisfy project protection needs.
IF-2.2	Identify and provide security improvements or changes to the infrastructure resources as the project requirements change.
PM	**Portfolio Management**
PM-1	DEFINE AND AUTHORIZE THE SECURITY ASPECTS OF PROJECTS
PM-1.1	Identify potential new or modified security capabilities or security aspects of missions or business opportunities.
PM-1.2	Prioritize, select, and establish new business opportunities, ventures, or undertakings with consideration for security objectives and concerns.
PM-1.3	Define the security aspects of projects, accountabilities, and authorities.
PM-1.4	Identify the security aspects of goals, objectives, and outcomes of each project.
PM-1.5	Identify and allocate resources for the achievement of the security aspects of project goals and objectives.
PM-1.6	Identify the security aspects of any multi-project interfaces and dependencies to be managed or supported by each project.

ORGANIZATION PROJECT-ENABLING PROCESSES	
PM-1.7	Specify the security aspects of project reporting requirements and review milestones that govern the execution of each project.
PM-1.8	Authorize each project to commence execution with consideration of the security aspects of project plans.
PM-2	EVALUATE THE SECURITY ASPECTS OF THE PORTFOLIO OF PROJECTS
PM-2.1	Evaluate the security aspects of projects to confirm ongoing viability.
PM-2.2	Continue or redirect projects that are satisfactorily progressing or can be expected to progress satisfactorily by appropriate redirection in consideration of project security aspects.
PM-3	TERMINATE PROJECTS
PM-3.1	Cancel or suspend projects whose security-driven disadvantages or security-driven risks to the organization outweigh the benefits of continued investments.
PM-3.2	After completion of agreements for products or services, act to close the projects in accordance with established security criteria, constraints, and considerations.
HR	Human Resource Management
HR-1	IDENTIFY SYSTEMS SECURITY ENGINEERING SKILLS
HR-1.1	Identify systems security engineering skills needed based on current and expected projects.
HR-1.2	Identify existing systems security engineering skills of personnel.
HR-2	DEVELOP SYSTEMS SECURITY ENGINEERING SKILLS
HR-2.1	Establish a plan for systems security engineering skills development.
HR-2.2	Obtain systems security engineering training, education, or mentoring resources.
HR-2.3	Provide and document records of systems security engineering skills development.
HR-3	ACQUIRE AND PROVIDE SYSTEMS SECURITY ENGINEERING SKILLS TO PROJECTS
HR-3.1	Obtain qualified systems security engineering personnel to meet project needs.
HR-3.2	Maintain and manage the pool of skilled systems security engineering personnel to staff ongoing projects.
HR-3.3	Make personnel assignments based on the specific systems security engineering needs of the project and staff development needs.
QM	Quality Management
QM-1	PLAN SECURITY QUALITY MANAGEMENT
QM-1.1	Establish security quality management objectives.
QM-1.2	Establish security quality management policies, standards, and procedures.
QM-1.3	Define responsibilities and authority for the implementation of security quality management.
QM-1.4	Define security quality evaluation criteria and methods.
QM-1.5	Provide resources, data, and information for security quality management.
QM-2	ASSESS SECURITY QUALITY MANAGEMENT
QM-2.1	Obtain and analyze quality assurance evaluation results in accordance with the defined security quality evaluation criteria.
QM-2.2	Assess customer security quality satisfaction.

	ORGANIZATION PROJECT-ENABLING PROCESSES	
QM-2.3	Conduct periodic reviews of project quality assurance activities for compliance with the security quality management policies, standards, and procedures.	
QM-2.4	Monitor the status of security quality improvements on processes, products, and services.	
QM-3	PERFORM SECURITY QUALITY MANAGEMENT CORRECTIVE AND PREVENTIVE ACTIONS	
QM-3.1	Plan corrective actions when security quality management objectives are not achieved.	
QM-3.2	Plan preventive actions when there is a sufficient risk that security quality management objectives will not be achieved.	
QM-3.3	Monitor security quality management corrective and preventive actions to completion and inform relevant stakeholders.	
KM	Knowledge Management	
KM-1	PLAN SECURITY KNOWLEDGE MANAGEMENT	
KM-1.1	Define the security aspects of the knowledge management strategy.	
KM-1.2	Identify the security knowledge, skills, and knowledge assets to be managed.	
KM-1.3	Identify projects that can benefit from the application of the security knowledge, skills, and knowledge assets.	
KM-2	SHARE SECURITY KNOWLEDGE AND SKILLS THROUGHOUT THE ORGANIZATION	
KM-2.1	Establish and maintain a classification for capturing and sharing security knowledge and skills.	
KM-2.2	Capture or acquire security knowledge and skills.	
KM-2.3	Share security knowledge and skills across the organization.	
KM-3	SHARE SECURITY KNOWLEDGE ASSETS THROUGHOUT THE ORGANIZATION	
KM-3.1	Establish a taxonomy to organize security knowledge assets.	
KM-3.2	Develop or acquire security knowledge assets.	
KM-3.3	Securely share knowledge assets across the organization.	
KM-4	MANAGE SECURITY KNOWLEDGE, SKILLS, AND KNOWLEDGE ASSETS	
KM-4.1	Maintain security knowledge, skills, and knowledge assets.	
KM-4.2	Monitor and record the use of security knowledge, skills, and knowledge assets.	
KM-4.3	Periodically reassess the currency of the security aspects of technology and market needs of the security knowledge assets.	

TABLE D-3: SSE ACTIVITIES AND TASKS IN THE TECHNICAL MANAGEMENT PROCESSES

	TECHNICAL MANAGEMENT PROCESSES
PL	**Project Planning**
PL-1	DEFINE THE SECURITY ASPECTS OF THE PROJECT
PL-1.1	Identify the security objectives and security constraints for the project.
PL-1.2	Define the security aspects of the project scope as established in agreements.
PL-1.3	Define and maintain a security view of the life cycle model and its constituent stages.
PL-1.4	Identify the security activities and tasks of the work breakdown structure.
PL-1.5	Define and maintain the security aspects of processes that will be applied on the project.
PL-2	PLAN THE SECURITY ASPECTS OF THE PROJECT AND TECHNICAL MANAGEMENT
PL-2.1	Define and maintain the security aspects of a project schedule based on management and technical objectives and work estimates.
PL-2.2	Define the security achievement criteria and major dependencies on external inputs and outputs for life cycle stage decision gates.
PL-2.3	Define the security-related costs for the project and plan the budget informed by those projected costs.
PL-2.4	Define the systems security engineering roles, responsibilities, accountabilities, and authorities.
PL-2.5	Define the security aspects of infrastructure and services required.
PL-2.6	Plan the security aspects of acquisition of materials and enabling systems and services supplied from outside the project.
PL-2.7	Generate and communicate a plan for the project and technical management and execution, including reviews that address all security considerations.
PL-3	ACTIVATE THE SECURITY ASPECTS OF THE PROJECT
PL-3.1	Obtain authorization for the security aspects of the project.
PL-3.2	Submit requests and obtain commitments for the resources required to perform the security aspects of the project.
PL-3.3	Implement the security aspects of the project plan.
PA	**Project Assessment and Control**
PA-1	PLAN FOR THE SECURITY ASPECTS OF PROJECT ASSESSMENT AND CONTROL
PA-1.1	Define the security aspects of the project assessment strategy.
PA-1.2	Define the security aspects of the project control strategy.
PA-2	ASSESS THE SECURITY ASPECTS OF THE PROJECT
PA-2.1	Assess the alignment of the security aspects of project objectives and plans with the project context.
PA-2.2	Assess the security aspects of the management and technical plans against objectives to determine adequacy and feasibility.
PA-2.3	Assess the security aspects of the project and its technical status against appropriate plans to determine actual and projected cost, schedule, and performance variances.
PA-2.4	Assess the adequacy of the security roles, responsibilities, accountabilities, and authorities associated with the project.

	TECHNICAL MANAGEMENT PROCESSES	
PA-2.5	Assess the adequacy and availability of resources allocated to the security aspects of the project.	
PA-2.6	Assess progress using measured security achievement and milestone completion.	
PA-2.7	Conduct required management and technical reviews, audits, and inspections with full consideration for the security aspects of the project.	
PA-2.8	Monitor the security aspects of critical processes and new technologies.	
PA-2.9	Analyze security measurement results and make recommendations.	
PA-2.10	Record and provide security status and security findings from the assessment tasks.	
PA-2.11	Monitor the security aspects of process execution within the project.	
PA-3	**CONTROL THE SECURITY ASPECTS OF THE PROJECT**	
PA-3.1	Initiate the actions needed to address identified security issues.	
PA-3.2	Initiate the security aspects of necessary project replanning.	
PA-3.3	Initiate change actions when there is a contractual change to cost, time, or quality due to the security impact of an acquirer or supplier request.	
PA-3.4	Recommend the project to proceed toward the next milestone or event, if justified, based on the achievement of security objectives and performance measures.	
DM	**Decision Management**	
DM-1	**PREPARE FOR DECISIONS WITH SECURITY IMPLICATIONS**	
DM-1.1	Define the security aspects of the decision management strategy.	
DM-1.2	Identify the security aspects of the circumstances and need for a decision.	
DM-1.3	Involve stakeholders with relevant security expertise in the decision making in order to draw on their experience and knowledge.	
DM-2	**ANALYZE THE SECURITY ASPECTS OF DECISION INFORMATION**	
DM-2.1	Select and declare the security aspects of the decision management strategy for each decision.	
DM-2.2	Determine the desired security outcomes and measurable security selection criteria.	
DM-2.3	Identify the security aspects of the trade space and alternatives.	
DM-2.4	Evaluate each alternative against the security evaluation criteria.	
DM-3	**MAKE AND MANAGE SECURITY DECISIONS**	
DM-3.1	Determine preferred alternative for each security-informed and security-based decision.	
DM-3.2	Record the security-informed or security-based resolution, decision rationale, and assumptions.	
DM-3.3	Record, track, evaluate, and report the security aspects of security-informed and security-based decisions.	
RM	**Risk Management**	
RM-1	**PLAN SECURITY RISK MANAGEMENT**	
RM-1.1	Define the security aspects of the risk management strategy.	
RM-1.2	Define and record the security context of the risk management process.	
RM-2	**MANAGE THE SECURITY ASPECTS OF THE RISK PROFILE**	

	TECHNICAL MANAGEMENT PROCESSES
RM-2.1	Define and record the security risk thresholds and conditions under which a level of risk may be accepted.
RM-2.2	Establish and maintain the security aspects of the risk profile.
RM-2.3	Provide the security aspects of the risk profile to stakeholders based on their needs.
RM-3	ANALYZE SECURITY RISK
RM-3.1	Identify security risks in the categories described in the security risk management context.
RM-3.2	Estimate the likelihood of occurrence and consequences of each identified security risk.
RM-3.3	Evaluate each security risk against its security risk thresholds.
RM-3.4	Define risk treatment strategies and measures for each security risk that does not meet its security risk threshold.
RM-4	TREAT SECURITY RISK
RM-4.1	Identify recommended alternatives for security risk treatment.
RM-4.2	Implement the security risk treatment alternatives selected by stakeholders.
RM-4.3	Identify and monitor those security risks accepted by stakeholders to determine if any future risk treatment actions are necessary.
RM-4.4	Coordinate management action for the identified security risk treatments.
RM-5	MONITOR SECURITY RISK
RM-5.1	Continually monitor all risks and the security risk management context for changes and evaluate the security risks when their state has changed.
RM-5.2	Implement and monitor measures to evaluate the effectiveness of security risk treatments.
RM-5.3	Monitor on an ongoing basis, the emergence of new security risks and sources of risk throughout the life cycle.
CM	**Configuration Management**
CM-1	PLAN FOR THE SECURITY ASPECTS OF CONFIGURATION MANAGEMENT
CM-1.1	Define the security aspects of a configuration management strategy.
CM-1.2	Define the approach for the secure archive and retrieval for configuration items, configuration management artifacts, data, and information.
CM-2	PERFORM THE SECURITY ASPECTS OF CONFIGURATION IDENTIFICATION
CM-2.1	Identify the security aspects of system elements and information items that are configuration items.
CM-2.2	Identify the security aspects of the hierarchy and structure of system information.
CM-2.3	Establish the security nomenclature for system, system element, and information item identifiers.
CM-2.4	Define the security aspects of baseline identification throughout the system life cycle.
CM-2.5	Obtain acquirer and supplier agreement for security aspects to establish a baseline.
CM-3	PERFORM SECURITY CONFIGURATION CHANGE MANAGEMENT
CM-3.1	Identify security aspects of requests for change and requests for variance.
CM-3.2	Determine the security aspects of action to coordinate, evaluate, and disposition requests for change or requests for variance.
CM-3.3	Incorporate security aspects in requests submitted for review and approval.

	TECHNICAL MANAGEMENT PROCESSES	
CM-3.4	Track and manage the security aspects of approved changes to the baseline, requests for change, and requests for variance.	
CM-4	PERFORM SECURITY CONFIGURATION STATUS ACCOUNTING	
CM-4.1	Develop and maintain security-relevant configuration management status information for system elements, baselines, approved changes, and releases.	
CM-4.2	Capture, store, and report security-relevant configuration management data.	
CM-5	PERFORM SECURITY CONFIGURATION EVALUATION	
CM-5.1	Identify the need for security-focused configuration management audits.	
CM-5.2	Verify that the system configuration satisfies the security-relevant configuration requirements.	
CM-5.3	Monitor the security aspects of incorporation of approved configuration changes.	
CM-5.4	Assess whether the system meets baseline security functional and performance capabilities.	
CM-5.5	Assess whether the system conforms to the security aspects of the operational and configuration information items.	
CM-5.6	Record the security aspects of configuration management audit results and disposition actions.	
CM-6	PERFORM THE SECURITY ASPECTS OF RELEASE CONTROL	
CM-6.1	Approve the security aspects of system releases and deliveries.	
CM-6.2	Track and manage the security aspects of system releases.	
IM	Information Management	
IM-1	PREPARE FOR THE SECURITY ASPECTS OF INFORMATION MANAGEMENT	
IM-1.1	Define the security aspects of the information management strategy.	
IM-1.2	Define protections for information items that will be managed.	
IM-1.3	Designate authorities and responsibilities for the security aspects of information management.	
IM-1.4	Define protections for specific information item content, formats, and structure.	
IM-1.5	Define the security aspects of information maintenance actions.	
IM-2	PERFORM THE SECURITY ASPECTS OF INFORMATION MANAGEMENT	
IM-2.1	Securely obtain, develop, or transform the identified information items.	
IM-2.2	Securely maintain information items and their storage records, and record the security status of information.	
IM-2.3	Securely publish, distribute, or provide access to information and information items to designated stakeholders.	
IM-2.4	Securely archive designated information.	
IM-2.5	Securely dispose of unwanted or invalid information or information that has not been validated.	
MS	Measurement	
MS-1	PREPARE FOR SECURITY MEASUREMENT	
MS-1.1	Define the security aspects of the measurement strategy.	
MS-1.2	Describe the characteristics of the organization that are relevant to security measurement.	
MS-1.3	Identify and prioritize the security-relevant information needs.	

TECHNICAL MANAGEMENT PROCESSES	
MS-1.4	Select and specify measures that satisfy the security-relevant information needs.
MS-1.5	Define procedures for the collection, analysis, access, and reporting of security-relevant data.
MS-1.6	Define criteria for evaluating the security-relevant information items and the process used for the security aspects of measurement.
MS-1.7	Identify, plan for, and obtain enabling systems or services to support the security aspects of measurement.
MS-2	PERFORM SECURITY MEASUREMENT
MS-2.1	Integrate procedures for the generation, collection, analysis, and reporting of security-relevant data into the relevant processes.
MS-2.2	Collect, store, and verify security-relevant data.
MS-2.3	Analyze security-relevant data and develop security-informed information items.
MS-2.4	Record security measurement results and inform the measurement users.
QA	Quality Assurance
QA-1	PREPARE FOR SECURITY QUALITY ASSURANCE
QA-1.1	Define the security aspects of the quality assurance strategy.
QA-1.2	Establish independence of security quality assurance from other life cycle processes.
QA-2	PERFORM PRODUCT OR SERVICE SECURITY EVALUATIONS
QA-2.1	Evaluate products and services for conformance to established security criteria, contracts, standards, and regulations.
QA-2.2	Perform the security aspects of verification and validation of the outputs of the life cycle processes to determine conformance to specified security requirements.
QA-3	PERFORM PROCESS SECURITY EVALUATIONS
QA-3.1	Evaluate project life cycle processes for conformance to established security criteria, contracts, standards, and regulations.
QA-3.2	Evaluate tools and environments that support or automate the process for conformance to established security criteria, contracts, standards, and regulations.
QA-3.3	Evaluate supplier processes for conformance to process security requirements.
QA-4	MANAGE QUALITY ASSURANCE SECURITY RECORDS AND REPORTS
QA-4.1	Create records and reports related to the security aspects of quality assurance activities.
QA-4.2	Securely maintain, store, and distribute records and reports.
QA-4.3	Identify the security aspects of incidents and problems associated with product, service, and process evaluations.
QA-5	TREAT SECURITY INCIDENTS AND PROBLEMS
QA-5.1	The security aspects of incidents are recorded, analyzed, and classified.
QA-5.2	The security aspects of incidents are resolved or elevated to problems.
QA-5.3	The security aspects of problems are recorded, analyzed, and classified.
QA-5.4	Treatments for the security aspects of problems are prioritized and implementation is tracked.
QA-5.5	Trends in the security aspects of incidents and problems are noted and analyzed.

TECHNICAL MANAGEMENT PROCESSES	
QA-5.6	Stakeholders are informed of the status of the security aspects of incidents and problems.
QA-5.7	The security aspects of incidents and problems are tracked to closure.

TABLE D-4: SSE ACTIVITIES AND TASKS IN THE TECHNICAL PROCESSES

	TECHNICAL PROCESSES
BA	**Business or Mission Analysis**
BA-1	PREPARE FOR THE SECURITY ASPECTS OF BUSINESS OR MISSION ANALYSIS
BA-1.1	Identify stakeholders who will contribute to the identification and assessment of any mission, business, or operational problems or opportunities.
BA-1.2	Review organizational problems and opportunities with respect to desired security objectives.
BA-1.3	Define the security aspects of the business or mission analysis strategy.
BA-1.4	Identify, plan for, and obtain access to enabling systems or services to support the security aspects of the business or mission analysis process.
BA-2	DEFINE THE SECURITY ASPECTS OF THE PROBLEM OR OPPORTUNITY SPACE
BA-2.1	Analyze the problems or opportunities in the context of the security objectives and measures of success to be achieved.
BA-2.2	Define the security aspects and considerations of the mission, business, or operational problem or opportunity.
BA-3	CHARACTERIZE THE SECURITY ASPECTS OF THE SOLUTION SPACE
BA-3.1	Define the security aspects of the preliminary operational concepts and other concepts in life cycle stages.
BA-3.2	Identify alternative solution classes that can achieve the security objectives within limitations, constraints, and other considerations.
BA-4	EVALUATE AND SELECT SOLUTION CLASSES
BA-4.1	Assess each alternative solution class taking into account the security objectives, limitations, constraints, and other relevant security considerations.
BA-4.2	Select the preferred alternative solution class (or classes) based on the identified security objectives, trade space factors, and other criteria defined by the organization.
BA-5	MANAGE THE SECURITY ASPECTS OF BUSINESS OR MISSION ANALYSIS
BA-5.1	Maintain traceability of the security aspects of business or mission analysis.
BA-5.2	Provide security-relevant information items required for business or mission analysis to baselines.
SN	**Stakeholder Needs and Requirements Definition**
SN-1	PREPARE FOR STAKEHOLDER PROTECTION NEEDS AND SECURITY REQUIREMENTS DEFINITION
SN-1.1	Identify the stakeholders who have a security interest in the system throughout its life cycle.
SN-1.2	Define the stakeholder protection needs and security requirements definition strategy.
SN-1.3	Identify, plan for, and obtain access to enabling systems or services to support the security aspects of the stakeholder needs and requirements definition process.
SN-2	DEFINE STAKEHOLDER PROTECTION NEEDS
SN-2.1	Define the security context of use across all preliminary life cycle concepts.
SN-2.2	Identify stakeholder assets and asset classes.
SN-2.3	Prioritize assets based on the adverse consequence of asset loss.
SN-2.4	Determine asset susceptibility to adversity and uncertainty.

TECHNICAL PROCESSES	
SN-2.5	Identify stakeholder protection needs.
SN-2.6	Prioritize and down-select the stakeholder protection needs.
SN-2.7	Define the stakeholder protection needs and rationale.
SN-3	DEVELOP THE SECURITY ASPECTS OF OPERATIONAL AND OTHER LIFE CYCLE CONCEPTS
SN-3.1	Define a representative set of scenarios to identify all required protection capabilities and security measures that correspond to anticipated operational and other life cycle concepts.
SN-3.2	Identify the security-relevant interaction between users and the system.
SN-4	TRANSFORM STAKEHOLDER PROTECTION NEEDS INTO SECURITY REQUIREMENTS
SN-4.1	Identify the security-oriented constraints on a system solution.
SN-4.2	Identify the stakeholder security requirements and security functions.
SN-4.3	Define stakeholder security requirements, consistent with life cycle concepts, scenarios, interactions, constraints, and critical quality characteristics.
SN-4.4	Apply security metadata tagging to identify stakeholder security requirements and security-driven constraints.
SN-5	ANALYZE STAKEHOLDER SECURITY REQUIREMENTS
SN-5.1	Analyze the complete set of stakeholder security requirements.
SN-5.2	Define critical security-relevant performance and assurance measures that enable the assessment of technical achievement.
SN-5.3	Validate that stakeholder protection needs and expectations have been adequately captured and expressed by the analyzed security requirements.
SN-5.4	Resolve stakeholder security requirements issues.
SN-6	MANAGE STAKEHOLDER PROTECTION NEEDS AND SECURITY REQUIREMENTS DEFINITION
SN-6.1	Obtain explicit agreement on the stakeholder security requirements.
SN-6.2	Record asset protection data.
SN-6.3	Maintain traceability between stakeholder protection needs and stakeholder security requirements.
SN-6.4	Provide security-relevant information items required for stakeholder needs and requirements definition to baselines.
SR	**System Requirements Definition**
SR-1	PREPARE FOR SYSTEM SECURITY REQUIREMENTS DEFINITION
SR-1.1	Define the security aspects of the functional boundary of the system in terms of the security behavior and security properties to be provided.
SR-1.2	Define the security domains of the system and their correlation to the functional boundaries of the system.
SR-1.3	Define the security aspects of the system requirements definition strategy.
SR-1.4	Identify, plan for, and obtain access to enabling systems or services to support the security aspects of the system requirements definition process.
SR-2	DEFINE SYSTEM SECURITY REQUIREMENTS
SR-2.1	Define each security function that the system is required to perform.

	TECHNICAL PROCESSES
SR-2.2	Define system security requirements, security constraints on system requirements, and rationale.
SR-2.3	Incorporate system security requirements and associated constraints into system requirements and define rationale.
SR-2.4	Apply security metadata tagging to identify system security requirements and security-driven constraints.
SR-3	ANALYZE SYSTEM SECURITY IN SYSTEM REQUIREMENTS
SR-3.1	Analyze the complete set of system requirements in consideration of security concerns.
SR-3.2	Define security-driven performance and assurance measures that enable the assessment of technical achievement.
SR-3.3	Provide the analyzed system security requirements and security-driven constraints to applicable stakeholders for review.
SR-3.4	Resolve system security requirements and security-driven constraints issues.
SR-4	MANAGE SYSTEM SECURITY REQUIREMENTS
SR-4.1	Obtain explicit agreement on the system security requirements and security-driven constraints.
SR-4.2	Maintain traceability of system security requirements and security-driven constraints.
SR-4.3	Provide security-relevant information items required for systems requirements definition to baselines.
AR	**Architecture Definition**
AR-1	PREPARE FOR ARCHITECTURE DEFINITION FROM THE SECURITY VIEWPOINT
AR-1.1	Identify the key drivers that impact the security aspects of the system architecture.
AR-1.2	Identify stakeholder security concerns.
AR-1.3	Define the security aspects of the architecture definition roadmap, approach, and strategy.
AR-1.4	Define evaluation criteria based on stakeholder security concerns and security-relevant requirements.
AR-1.5	Identify, plan for, and obtain access to enabling systems or services to support the security aspects of the architecture definition process.
AR-2	DEVELOP SECURITY VIEWPOINTS OF THE ARCHITECTURE
AR-2.1	Define the concept of secure function for the system at the architecture level.
AR-2.2	Select, adapt, or develop the security viewpoints and model kinds based on stakeholder security concerns.
AR-2.3	Identify the security architecture frameworks to be used in developing the security models and security views of the system architecture.
AR-2.4	Record the rationale for the selection of architecture frameworks that address security concerns, security viewpoints, and security model types.
AR-2.5	Select or develop supporting security modeling techniques and tools.
AR-3	DEVELOP SECURITY MODELS AND SECURITY VIEWS OF CANDIDATE ARCHITECTURES
AR-3.1	Define the security context and boundaries of the system in terms of interfaces, interconnections, and interactions with external entities.
AR-3.2	Identify architectural entities and relationships between entities that address key stakeholder security concerns and system security requirements.

	TECHNICAL PROCESSES
AR-3.3	Allocate security concepts, properties, characteristics, behavior, functions, or constraints to architectural entities.
AR-3.4	Select, adapt, or develop security models of the candidate architectures.
AR-3.5	Compose views in accordance with security viewpoints to express how the architecture addresses stakeholder security concerns and meets stakeholder and system security requirements.
AR-3.6	Harmonize the security models and security views with each other and with the concept of secure function.
AR-4	RELATE SECURITY VIEWS OF THE ARCHITECTURE TO DESIGN
AR-4.1	Identify the security-relevant system elements that relate to architectural entities and the nature of these relationships.
AR-4.2	Define the security interfaces, interconnections, and interactions between the system elements and with external entities.
AR-4.3	Allocate system security requirements to architectural entities and system elements.
AR-4.4	Map security-relevant system elements and architectural entities to security design characteristics.
AR-4.5	Define the security design principles for the system design and evolution that reflect the concept of secure function.
AR-5	SELECT CANDIDATE ARCHITECTURE
AR-5.1	Assess each candidate architecture against the security requirements and security-related constraints.
AR-5.2	Assess each candidate architecture against stakeholder security concerns using evaluation criteria.
AR-5.3	Select the preferred architecture(s) and capture key security decisions and rationale for those decisions.
AR-5.4	Establish the security aspects of the architecture baseline of the selected architecture.
AR-6	MANAGE THE SECURITY VIEW OF THE SELECTED ARCHITECTURE
AR-6.1	Formalize the security aspects of the architecture governance approach and specify security governance-related roles and responsibilities, accountabilities, and authorities.
AR-6.2	Obtain explicit acceptance of the security aspects of the architecture by stakeholders.
AR-6.3	Maintain concordance and completeness of the security architectural entities and their security-related architectural characteristics.
AR-6.4	Organize, assess, and control the evolution of the security models and security views of the architecture.
AR-6.5	Maintain the security aspects of the architecture definition and evaluation strategy.
AR-6.6	Maintain traceability of the security aspects of the architecture.
AR-6.7	Provide security-relevant information items required for architecture definition to baselines.
DE	**Design Definition**
DE-1	PREPARE FOR SECURITY DESIGN DEFINITION
DE-1.1	Apply the concept of secure function for the system at the design level.
DE-1.2	Determine the security technologies required for each system element composing the system.
DE-1.3	Determine the types of security design characteristics.

	TECHNICAL PROCESSES	
DE-1.4	Define the principles for secure evolution of the system design.	
DE-1.5	Define the security aspects of the design definition strategy.	
DE-1.6	Identify, plan for, and obtain access to enabling systems or services to support the security aspects of the design definition process.	
DE-2	ESTABLISH SECURITY DESIGN CHARACTERISTICS AND ENABLERS FOR EACH SYSTEM ELEMENT	
DE-2.1	Allocate system security requirements to system elements.	
DE-2.2	Transform security architectural characteristics into security design characteristics.	
DE-2.3	Define the necessary security design enablers.	
DE-2.4	Examine security design alternatives.	
DE-2.5	Refine or define the security interfaces between the system elements and with external entities.	
DE-2.6	Develop the security design artifacts.	
DE-3	ASSESS THE ALTERNATIVES FOR OBTAINING SECURITY-RELEVANT SYSTEM ELEMENTS	
DE-3.1	Identify security-relevant nondevelopmental items (NDI) that may be considered for use.	
DE-3.2	Assess each candidate NDI and new design alternative against the criteria developed from expected security design characteristics or system element security requirements to determine suitability for the intended application.	
DE-3.3	Determine the preferred alternative among candidate NDI solutions and new design alternatives for a system element.	
DE-4	MANAGE THE SECURITY DESIGN	
DE-4.1	Map the security design characteristics to the system elements.	
DE-4.2	Capture the security design and rationale.	
DE-4.3	Maintain traceability of the security aspects of the system design.	
DE-4.4	Provide security-relevant information items required for the system design definition to baselines.	
SA	System Analysis	
SA-1	PREPARE FOR THE SECURITY ASPECTS OF SYSTEM ANALYSIS	
SA-1.1	Identify the security aspects of the problem or question that requires system analysis.	
SA-1.2	Identify the stakeholders of the security aspects of system analysis.	
SA-1.3	Define the objectives, scope, level of fidelity, and level of assurance of the security aspects of system analysis.	
SA-1.4	Select the methods associated with the security aspects of system analysis.	
SA-1.5	Define the security aspects of the system analysis strategy.	
SA-1.6	Identify, plan for, and obtain access to enabling systems or services to support the security aspects of the system analysis process.	
SA-1.7	Collect the data and inputs needed for the security aspects of system analysis.	
SA-2	PERFORM THE SECURITY ASPECTS OF SYSTEM ANALYSIS	
SA-2.1	Identify and validate the assumptions associated with the security aspects of system analysis.	

TECHNICAL PROCESSES	
SA-2.2	Apply the selected security analysis methods to perform the security aspects of required system analysis.
SA-2.3	Review the security aspects of the system analysis results for quality and validity.
SA-2.4	Establish conclusions, recommendations, and rational based on the results of the security aspects of system analysis.
SA-2.5	Record the results of the security aspects of system analysis.
SA-3	MANAGE THE SECURITY ASPECTS OF SYSTEM ANALYSIS
SA-3.1	Maintain traceability of the security aspects of the system analysis results.
SA-3.2	Provide security-relevant system analysis information items that have been selected for baselines.
IP	Implementation
IP-1	PREPARE FOR THE SECURITY ASPECTS OF IMPLEMENTATION
IP-1.1	Develop the security aspects of the implementation strategy.
IP-1.2	Identify constraints from the security aspects of the implementation strategy and technology on the system requirements, architecture, design, or implementation techniques.
IP-1.3	Identify, plan for, and obtain access to enabling systems or services to support the security aspects of implementation.
IP-2	PERFORM THE SECURITY ASPECTS OF IMPLEMENTATION
IP-2.1	Realize or adapt system elements in accordance with the security aspects of the implementation strategy, defined implementation procedures, and security-driven constraints.
IP-2.2	Develop initial training materials for users for operation, sustainment, and support.
IP-2.3	Securely package and store system elements.
IP-2.4	Record evidence that system elements meet the system security requirements.
IP-3	MANAGE RESULTS OF THE SECURITY ASPECTS OF IMPLEMENTATION
IP-3.1	Record the security aspects of implementation results and any security-related anomalies encountered.
IP-3.2	Maintain traceability of the security aspects of implemented system elements.
IP-3.3	Provide security-relevant information items required for implementation to baselines.
IN	Integration
IN-1	PREPARE FOR THE SECURITY ASPECTS OF INTEGRATION
IN-1.1	Identify and define checkpoints for the trustworthy secure operation of the assembled interfaces and selected system functions.
IN-1.2	Develop the security aspects of the integration strategy.
IN-1.3	Identify, plan for, and obtain access to enabling systems or services to support the security aspects of integration.
IN-1.4	Identify the constraints resulting from the security aspects of integration to be incorporated into the system requirements, architecture, or design.
IN-2	PERFORM THE SECURITY ASPECTS OF INTEGRATION

	TECHNICAL PROCESSES
IN-2.1	Obtain implemented system elements in accordance with security criteria and requirements established in agreements and schedules.
IN-2.2	Assemble the implemented systems elements to achieve secure configurations.
IN-2.3	Perform checks of the security characteristics of interfaces, functional behavior, and behavior across interconnections.
IN-3	MANAGE RESULTS OF THE SECURITY ASPECTS OF INTEGRATION
IN-3.1	Record the security aspects of integration results and any security anomalies encountered.
IN-3.2	Maintain traceability of the security aspects of integrated system elements.
IN-3.3	Provide security-relevant information items required for integration to baselines.
VE	Verification
VE-1	PREPARE FOR THE SECURITY ASPECTS OF VERIFICATION
VE-1.1	Identify the security aspects within the verification scope and corresponding security-focused verification actions.
VE-1.2	Identify the constraints that can potentially limit the feasibility of the security-focused verification actions.
VE-1.3	Select the appropriate methods or techniques for the security aspects of verification and the associated security criteria for each security-focused verification action.
VE-1.4	Define the security aspects of the verification strategy.
VE-1.5	Identify the system constraints resulting from the security aspects of the verification strategy to be incorporated into the system requirements, architecture, or design.
VE-1.6	Identify, plan for, and obtain access to enabling systems or services to support the security aspects of verification.
VE-2	PERFORM SECURITY-FOCUSED VERIFICATION
VE-2.1	Define the security aspects of the verification procedures, each supporting one or a set of security-focused verification actions.
VE-2.2	Perform security verification procedures.
VE-2.3	Analyze security-focused verification results against any established expectations and success criteria.
VE-3	MANAGE RESULTS OF SECURITY-FOCUSED VERIFICATION
VE-3.1	Record the security aspects of verification results and any security anomalies encountered.
VE-3.2	Record the security characteristics of operational incidents and problems and track their resolution.
VE-3.3	Obtain stakeholder agreement that the system or system element meets the specified system security requirements and characteristics.
VE-3.4	Maintain traceability of the security aspects of verified system elements.
VE-3.5	Provide security-relevant information items required for verification to baselines.
TR	Transition
TR-1	PREPARE FOR THE SECURITY ASPECTS OF TRANSITION
TR-1.1	Develop the security aspects of the transition strategy.
TR-1.2	Identify the facility or site changes needed for security purposes.

TECHNICAL PROCESSES	
TR-1.3	Identify the constraints resulting from the security aspects of transition to be incorporated into the system requirements, architecture, and design.
TR-1.4	Identify and arrange the training necessary for secure system utilization, sustainment, and support.
TR-1.5	Identify, plan for, and obtain access to enabling systems or services to support the security aspects of transition.
TR-2	PERFORM THE SECURITY ASPECTS OF TRANSITION
TR-2.1	Prepare the facility or site in accordance with the secure installation requirements.
TR-2.2	Securely deliver the system for installation.
TR-2.3	Install the system at its specified location and establish secure interconnections to its environment.
TR-2.4	Demonstrate proper achievement of the security aspects of system installation.
TR-2.5	Provide security training for stakeholders that interact with the system.
TR-2.6	Perform activation and checkout of the security aspects of the system.
TR-2.7	Demonstrate that the installed system is capable of delivering the required protection capability.
TR-2.8	Demonstrate that the security functions provided by the system are sustainable by the enabling systems.
TR-2.9	Review the security aspects of the system for operational readiness.
TR-2.10	Commission the system for secure operation.
TR-3	MANAGE RESULTS OF THE SECURITY APECTS OF TRANSITION
TR-3.1	Record the security aspects of transition results and any security anomalies encountered.
TR-3.2	Record the security aspects of operational incidents and problems and track their resolution.
TR-3.3	Maintain traceability of the security aspects of transitioned system elements.
TR-3.4	Provide security-relevant information items required for transition to baselines.
VA	Validation
VA-1	PREPARE FOR THE SECURITY ASPECTS OF VALIDATION
VA-1.1	Identify the security aspects of the validation scope and corresponding security-focused validation actions.
VA-1.2	Identify the constraints that can potentially limit the feasibility of the security-focused validation actions.
VA-1.3	Select the appropriate methods or techniques for the security aspects of validation and the associated security criteria for each security-focused validation action.
VA-1.4	Develop the security aspects of the validation strategy.
VA-1.5	Identify system constraints resulting from the security aspects of validation to be incorporated into the stakeholder security requirements.
VA-1.6	Identify, plan for, and obtain access to enabling systems or services to support the security aspects of validation.
VA-2	PERFORM SECURITY-FOCUSED VALIDATION
VA-2.1	Define the security aspects of the validation procedures, each supporting one or a set of security-focused validation actions.

	TECHNICAL PROCESSES
VA-2.2	Perform security validation procedures in the defined environment.
VA-2.3	Review security-focused validation results to confirm that the protection services of the system that are required by stakeholders are available.
VA-3	MANAGE RESULTS OF SECURITY-FOCUSED VALIDATION
VA-3.1	Record the security aspects of validation results and any security anomalies encountered.
VA-3.2	Record the security characteristics of operational incidents and problems and track their resolution.
VA-3.3	Obtain stakeholder agreement that the system or system element meets the stakeholder protection needs.
VA-3.4	Maintain traceability of the security aspects of validated system elements.
VA-3.5	Provide security-relevant information items required for validation to baselines.
OP	**Operation**
OP-1	PREPARE FOR SECURE OPERATION
OP-1.1	Develop the security aspects of the operation strategy.
OP-1.2	Identify the constraints resulting from the security aspects of operation to be incorporated into the system requirements, architecture, and design.
OP-1.3	Identify, plan for, and obtain access to enabling systems or services to support the security aspects of operation.
OP-1.4	Identify or define security training and qualification requirements; train, and assign personnel needed for system operation.
OP-2	PERFORM SECURE OPERATION
OP-2.1	Securely use the system in its intended operational environment.
OP-2.2	Apply materials and other resources, as required, to operate the system in a secure manner and sustain its security services.
OP-2.3	Monitor the security aspects of system operation.
OP-2.4	Identify and record when system security performance is not within acceptable parameters.
OP-2.5	Perform system security contingency operations, if necessary.
OP-3	MANAGE RESULTS OF SECURE OPERATION
OP-3.1	Record results of secure operation and any security anomalies encountered.
OP-3.2	Record the security aspects of operational incidents and problems and track their resolution.
OP-3.3	Maintain traceability of the security aspects of the operations elements.
OP-3.4	Provide security-relevant information items required for operation to baselines.
OP-4	SUPPORT SECURITY NEEDS OF CUSTOMERS
OP-4.1	Provide security assistance and consultation to customers as requested.
OP-4.2	Record and monitor requests and subsequent actions for security support.
OP-4.3	Determine the degree to which the delivered system security services satisfy the needs of the customers.
MA	**Maintenance**

TECHNICAL PROCESSES	
MA-1	**PREPARE FOR THE SECURITY ASPECTS OF MAINTENANCE**
MA-1.1	Define the security aspects of the maintenance strategy.
MA-1.2	Identify the system constraints resulting from the security aspects of maintenance and logistics to be incorporated into the system requirements, architecture, and design.
MA-1.3	Identify trades such that the security aspects of system maintenance and logistics result in a solution that is trustworthy, secure, affordable, operable, supportable, and sustainable.
MA-1.4	Identify, plan for, and obtain enabling systems or services to support the security aspects of system maintenance and logistics.
MA-2	**PERFORM THE SECURITY ASPECTS OF MAINTENANCE**
MA-2.1	Review incident and problem reports to identify security relevance and associated maintenance needs.
MA-2.2	Record the security aspects of maintenance incidents and problems and track their resolution.
MA-2.3	Implement the procedures for the correction of random faults or scheduled replacement of system elements to ensure the ability to deliver system security functions and services.
MA-2.4	Implement action to restore the system to secure operational status when a random fault causes a system failure.
MA-2.5	Perform preventive maintenance by replacing or servicing system elements prior to failure with security-related impact.
MA-2.6	Perform failure identification actions when security noncompliance has occurred in the system.
MA-2.7	Identify when security-relevant adaptive or perfective maintenance is required.
MA-3	**PERFORM THE SECURITY ASPECTS OF LOGISTICS SUPPORT**
MA-3.1	Perform the security aspects of acquisition logistics.
MA-3.2	Perform the security aspects of operational logistics.
MA-3.3	Implement any secure packaging, handling, storage, and transportation needed during the life cycle of the system.
MA-3.4	Confirm that security aspects incorporated into logistics actions satisfy the required protection levels so that system elements are securely stored and able to meet repair rates and planned schedules.
MA-3.5	Confirm that the security aspects of logistics actions include security supportability requirements that are planned, resourced, and implemented.
MA-4	**MANAGE RESULTS OF THE SECURITY ASPECTS OF MAINTENANCE AND LOGISTICS**
MA-4.1	Record the security aspects of maintenance and logistics results and any security anomalies encountered.
MA-4.2	Record operational security incidents and security problems and track their resolution.
MA-4.3	Identify and record the security-related trends of incidents, problems, and maintenance and logistics actions.
MA-4.4	Maintain traceability of system elements and the security aspects of maintenance actions and logistics actions performed.
MA-4.5	Provide security-relevant configuration items from system maintenance to baselines.
MA-4.6	Monitor customer satisfaction with the security aspects of system performance and maintenance support.

TECHNICAL PROCESSES	
DS	**Disposal**
DS-1	PREPARE FOR THE SECURITY ASPECTS OF DISPOSAL
DS-1.1	Develop the security aspects of the disposal strategy.
DS-1.2	Identify the system constraints resulting from the security aspects of disposal to be incorporated into the system requirements, architecture, and design.
DS-1.3	Identify, plan for, and obtain the enabling systems or services to support the secure disposal of the system.
DS-1.4	Specify secure storage criteria for the system if it is to be stored.
DS-1.5	Identify and preclude terminated personnel or disposed system elements and materials from being returned to service.
DS-2	PERFORM THE SECURITY ASPECTS OF DISPOSAL
DS-2.1	Deactivate the system or system element to prepare it for secure removal from operation.
DS-2.2	Securely remove the system or system element from use for appropriate secure disposition and action.
DS-2.3	Securely withdraw impacted operating staff from the system and record relevant secure operation knowledge.
DS-2.4	Disassemble the system or system element into manageable components and ensure that appropriate protections are in place for those components during removal for reuse, recycling, reconditioning, overhaul, archiving, or destruction.
DS-2.5	Sanitize system elements and life cycle artifacts in a manner appropriate to the disposition action.
DS-2.6	Manage system elements and their parts that are not intended for reuse to prevent them from re-entering the supply chain.
DS-3	FINALIZE THE SECURITY ASPECTS OF DISPOSAL
DS-3.1	Confirm that no unresolved security factors exist following disposal of the system.
DS-3.2	Return the environment to its original state or to a secure state specified by agreement.
DS-3.3	Archive and protect information generated during the life cycle of the system.

APPENDIX E

ROLES, RESPONSIBILITIES, AND SKILLS
THE CHARACTERISTICS AND EXPECTATIONS OF A SYSTEMS SECURITY ENGINEER

The role of a systems security engineer is to participate in a multidisciplinary systems engineering team, applying fundamental systems security understanding, skills, expertise, and experience to develop a system that satisfies organizational mission and/or business requirements, including stakeholder protection needs and security requirements.[41] The systems security engineer is expected to have expertise and experience in multiple areas (e.g., protection needs assessment, requirements elicitation, security architecture, threat assessment, computer security, communication security, networking, security technologies, hardware and software development, test and evaluation, vulnerability assessment, penetration testing, and supply chain risk).[42] Systems security engineer responsibilities include:

- Maintaining a comprehensive and holistic system view while addressing stakeholder security and risk concerns;

- Ensuring the effectiveness and suitability of the security elements of the system as an enabler to mission/business success;

- Ensuring that relevant threat and vulnerability data is considered in support of security-relevant decisions;

- Providing input to analyses of alternatives and to requirements, engineering, and risk trade-off analyses to achieve a cost-effective security architectural design for protections that enable mission/business success;

- Providing the evidence necessary to support assurance claims and to substantiate the determination that the system is sufficiently trustworthy; and

- Conducting security risk management activities, producing related security risk management information, and advising the engineering team and key stakeholders on the security-relevant impact of threats and vulnerabilities to the mission/business supported by the system.

The systems security engineer has a foundational understanding of systems engineering, to include the processes and roles for which the systems engineer is responsible. This understanding is necessary for effective participation on a systems engineering team. However, it is imperative in cases where systems security engineering activities are conducted in the absence of a systems engineering effort. This situation can occur at any stage in the system life cycle and may require the systems security engineer to assume additional responsibilities to ensure that the broader systems engineering concerns are identified and communicated to key stakeholders for action or resolution.

---

[41] The size of the systems engineering team is determined by factors such as scope, size, duration, and complexity of the engineering effort. As the size of the team increases, there may be multiple sub-teams with clearly defined scopes and responsibilities. Typically, each sub-team has a leader. Ultimately, one individual assumes responsibility for the entire engineering effort. That individual may be referred to as the lead or chief systems engineer.

[42] The National Cybersecurity Workforce Framework [SP 800-181] provides a blueprint to categorize, organize, and describe security work into specialty areas, tasks, and knowledge, skills and abilities (KSAs). The framework also provides a common language to describe cyber roles and jobs and helps define professional requirements in cybersecurity.

A systems security engineer may serve as the lead systems security engineer with responsibility for all systems security engineering activities reporting directly to the systems engineering team lead.[43] A systems security engineer may also participate as a member of a focused sub-team or to direct the systems security activities within a focused sub-team (e.g., an integrated product team). Finally, a systems security engineer may, in certain situations, serve as a consultant to another systems engineering team, providing security-relevant subject-matter expertise in support of the team's engineering efforts.

Systems Security Engineer Skills

Systems security engineering skills are a combination of core systems engineering and security specialty skills. Those foundational skills are then supplemented with specialty needs that might be project-dependent. For example, you want anyone working in a systems security engineering role to have an understanding of the basic systems engineering and system life cycle processes and how the contributions in NIST SP 800-160 work within those processes. That capability and skill set would suffice in most cases. However, in certain situations, you might need the systems security engineering role to be filled by someone with a financial or banking background, a submarine background, a biometrics background, a medical background, or cryptography background. The optimal systems security engineer would be someone with a broad understanding of systems engineering; a broad understanding of security; a technology specific understanding; a domain specific understanding; and all refined by the level of assurance to which the system is being engineered.

There are cases where a systems security engineer may participate on or provide consultation to teams performing system life cycle processes and activities that are not part of the developmental or field/sustainment engineering effort. Participation in such activities is best conducted under direction of management authority that is separate from that of the engineering effort to prevent conflict-of-interest concerns. Examples of teams that may be supported by a systems security engineer include:

- Independent verification and validation, assessment, audit, certification, test and evaluation;

- Security authorization, system approval to operate/connect, engineering project milestone decision; and

- Organizational security risk management.

Systems security engineers interact with a variety of stakeholders throughout the system life cycle. Stakeholders and their roles and responsibilities related to the engineering effort are identified at the start of a systems security engineering effort. These roles and responsibilities may vary over the course of the systems engineering technical and nontechnical processes.

Systems security engineers are capable of communicating with stakeholders at various levels of abstraction and in a variety of contexts including, for example: using high-level mission or business terms understood by senior executives; using more detailed technical terms understood by scientists and engineers; and using management terms understood by program or project

---

[43] Where the solution is a security system, the systems security engineer may serve as both the lead engineer and lead systems security engineer.

managers. The systems security engineer builds strong relationships with the stakeholders and is sensitive to understanding each stakeholder's perspective of the issues, priorities, and constraints that drive the engineering effort, including stakeholder expectations, concerns, and perspectives on indicators of success.

Bringing together systems security engineering roles, responsibilities, and skills allows for more clarity in the systems engineering perspective of need. Most security roles are oriented toward information system operations, policy, directives, regulatory needs (e.g., assessment, certification, authorization). Those roles are effective as long as the individuals are operating in that *domain space*. Ultimately, it is important to be more cognizant of and understand the purpose of the roles and associate specific responsibilities with those roles. It is subsequently possible to link those responsibilities to individual skills necessary to carry out the responsibilities.

Systems Security Engineering — An Organizational Mindset

Organizations desiring to fundamentally increase the trustworthiness of the systems they deploy in support of their missions or business operations must understand the importance of the discipline of systems security engineering—and how that specialty discipline can be effectively integrated into a comprehensive, system life cycle-based systems engineering effort. The objective is to have security-related activities and considerations tightly integrated into the mainstream technical and management processes of an organization—in effect, *institutionalizing* and *operationalizing* security at every organizational level from development to governance to operations. The most effective organizations consider security as a key corporate investment in their mission/business success—and not as a separate activity or programmatic element disconnected from the mission or business context and operational requirements. A proactive approach to security ensures that the protection needs of the organization and its stakeholders are clearly articulated and sufficient to produce the appropriate protection capabilities within the system and the environment in which it operates.

APPENDIX F

DESIGN PRINCIPLES FOR SECURITY

PROVIDING THE FOUNDATION FOR SYSTEMS SECURITY ENGINEERING[44]

Security design principles and concepts serve as the foundation for engineering trustworthy secure systems, including their constituent subsystems and components. These principles and concepts represent research, development, and application experience starting with the early incorporation of security mechanisms for trusted operating systems, to today's wide variety of fully networked, distributed, mobile, and virtual computing components, environments, and systems. The principles and concepts are intended to be universally applicable across this broad range of systems, as well as new systems as they emerge and mature.

The threat to be addressed is pervasive and can impact the trustworthiness of a system at any point during its life cycle. The principles are of particular interest to system developers who wish to mitigate the threat of insiders attempting to subvert systems at the hardware or software levels. Given the ubiquitous and increasing reliance on computing platforms and infrastructures to provide and enable mission and business capabilities, as well as data and information access and sharing, a shift toward robust, principles-based systems security engineering is both timely and relevant.

The security design principles are organized in a taxonomy that includes: *Security Architecture and Design* (i.e., organization, structure, interconnections, and interfaces); *Security Capability and Intrinsic Behaviors* (i.e., what the protections are and how they are provided); and *Life Cycle Security* (i.e., security process definition, conduct, and management). Application of these principles is intended to permit a demonstration of system trustworthiness through assurance based on reasoning about relevant and credible evidence. By applying the principles at different levels of abstraction (e.g., component design and composition), a sound security architecture based on trustworthy building blocks and a constructive approach can be developed. Definitions, underlying concepts, and other factors relevant to each principle and its application are also provided.

The security design principles and concepts presented in this appendix are intended to provide a basis for reasoning about a component or system. As reasoning tools, the inherent suitability of the principles and concepts in a particular situation will depend upon the practitioner's judgment. At times, the principles may be in conflict and their method of application may require tailoring. Within the overall system development process, the applicability of a particular principle may change due to evolving stakeholder requirements, protection needs, or constraints; architecture and design decisions and trade-offs; or by changes in risk tolerance. The security design principles and concepts should be an integral part of the total system solution. Their application should be planned for, scoped, and revisited throughout the engineering effort. Failure to properly apply these design principles and concepts may incur developmental, operational, or sustainment-driven risk.

[44] NIST acknowledges and appreciates the contribution of the U.S. Naval Postgraduate School (NPS) and the NPS Center for Information Systems Security Studies and Research (CISR) including principal investigators Paul Clark, Cynthia Irvine, and Thuy Nguyen, in providing the content for this appendix.

Table F-1 summarizes the taxonomy of security design principles. Each will be described in subsequent sections.

TABLE F-1: TAXONOMY OF SECURITY DESIGN PRINCIPLES

SECURITY DESIGN PRINCIPLES	
Security Architecture and Design	
Clear Abstraction	Hierarchical Trust
Least Common Mechanism	Inverse Modification Threshold
Modularity and Layering	Hierarchical Protection
Partially Ordered Dependencies	Minimized Security Elements
Efficiently Mediated Access	Least Privilege
Minimized Sharing	Predicate Permission
Reduced Complexity	Self-Reliant Trustworthiness
Secure Evolvability	Secure Distributed Composition
Trusted Components	Trusted Communication Channels
Security Capability and Intrinsic Behaviors	
Continuous Protection	Secure Failure and Recovery
Secure Metadata Management	Economic Security
Self-Analysis	Performance Security
Accountability and Traceability	Human Factored Security
Secure Defaults	Acceptable Security
Life Cycle Security	
Repeatable and Documented Procedures	Secure System Modification
Procedural Rigor	Sufficient Documentation

F.1 SECURITY ARCHITECTURE AND DESIGN

The following *structural design principles* affect the fundamental architecture of the system. This includes how the *system* is decomposed into its constituent *system elements*; and how the system elements relate to each other and the nature of the interfaces between elements.

F.1.1 Clear Abstractions

The principle of *clear abstractions* states that a system should have simple, well-defined interfaces and functions that provide a consistent and intuitive view of the data and how it is managed. The elegance (e.g., clarity, simplicity, necessity, sufficiency) of the system interfaces, combined with a precise definition of their functional behavior promotes ease of analysis, inspection, and testing as well as the correct and secure use of the system. The clarity of an abstraction is subjective. Examples reflecting application of this principle include avoidance of redundant, unused interfaces; *information hiding*; and avoidance of semantic overloading of interfaces or their parameters (e.g., not using one function to provide different functionality, depending on how it is used). Information hiding, also called *representation-independent programming*, is a design discipline to ensure that the internal representation of information in one system component is not visible to another system component invoking or calling the first component, such that the published abstraction is not influenced by how the data may be managed internally.

F.1.2 Least Common Mechanism

The principle of *least common mechanism*[45] states that, if multiple components in the system require the same function or mechanism, the function or mechanism should be factored into a single mechanism that can be used by all of them. The use of least common mechanism helps to minimize the complexity of the system by avoiding unnecessary duplicate functions and mechanisms. This has the distinct advantage of facilitating the construction and analysis of the non-bypassability of policy-enforcing system functions and mechanisms. It also simplifies maintainability since a necessary modification to a common function or mechanism can be performed once and the impact of modifications can be more easily understood in advance through analysis. Security considerations presented by least common mechanism include the potential for shared state and shared data among users of the common mechanism. Care is required to distinguish between functionality provided by the mechanism (e.g., a library) and implementations that require shared data or shared state. The former can be shared, whereas sharing of data or state risks creation of information flow channels in violation of security policy. An additional security concern is overloading a common mechanism with additional functionality intended to support a subset of its users. To avoid possible increased risk, designers should consider placing new mechanisms into separate components, thus avoiding increased complexity and divergent expectations for the original mechanism.

F.1.3 Modularity and Layering

The principles of *modularity* and *layering* are fundamental across system engineering disciplines. Modularity and layering derived from functional decomposition are effective in managing system complexity, by making it possible to comprehend the structure of the system. Yet, good modular decomposition, or refinement in system design is challenging and resists general statements of principle.

Modularity serves to isolate functions and related data structures into well-defined logical units. Layering allows the relationships of these units to be better understood, so that dependencies are clear and undesired complexity can be avoided. The security design principle of modularity extends functional modularity to include considerations based on trust, trustworthiness, privilege, and security policy. Security-informed modular decomposition includes the following: allocation of policies to systems in a network; allocation of system policies to layers; separation of system applications into processes with distinct address spaces; and separation of processes into subjects with distinct privileges based on hardware-supported privilege domains. The security design principles of modularity and layering are not the same as the concept of *defense in depth*, which is discussed in Section F.4.

F.1.4 Partially Ordered Dependencies

The principle of *partially ordered dependencies* states that the calling, synchronization, and other dependencies in the system should be partially ordered. A fundamental concept in system design is layering, whereby the system is organized into well-defined, functionally related modules or components. The layers are linearly ordered with respect to inter-layer dependencies, such that higher layers are dependent on lower layers. While providing functionality to higher layers, some layers can be self-contained and not dependent upon lower layers. While a partial ordering of all

---

[45] Least common mechanism refers to *functionality* rather than *state*.

functions in a given system may not be possible, if circular dependencies are constrained to occur within layers, the inherent problems of circularity can be more easily managed. Partially ordered dependencies and system layering contribute significantly to the simplicity and coherency of the system design. Partially ordered dependencies also facilitate system testing and analysis.

F.1.5 Efficiently Mediated Access

The principle of *efficiently mediated access* states that policy-enforcement mechanisms should utilize the least common mechanism available while satisfying stakeholder requirements within expressed constraints. The mediation of access to system resources (i.e., CPU, memory, devices, communication ports, services, infrastructure, data and information) is often the predominant security function of secure systems. It also enables the realization of protections for the capability provided to stakeholders by the system. Mediation of resource access can result in performance bottlenecks if the system is not designed correctly. For example, by using hardware mechanisms, efficiently mediated access can be achieved. Once access to a low-level resource such as memory has been obtained, hardware protection mechanisms can ensure that out-of-bounds access does not occur.

F.1.6 Minimized Sharing

The principle of *minimized sharing* states that no computer resource should be shared between system components (e.g., subjects, processes, functions) unless it is absolutely necessary to do so. Minimized sharing helps to simplify design and implementation. In order to protect user-domain resources from arbitrary active entities, no resource should be shared unless that sharing has been explicitly requested and granted. The need for resource sharing can be motivated by the principle of least common mechanism in the case internal entities, or driven by stakeholder requirements. However, internal sharing must be carefully designed to avoid performance and covert storage- and timing-channel problems. Sharing via common mechanism can increase the susceptibility of data and information to unauthorized access, disclosure, use, or modification and can adversely affect the inherent capability provided by the system. To help minimize the sharing induced by common mechanisms, such mechanisms can be designed to be reentrant or virtualized to preserve separation. Moreover, use of global data to share information should be carefully scrutinized. The lack of encapsulation may obfuscate relationships among the sharing entities.

F.1.7 Reduced Complexity

The principle of *reduced complexity* states that the system design should be as simple and small as possible. A small and simple design will be more understandable, more analyzable, and less prone to error. This principle applies to any aspect of a system, but it has particular importance for security due to the various analyses performed to obtain evidence about the emergent security property of the system. For such analyses to be successful, a small and simple design is essential. Application of the principle of reduced complexity contributes to the ability of system developers to understand the correctness and completeness of system security functions. It also facilitates identification of potential vulnerabilities. The corollary of reduced complexity states that the simplicity of the system is directly related to the number of vulnerabilities it will contain—that is, simpler systems contain fewer vulnerabilities. An important benefit of reduced complexity is that it is easier to understand whether the intended security policy has been captured in the system design, and that fewer vulnerabilities are likely to be introduced during engineering development. An additional benefit is that any such conclusion about correctness, completeness, and existence of vulnerabilities can be reached with a higher degree of assurance in contrast to conclusions reached in situations where the system design is inherently more complex.

F.1.8 Secure Evolvability

The principle of *secure evolvability* states that a system should be developed to facilitate the maintenance of its security properties when there are changes to its functionality structure, interfaces, and interconnections (i.e., system architecture) or its functionality configuration (i.e., security policy enforcement). These changes may include for example: new, enhanced, and upgraded system capability; maintenance and sustainment activities; and reconfiguration. Although it is not possible to plan for every aspect of system evolution, system upgrades and changes can be anticipated by analyses of mission or business strategic direction; anticipated changes in the threat environment; and anticipated maintenance and sustainment needs. It is unrealistic to expect that complex systems will remain secure in contexts not envisioned during development, whether such contexts are related to the operational environment or to usage. A system may be secure in some new contexts, but there is no guarantee that its emergent behavior will always be secure. It is easier to build trustworthiness into a system from the outset, and it follows that the sustainment of system trustworthiness requires planning for change as opposed to adapting in an ad hoc or non-methodical manner. The benefits of this principle include reduced vendor life-cycle costs; reduced cost of ownership; improved system security; more effective management of security risk; and less risk uncertainty.

F.1.9 Trusted Components

The principle of *trusted components* states that a component must be trustworthy to at least a level commensurate with the security dependencies it supports (i.e., how much it is trusted to perform its security functions by other components). This principle enables the composition of components such that trustworthiness is not inadvertently diminished and where consequently the trust is not misplaced. Ultimately this principle demands some metric by which the trust in a component and the trustworthiness of a component can be measured on the same abstract scale. This principle is particularly relevant when considering systems and components in which there are complex chains of trust dependencies.[46] The principle also applies to a compound component that consists of several subcomponents (e.g., a subsystem), which may have varying levels of trustworthiness. The conservative assumption is that the overall trustworthiness of a compound component is that of its least trustworthy subcomponent. It may be possible to provide a security engineering rationale that the trustworthiness of a particular compound component is greater than the conservative assumption; however, any such rationale should reflect logical reasoning based on a clear statement of the trustworthiness goals, and relevant and credible evidence.[47]

F.1.10 Hierarchical Trust

The principle of *hierarchical trust* for components builds on the principle of trusted components and states that the security dependencies in a system will form a partial ordering if they preserve the principle of trusted components. The partial ordering provides the basis for trustworthiness reasoning when composing a secure system from heterogeneously trustworthy components. To be able to analyze a system composed of heterogeneously trustworthy components for its overall trustworthiness, it is essential to eliminate circular dependencies with regard to trustworthiness. If a more trustworthy component located in a lower layer of the system were to depend upon a less trustworthy component in a higher layer, this would in effect, put the components in the same "less trustworthy" equivalence class per the principle of trusted components. Trust relationships,

---

[46] A trust dependency is also referred to as a *trust relationship* and there may be chains of trust relationships.

[47] The trustworthiness of a compound component is not the same as increased application of *defense–in–depth* layering within the component, or replication of components. Defense in depth techniques do not increase the trustworthiness of the whole above that of the least trustworthy component.

or chains of trust, have various manifestations. For example, the root certificate of a certificate hierarchy is the most trusted node in the hierarchy, whereas the leaves in the hierarchy may be the least trustworthy nodes. Another example occurs in a layered high-assurance system where the security kernel (including the hardware base), which is located at the lowest layer of the system, is the most trustworthy component. This principle, however, does not prohibit the use of overly trustworthy components. There may be cases in a system of low trustworthiness, where it is reasonable to employ a highly trustworthy component rather than one that is less trustworthy (e.g., due to availability or other cost-benefit driver). For such a case, any dependency of the highly trustworthy component upon a less trustworthy component does not degrade the overall trustworthiness of the resulting low-trust system.

F.1.11 Inverse Modification Threshold

The principle of *inverse modification threshold* builds on the principle of trusted components and the principle of hierarchical trust, and states that the degree of protection provided to a component must be commensurate with its trustworthiness. As the trust placed in a component increases, the protection against unauthorized modification of the component should also increase to the same degree. This protection can come in the form of the component's own self-protection and innate trustworthiness, or from protections afforded to the component from other elements or attributes of the architecture (to include protections in the environment of operation).

F.1.12 Hierarchical Protection

The principle of *hierarchical protection* states that a component need not be protected from more trustworthy components. In the degenerate case of the most trusted component, it must protect itself from all other components. For example, if an operating system kernel is deemed the most trustworthy component in a system, then it must protect itself from all untrusted applications it supports, but the applications, conversely, do not need to protect themselves from the kernel. The trustworthiness of users is a consideration for applying the principle of hierarchical protection. A trusted computer system need not protect itself from an equally trustworthy user, reflecting use of untrusted systems in "system high" environments where users are highly trustworthy and where other protections are put in place to bound and protect the "system high" execution environment.

F.1.13 Minimized Security Elements

The principle of *minimized security elements* states that the system should not have extraneous trusted components. This principle has two aspects: the overall cost of security analysis and the complexity of security analysis. Trusted components, necessarily being trustworthy, are generally costlier to construct, owing to increased rigor of development processes. They also require greater security analysis to qualify their trustworthiness. Thus, to reduce the cost and decrease the complexity of the security analysis, a system should contain as few trustworthy components as possible. The analysis of the interaction of trusted components with other components of the system is one of the most important aspects of the verification of system security. If these interactions are unnecessarily complex, the security of the system will also be more difficult to ascertain than one whose internal trust relationships are simple and elegantly constructed. In general, fewer trusted components will result in fewer internal trust relationships and a simpler system.

F.1.14 Least Privilege

The principle of *least privilege* states that each component should be allocated sufficient privileges to accomplish its specified functions, but no more. This limits the scope of the component's actions, which has two desirable effects: the security impact of a failure, corruption, or misuse of the component will have a minimized security impact; and the security analysis of the component will be simplified. Least privilege is a pervasive principle that is reflected in all aspects of the secure system design. Interfaces used to invoke component capability should be available to only certain subsets of the user population, and component design should support a sufficiently fine granularity of privilege decomposition. For example, in the case of an audit mechanism, there may be an interface for the audit manager, who configures the audit settings; an interface for the audit operator, who ensures that audit data is safely collected and stored; and, finally, yet another interface for the audit reviewer, who has need only to view the audit data that has been collected but no need to perform operations on that data.

In addition to its manifestations at the system interface, least privilege can be used as a guiding principle for the internal structure of the system itself. One aspect of internal least privilege is to construct modules so that only the elements encapsulated by the module are directly operated upon by the functions within the module. Elements external to a module that may be affected by the module's operation are indirectly accessed through interaction (e.g., via a function call) with the module that contains those elements. Another aspect of internal least privilege is that the scope of a given module or component should include only those system elements that are necessary for its functionality, and that the modes (e.g., read, write) by which the elements are accessed should also be minimal.

F.1.15 Predicate Permission

The principle of *predicate permission*[48] states that system designers should consider requiring multiple authorized entities to provide consent before a highly critical operation or access to highly sensitive data, information, or resources is allowed to proceed. The division of privilege among multiple parties decreases the likelihood of abuse and provides the safeguard that no single accident, deception, or breach of trust is sufficient to enable an unrecoverable action that can lead to significantly damaging consequences. The design options for such a mechanism may require simultaneous action (e.g., the firing of a nuclear weapon requires two different authorized individuals to give the correct command within a small time window) or a sequence of operations where each successive action is enabled by some prior action, but no single individual is able to enable more than one action.

F.1.16 Self-Reliant Trustworthiness

The principle of *self-reliant trustworthiness* states that systems should minimize their reliance on other systems for their own trustworthiness. A system should be trustworthy by default with any connection to an external entity used to supplement its function. If a system were required to maintain a connection with another external entity in order to maintain its trustworthiness, then that system would be vulnerable to malicious and non-malicious threats that result in loss or degradation of that connection. The benefit to this principle is that the isolation of a system will make it less vulnerable to attack. A corollary to this principle relates to the ability of the system (or system element) to operate in isolation and then resynchronize with other components when it is rejoined with them.

F.1.17 Secure Distributed Composition

The principle of *secure distributed composition* states that the composition of distributed components that enforce the same security policy should result in a system that enforces that policy at least as well as the individual components do. Many of the design principles for secure

---

[48] [Saltzer75] originally named this the *separation of privilege*. It is also equivalent to separation of duty.

systems deal with how components can or should interact. The need to create or enable capability from the composition of distributed components can magnify the relevancy of these principles. In particular, the translation of security policy from a stand-alone to a distributed system or a system-of-systems can have unexpected or emergent results. Communication protocols and distributed data consistency mechanisms help to ensure consistent policy enforcement across a distributed system. To ensure a system-wide level of assurance of correct policy enforcement, the security architecture of a distributed composite system must be thoroughly analyzed.

F.1.18 Trusted Communication Channels

The principle of *trusted communication channels* states that when composing a system where there is a potential threat to communications between components (i.e., the interconnections between components), each communication channel must be trustworthy to a level commensurate with the security dependencies it supports (i.e., how much it is trusted by other components to perform its security functions). Trusted communication channels are achieved by a combination of restricting access to the communication channel (to help ensure an acceptable match in the trustworthiness of the endpoints involved in the communication) and employing end-to-end protections for the data transmitted over the communication channel (to help protect against interception, modification, and to further increase the overall assurance of proper end-to-end communication).

F.2 SECURITY CAPABILITY AND INTRINSIC BEHAVIORS

Security capability and intrinsic behavior design principles describe protection behavior that must be specified, designed, and implemented to achieve the emergent system property of security. The principles are applicable at the system, subsystem, and component levels of abstraction, and in general, are largely reflected in the system security requirements.

F.2.1 Continuous Protection

The principle of *continuous protection* states that all components and data used to enforce the security policy must have uninterrupted protection that is consistent with the security policy and the security architecture assumptions. No assurances that the system can provide the specified confidentiality, integrity, availability, and privacy protections for its design capability can be made if there are gaps in the protection. More fundamentally, any assurances about the ability to secure a delivered capability require that data and information are continuously protected. That is, there are no time periods during which data and information are left unprotected while under control of the system (i.e., during the creation, storage, processing, or communication of the data and information, as well as during system initialization, execution, failure, interruption, and shutdown). Continuous protection requires adherence to the precepts of the *reference monitor concept* (i.e., every request is validated by the reference monitor, the reference monitor is able to protect itself from tampering, and sufficient assurance of the correctness and completeness of the mechanism can be ascertained from analysis and testing), and the *principle of secure failure and recovery* (i.e., preservation of a secure state during error, fault, failure, and successful attack; preservation of a secure state during recovery to normal, degraded, or alternative operational modes).

Continuous protection also applies to systems designed to operate in varying configurations including those that deliver full operational capability and other degraded-mode configurations that deliver partial operational capability. The continuous protection principle requires that changes to the system security policies be traceable to the operational need that drives the configuration and be verifiable (i.e., it must be possible to verify that the proposed changes will not put the system into an insecure state). Insufficient traceability and verification may lead to inconsistent states or protection discontinuities due to the complex or undecidable nature of the problem. The use of pre-verified configuration definitions that reflect the new security policy enables analysis to determine that a transition from old to new policies is essentially atomic, and that any residual effects from the old policy are guaranteed to not conflict with the new policy. The ability to demonstrate continuous protection is rooted in the clear articulation of life cycle protection needs as stakeholder security requirements.

F.2.2 Secure Metadata Management

The principle of *secure metadata management* states that metadata must be considered as first class objects with respect to security policy when the policy requires complete protection of information or it requires the security subsystem to be self-protecting. This principle is driven by the recognition that a system, subsystem, or component cannot achieve self-protection unless it protects the data it relies upon for correct execution. Data is generally not interpreted by the system that stores it. It may have semantic value (i.e., it comprises information) to users and programs that process the data. In contrast, metadata is information about data, such as a file name or the date when the file was created. Metadata is bound to the target data that it describes in a way that the system can interpret, but it need not be stored inside of or proximate to its target data. There may be metadata whose target is itself metadata (e.g., the sensitivity level of a file name), to include self-referential metadata.

The apparent secondary nature of metadata can lead to a neglect of its legitimate need for protection, resulting in violation of the security policy that includes the exfiltration of information in violation of security policy. A particular concern associated with insufficient protections for metadata is associated with multilevel secure (MLS) computing systems. MLS computing systems mediate access by a subject to an object based on their relative sensitivity levels. It follows that all subjects and objects in the scope of control of the MLS system must be directly labeled or indirectly attributed with sensitivity levels. The *corollary of labeled metadata* for MLS systems states that objects containing metadata must be labeled. As with the protection needs assessment for data, attention should be given to ensure that appropriate confidentiality and integrity protections are individually assessed, specified, and allocated to metadata, as would be done for mission, business, and system data.

F.2.3 Self-Analysis

The principle of *self-analysis* states that a component must be able to assess its internal state and functionality to a limited extent at various stages of execution, and that this self-analysis capability must be commensurate with the level of trustworthiness invested in the system. At the system level, self-analysis can be achieved via hierarchical trustworthiness assessments established in a bottom up fashion. In this approach, the lower-level components check for *data integrity* and correct functionality (to a limited extent) of higher-level components. For example, trusted boot sequences involve a trusted lower-level component attesting to the trustworthiness of the next higher-level components so that a transitive chain of trust can be established. At the root, a component attests to itself, which usually involves an axiomatic or environmentally enforced assumption about its integrity. These tests can be used to guard against externally induced errors, or internal malfunction or transient errors. By following this principle, some simple errors or malfunctions can be detected without allowing the effects of the error or malfunction to propagate outside the component. Further, the self-test can also be used to attest to the configuration of the component, detecting any potential conflicts in configuration with respect to the expected configuration.

F.2.4 Accountability and Traceability

The principle of *accountability and traceability* states that it must be possible to trace security-relevant actions (i.e., subject-object interactions) to the entity on whose behalf the action is being taken. This principle requires a trustworthy infrastructure that can record details about actions that affect system security (e.g., an audit subsystem). To do this, the system must not only be able to uniquely identify the entity on whose behalf the action is being carried out, but also record the relevant sequence of actions that are carried out. Further, the accountability policy must require the audit trail itself be protected from unauthorized access and modification. The principle of least privilege aids in tracing the actions to particular entities, as it increases the granularity of accountability. Associating actions with system entities, and ultimately with users, and making the audit trail secure against unauthorized access and modifications provides non-repudiation, because once an action is recorded, it is not possible to change the audit trail. Another important function that accountability and traceability serves is in the routine and forensic analysis of events associated with the violation of security policy. Analysis of the audit logs may provide additional information that may be helpful in determining the path or component that allowed the violation of security policy, and the actions of individuals associated with the violation of security policy.

F.2.5 Secure Defaults

The principle of *secure defaults* states that the default configuration of a system (to include its constituent subsystems, components, and mechanisms) reflects a restrictive and conservative enforcement of security policy. The principle of secure defaults applies to the initial (i.e., default) configuration of a system as well as to the security engineering and design of access control and other security functions that should follow a "deny unless explicitly authorized" strategy. The initial configuration aspect of this principle requires that any "as shipped" configuration of a system, subsystem, or component should not aid in the violation of the security policy, and can prevent the system from operating in the default configuration for those cases where the security policy itself requires configuration by the operational user. Restrictive defaults mean that the system will operate "as-shipped" with adequate self-protection, and is able to prevent security breaches before the intended security policy and system configuration is established. In cases where the protection provided by the "as-shipped" product is inadequate, the stakeholder must assess the risk of using it prior to establishing a secure initial state. Adherence to the principle of secure defaults guarantees a system is established in a secure state upon successfully completing initialization. Moreover, in situations where the system fails to complete initialization, either it will perform a requested operation using secure defaults or it will not perform the operation. Refer also to the principles of continuous protection and secure failure and recovery which parallel this principle to provide the ability to detect and recover from failure.

The security engineering approach to this principle states that security mechanisms should deny requests unless the request is found to be well-formed and consistent with the security policy. The insecure alternative is to allow a request unless it is shown to be inconsistent with the policy. In a large system, the conditions that must be satisfied to grant a request that is by default denied are often far more compact and complete than those that would need to be checked in order to deny a request that is by default granted.

F.2.6 Secure Failure and Recovery

The principle of *secure failure and recovery* states that neither a failure in a system function or mechanism nor any recovery action in response to failure should lead to a violation of security policy. This principle parallels the principle of continuous protection to ensure that a system is capable of detecting (within limits) actual and impending failure at any stage of its operation (i.e., initialization, normal operation, shutdown, and maintenance) and to take appropriate steps to ensure that security policies are not violated. In addition, when specified, the system is capable of recovering from impending or actual failure to resume normal, degraded, or alternative secure operation while ensuring that a secure state is maintained such that security policies are not violated.

Failure is a condition in which a component's behavior deviates from its specified or expected behavior for an explicitly documented input. Once a failed security function is detected, the system may reconfigure itself to circumvent the failed component, while maintaining security, and still provide all or part of the functionality of the original system, or completely shut itself down to prevent any (further) violation of security policies. For this to occur, the reconfiguration functions of the system should be designed to ensure continuous enforcement of security policy during the various phases of reconfiguration. Another technique that can be used to recover from failures is to perform a *rollback* to a secure state (which may be the initial state) and then either shutdown or replace the service or component that failed such that secure operation may resume. Failure of a component may or may not be detectable to the components using it. The principle of secure failure indicates that components should fail in a state that denies rather than grants access. For example, a nominally "atomic" operation interrupted before completion should not violate security policy and hence must be designed to handle interruption events by employing higher-level atomicity and rollback mechanisms (e.g., transactions). If a service is being used, its atomicity properties must be well-documented and characterized so that the component availing itself of that service can detect and handle interruption events appropriately. For example, a system should be designed to gracefully respond to disconnection and support resynchronization and data consistency after disconnection.

Failure protection strategies that employ replication of policy enforcement mechanisms, sometimes called *defense in depth*, can allow the system to continue in a secure state even when one mechanism has failed to protect the system. If the mechanisms are similar, however, the additional protection may be illusory, as the adversary can simply *attack in series*. Similarly, in a networked system, breaking the security on one system or service may enable an attacker to do the same on other similar replicated systems and services. By employing multiple protection mechanisms, whose features are significantly different, the possibility of attack replication or repetition can be reduced. Analyses should be conducted to weigh the costs and benefits of such redundancy techniques against increased resource usage and adverse effects on the overall system performance. Additional analyses should be conducted as the complexity of these mechanisms increases, as could be the case for dynamic behaviors. Increased complexity generally reduces trustworthiness. When a resource cannot be continuously protected, it is critical to detect and repair any security breaches before the resource is once again used in a secure context.

F.2.7 Economic Security

The principle of *economic security* states that security mechanisms should not be costlier than the potential damage that could occur from a security breach. This is the security-relevant form of the cost-benefit analyses used in risk management. The cost assumptions of this analysis will prevent the system designer from incorporating security mechanisms of greater strength than necessary, where strength of mechanism is proportional to cost. It also requires analysis of the benefits of assurance relative to the cost of that assurance in terms of the effort expended to obtain relevant and credible evidence, and to perform the analyses necessary to assess and draw trustworthiness and risk conclusions from the evidence.

F.2.8 Performance Security

The principle of *performance security* states that security mechanisms should be constructed so that they do not degrade system performance unnecessarily. Both stakeholder and system design requirements for performance and security must be precisely articulated and prioritized. For the system implementation to meet its design requirements and be found acceptable to stakeholders (i.e., validation against stakeholder requirements), the designers must adhere to the specified constraints that capability performance needs place on protection needs. The overall impact of computationally intensive security services (e.g., cryptography) should be assessed and be demonstrated to pose no significant impact to higher-priority performance considerations or deemed to be providing an acceptable trade-off of performance for trustworthy protection. Trade-off considerations should include less computationally intensive security services unless they are unavailable or insufficient. The insufficiency of a security service is determined by functional capability and strength of mechanism. The strength of mechanism must be selected appropriately with respect to security requirements as well as performance-critical overhead issues (e.g., cryptographic key management) and an assessment of the capability of the threat.

The principle of performance security leads to the incorporation of features that help in the enforcement of security policy, but incur minimum overhead, such as low-level hardware mechanisms upon which higher-level services can be built. Such low-level mechanisms are usually very specific, have very limited functionality, and are heavily optimized for performance. For example, once access rights to a portion of memory is granted, many systems use hardware mechanisms to ensure that all further accesses involve the correct memory address and access mode. Application of this principle reinforces the need to design security into the system from the ground up, and to incorporate simple mechanisms at the lower layers that can be used as building blocks for higher-level mechanisms.

F.2.9 Human Factored Security

The principle of *human factored security* states that the user interface for security functions and supporting services should be intuitive, user friendly, and provide appropriate feedback for user actions that affect such policy and its enforcement. The mechanisms that enforce security policy should not be intrusive to the user and should be designed not to degrade user efficiency. They should also provide the user with meaningful, clear, and relevant feedback and warnings when insecure choices are being made. Particular attention must also be given to interfaces through which personnel responsible for system operation and administration configure and set up the security policies. Ideally, these personnel must be able to understand the impact of their choices. They must be able to configure systems before start-up and administer them during runtime, in both cases with confidence that their intent is correctly mapped to the system's mechanisms. Security services, functions, and mechanisms should not impede or unnecessarily complicate the intended use of the system. There is often a trade-off between system usability and the strictness necessitated for security policy enforcement. If security mechanisms are frustrating or difficult to use, then users may disable or avoid them, or use the mechanisms in ways inconsistent with the security requirements and protection needs the mechanisms were designed to satisfy.

F.2.10 Acceptable Security

The principle of *acceptable security* requires that the level of privacy and performance the system provides should be consistent with the users' expectations. The perception of personal privacy may affect user behavior, morale, and effectiveness. Based on the organizational privacy policy and the system design, users should be able to restrict their actions to protect their privacy. When systems fail to provide intuitive interfaces or meet privacy and performance expectations, users may either choose to completely avoid the system or use it in ways that may be inefficient or even insecure.

F.3 LIFE CYCLE SECURITY

Several principles guide and inform a definition of the system life cycle that incorporates the security perspective necessary to achieve the initial and continuing security of the system. A secure system life cycle contributes to system comprehensibility and maintainability, as well as system integrity.[49]

F.3.1 Repeatable and Documented Procedures

The principle of *repeatable and documented procedures* states that the techniques and methods employed to construct a system component should permit the same component to be completely and correctly reconstructed at a later time. Repeatable and documented procedures support the development of a component that is identical to the component created earlier that may be in widespread use. In the case of other system artifacts (e.g., documentation and testing results), repeatability supports consistency and ability to inspect the artifacts. Repeatable and documented procedures can be introduced at various stages within the system life cycle and can contribute to the ability to evaluate assurance claims for the system. Examples include systematic procedures for code development and review; procedures for configuration management of development tools and system artifacts; and procedures for system delivery.

F.3.2 Procedural Rigor

The principle of *procedural rigor* states that the rigor of a system life cycle process should be commensurate with its intended trustworthiness. Procedural rigor defines the scope, depth, and detail of the system life cycle procedures. These procedures contribute to the assurance that the system is correct and free of unintended functionality in several ways. First, they impose checks and balances on the life cycle process such that the introduction of unspecified functionality is prevented. Second, rigorous procedures applied to systems security engineering activities that produce specifications and other design documents contribute to the ability to understand the system as it has been built, rather than trusting that the component as implemented, is the authoritative (and potentially misleading) specification. Finally, modifications to an existing system component are easier when there are detailed specifications describing its current design, instead of studying source code or schematics to try to understand how it works. Procedural rigor helps to ensure that security functional and assurance requirements have been satisfied, and it contributes to a better-informed basis for the determination of trustworthiness and risk posture. Procedural rigor should always be commensurate with the degree of assurance desired for the system. If the required trustworthiness of the system is low, a high level of procedural rigor may add unnecessary cost, whereas when high trustworthiness is critical, the cost of high procedural rigor is merited.

F.3.3 Secure System Modification

The principle of *secure system modification* states that system modification must maintain system security with respect to the security requirements and risk tolerance of stakeholders. Upgrades or modifications to systems can transform a secure system into an insecure one. The procedures for system modification must ensure that, if the system is to maintain its trustworthiness, the same rigor that was applied to its initial development is applied to any changes. Because modifications

---

[49] [Myers80] provides examples of subversion throughout the system life cycle.

can affect the ability of the system to maintain its secure state, a careful security analysis of the modification is needed prior to its implementation and deployment. This principle parallels the principle of secure evolvability.

F.3.4 Sufficient Documentation

The principle of *sufficient documentation* states that personnel with responsibility to interact with the system should be provided with adequate documentation and other information such that they contribute to rather than detract from system security. Despite attempts to comply with principles such as human factored security and acceptable security, systems are inherently complex, and the design intent for the use of security mechanisms is not always intuitively obvious. Neither are the ramifications of their misuse or misconfiguration. Uninformed and insufficiently trained users can introduce new vulnerabilities due to errors of omission and commission. The ready availability of documentation and training can help to ensure a knowledgeable cadre of personnel, all of whom have a critical role in the achievement of principles such as continuous protection. Documentation must be written clearly and supported by appropriate training that provides security awareness and understanding of security-relevant responsibilities.

F.4 APPROACHES TO TRUSTWORTHY SECURE SYSTEM DEVELOPMENT

This section introduces three overarching strategies that may be applied in the development of trustworthy secure systems. These approaches may be used individually or in combination.

F.4.1 Reference Monitor Concept

The *reference monitor concept* provides an abstract security model of the necessary and sufficient properties that must be achieved by any system mechanism claiming to securely enforce access controls. The reference monitor concept does not refer to any particular policy to be enforced by a system, nor does it address any particular implementation. Instead, the intent of this concept is to help practitioners avoid *ad hoc* approaches to the development of security mechanisms intended to enforce critical policies and can also be used to provide assurance that the system has not been corrupted by an insider. The abstract instantiation of the reference monitor concept is an "ideal mechanism" characterized by three properties: the mechanism is tamper-proof (i.e., it is protected from modification so that it always is capable of enforcing the intended access control policy); the mechanism is always invoked (i.e., it cannot be bypassed so that every access to the resources it protects is mediated); and the mechanism can be subjected to analysis and testing to assure that it is correct (i.e., it is possible to validate that the mechanism faithfully enforces the intended security policy and that it is correctly implemented).

While abstract mechanisms can be ideal, actual systems are not. The reference monitor concept provides an "ideal" toward which system security engineers can strive in the basic design and implementation of the most critical components of their systems, given practical constraints and limitations. Those constraints and limitations translate to risk that is managed through analyses and decisions applied to the architecture and design of the particular reference monitor concept implementation, and subsequently to its integration into a broader system architecture for a component, subsystem, infrastructure, system, or system-of-systems. Therefore, although originally used to describe a monolithic system, a generalization of the reference monitor concept serves well as the fundamental basis for the design of individual security-relevant system elements, collections of elements, and for systems. The generalization also guides the activities that obtain evidence used to substantiate claims that trustworthiness objectives have been achieved and to support determinations of risk.

F.4.2 Defense in Depth

Defense in depth describes security architectures constructed through the application of multiple mechanisms to create a series of barriers to prevent, delay, or deter an attack by an adversary. The application of some security components in a defense in depth strategy may increase assurance, but there is no theoretical basis to assume that defense in depth alone could achieve a level of trustworthiness greater than that of the individual security components used. That is, a defense in depth strategy is not a substitute for or equivalent to a sound security architecture and design that leverages a balanced application of security concepts and design principles.

F.4.3 Isolation

Two forms of *isolation* are available to system security engineers: logical isolation and physical isolation. The former requires the use of underlying trustworthy mechanisms to create isolated processing environments. These can be constructed so that resource sharing among environments is minimized. Their utility can be realized in situations in which virtualized environments are sufficient to satisfy computing requirements. In other situations, the isolation mechanism can be constructed to permit sharing of resources, but under the control and mediation of the underlying security mechanisms, thus avoiding blatant violations of security policy. Researchers continue to demonstrate that isolation for processing environments can be extremely difficult to achieve, so stakeholders must determine the potential risk of incomplete isolation, the consequences of which can include covert channels and side channels. Another form of logical isolation can be realized within a process. Traditionally obtained through the use of hardware mechanisms, a hierarchy of protected privilege domains can be developed within a process. Course-grained hierarchical isolation, and consequently privilege domain separation, is in common use in many modern commercial systems, and separates the user domain from that of the operating system. More granular hierarchical isolation is less common today; however, examples exist in prior research-prototype and commercial systems.

Physical isolation involves separation of components, systems, and networks by hosting them on separate hardware. It may also include the use of specialized computing facilities and operational procedures to allow access to systems only by authorized personnel. In many situations, isolation objectives may be achieved by a combination of logical and physical isolation. Security architects and operational users must be cognizant of the co-dependencies between the logical and physical mechanisms and must ensure that their combination satisfies security and assurance objectives. A full discussion of isolation is beyond the scope of this appendix.

APPENDIX G

ENGINEERING AND SECURITY FUNDAMENTALS
THE BASIC BUILDING BLOCKS APPLIED TO SYSTEMS SECURITY ENGINEERING[50]

U nderstanding the foundational engineering and security concepts is essential to the conduct of a successful systems security engineering effort. These concepts also reinforce the importance of the security design principles in Appendix F and show how those principles are applied in the context of a system's life cycle. The key topics addressed in this section include protection needs; security requirements; requirements engineering;[51] the relationships among security requirements, policy, and mechanisms; security architecture; assurance and trustworthiness; and cost, performance, and effectiveness.

G.1 PROTECTION NEEDS

Understanding the nature and scope of *protection needs* is a foundational systems security engineering responsibility. Protection needs are determined from analyses of asset loss and associated consequences, the results of which serve as an informing basis to engineering a trustworthy secure system.[52] The analyses occur across three interrelated perspectives including:

- **Stakeholder perspective:** Mission/business needs; operational performance objectives and measures; life cycle concepts; laws; regulatory, statutory, and certification criteria; governing policies; loss and risk tolerance; accreditation, approval, and other independent authorization criteria; and all associated concerns and constraints.

- **System perspective:** System self-protection capability; system architecture, system design, and system implementation decisions; developmental, fabrication, manufacturing, and production standards; secure system management; technical performance objectives and measures; and all associated concerns and constraints.

- **Trades perspective:** Requirements trades; engineering trades; risk treatment trades; and other life cycle trades.

The *stakeholder* perspective of asset protection is based on those assets of value to stakeholders, and therefore warrants varying degrees of security protection. This includes, but is not limited to, those assets used to *execute* organizational missions or business functions, those assets consumed or produced by the execution of organizational missions and business functions, and those assets used to *manage* the execution of the missions or business functions.[53] The stakeholder perspective is typically derived from the mission or business operational and performance objectives and

---

[50] NIST acknowledges the contribution of the National Security Agency in providing selected content for this appendix.

[51] Requirements engineering includes a series of successive decomposition and derivation actions beginning with stakeholder requirements and moving through high-level design requirements to low-level design requirements to the implementation of the design. During requirements engineering, several requirements baselines are defined. These baselines include: a functional baseline that provides the basis for contracting and controlling the system design; an allocated baseline that provides performance requirements for each configuration item of the system; and a product baseline that provides a detailed design specification for system elements.

[52] Protection needs are expressed in terms of objectives for controlling asset loss.

[53] Some assets used by the mission or business are owned by or provided by non-mission/business stakeholders. These stakeholders may have protection needs that are different than the needs of the mission/business owners, and therefore, these stakeholders are consulted as part of the protection needs analyses.

measures, life cycle concepts, environments of operation, and all associated processes and procedures. The *system* perspective of asset protection is based on those assets that are deemed necessary for the system to execute correctly and securely; to manage its execution including secure execution; and to provide for its own protection.[54] The system perspective is driven by system and specialty engineering architecture, design, and implementation objectives and decisions—it is *not* driven by mission or business assets or asset protection needs. And finally, the *trades* perspective encompasses all forms of trades.[55] It considers protection need aspects associated with all feasible alternatives as well as those related to a specific decision.

Providing adequate security in a system is inherently a system design problem. It is achieved only through sound, purposeful engineering informed by the specialty discipline of systems security engineering [Ware70]. Having established an understanding of the basic need for protection across all contributing perspectives, the protection needs are then satisfied by the employment of specific *security functions*[56] that are deemed adequate to protect the stakeholder and system assets. The security functions represent the security-relevant portions of the system and the security-relevant aspects of the systems engineering effort. The selection of security functions is informed by adversity in the form of the disruptions, hazards, and threats anticipated across all stages of the system life cycle, stakeholder risk, and asset loss tolerance.

G.1.1 *Transformation of Protection Needs into Security Requirements and Policy*

Stakeholder protection needs are expressed and formalized in two distinctly different but related forms: *security requirements* and *security policy*. Security requirements specify security capability, performance, effectiveness, and the associated verification and validation measures. Security requirements also express constraints on system requirements.[57] Security requirements are developed in design-independent (i.e., stakeholder requirements) and design-dependent (i.e., system requirements) forms. Protection needs are also expressed in various abstractions of *security policy* at organizational and system levels.[58] Security policy consists of a well-defined set of rules that govern all aspects of the security-relevant behavior of system elements.

Protection needs are continuously reassessed and adjusted as variances, changes, and trades occur throughout the life cycle of the system. These include maturation of the system design and life cycle concepts; identification of new disruptions, hazards, threats, and vulnerabilities; and change in the assessment of the consequence of losing an asset. Revisiting protection needs is a necessary part of the iterative nature of systems security engineering—necessary to ensure completeness in understanding the problem space, exploring all feasible solutions, and engineering a trustworthy

---

[54] System self-protection is grounded in the fundamentals of computer security. The nucleus of a trustworthy secure system "…includes all the security protection mechanisms that are properly a part of a computer system, not just those necessary to control a user's capability to reference programs and data" [Anderson72].

[55] Engineering "trade space" refers to informed decision making whereby a set of candidate alternatives are considered for selection when each alternative is able to satisfy objectives within constraints such as performance, cost, schedule, and risk. The intent of the trade space decision is to select the optimal solution among the candidate alternatives.

[56] *A security function is* a capability provided by a system element. The capability may be expressed generally as a concept or specified precisely in requirements. A security mechanism is the implementation of a concept or security function and can be performed by machine/technology elements; human elements; physical elements; environmental elements; and all associated procedures and configurations.

[57] System requirements that are informed by security-driven constraints can be metadata tagged to indicate the nature of the security constraint.

[58] Security requirements determine the protection capability for a system, whereas security policy determines how the protection capability is intended to be used.

secure system. Figure G-1 illustrates the key input sources used to define protection needs and the outputs derived from the specification of those needs.

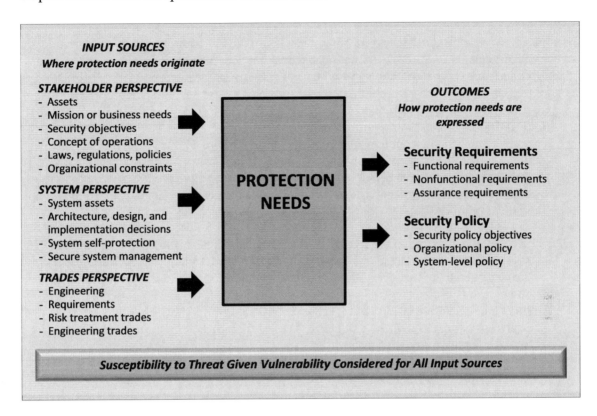

FIGURE G-1: DEFINING PROTECTION NEEDS

G.2 SECURITY REQUIREMENTS

A *requirement* is a condition or capability that must be met or possessed by a system or system element to satisfy a contract, standard, specification, or other formally imposed document [IEEE 610.12]. In general, requirements are considered to be functional or nonfunctional. Functional requirements specify capability and behavior while nonfunctional requirements specify quality attributes of the capability and behavior. The *Fundamentals* section in Chapter Two of this document differentiated security—an emergent property of the system, from protection—the active and passive capability and associated constraints on system function that composes to realize a trustworthy secure system. With that distinction in mind, security requirements have both functional and nonfunctional aspects. Security functional requirements specify *protection* and *policy enforcement* capability and behavior. Security non-functional requirements specify the quality attributes of the active protection capability. Security assurance requirements specify the verification and validation methods; the processes and procedures employed throughout the engineering effort, to include those used in verification and validation, and the evidence to be generated as an outcome of conducting verification and validation activities.

The systems security engineering framework identifies three contexts within which system security is addressed: the problem context; the solution context; and the trustworthiness context. Key to the determination of a system being trustworthy secure across *all* stakeholders and their asset loss concerns is having a common requirements basis to capture the stakeholder objectives for the protection of their assets. That foundation informs both the realization of the solution and the development of the assurance case as the basis for making the trustworthiness determination.

Security requirements provide the means for communicating and for reaching agreement on the problem to be solved, the realization of the solution in terms of the delivered system, and the security-driven claims used to make the trustworthiness determination.

The development of security requirements, similar to all requirements, is a continuous activity. Requirements engineering elicitation and analysis activities identify stakeholder protection needs, concerns, expectations, and constraints, and subsequently formalize those entities as objectives and stakeholder security requirements. The stakeholder security requirements are transformed into system security requirements as the engineering effort moves into realization of the solution. Security requirements analysis during realization is closely associated with development of the architecture, the allocation of functions to the architecture, and the design of system elements. Security requirements are iteratively decomposed and derived as design decisions, and as part of engineering, performance, risk, and other trades. This iterative process continues as the system architecture and design matures and enables implementation of the design and integration of the system.

Security requirements express the active security functions that exhibit behavior and their associated security architecture and security design needs. Security requirements also express concerns about the security of the intended functions of the system and the system architecture and design to ensure they are specified in a manner that is consistent with the active security functions. Therefore, some system requirements are informed by security constraints while not explicitly serving as a security function. These system requirements are metadata tagged to indicate their security relevance.

G.2.1 Stakeholder Requirements and Security Requirements

Systems engineering defines two primary categories of requirements: *stakeholder requirements*, which include stakeholder security requirements; and *system requirements*, which include system security requirements. Stakeholder requirements describe the stakeholder-oriented view of desired capability. These requirements include operational, protection, safety, and other needs[59] and expectations of stakeholders, including legal, policy, regulatory, statutory, certification, policy, and other constraints for solutions that support the mission or business. Requirements elicitation and analysis activities are used to transform the basic statements of stakeholder needs, expectations, concerns, and constraints into requirements and to ensure that the requirements are complete, consistent, and unambiguous. The requirements are reviewed with stakeholders and validated as representing what is required from any specific solution that is implemented. The requirements validated by the stakeholders establish the *stakeholder requirements baseline.*[60] The stakeholder requirements baseline is configuration controlled and used to develop the design requirements for specific solutions to be implemented. The baseline is also used to validate that a solution, when used as intended, correctly delivers the specified capability, is suitable for use, and is effective in addressing stakeholder objectives and concerns associated with the mission or business.

---

[59] Other needs include, for example: usability, human factors, form factor, and operational performance.

[60] A baseline is a specification or work product that has been formally reviewed and agreed upon, that thereafter serves as the basis for further development, and that can be changed only through formal change control procedures. Many different artifacts of the engineering process are used as a baseline during and after the completion of the engineering effort. Examples include stakeholder requirements baseline; design requirements baseline; and architecture and design baselines.

Stakeholder security requirements are those stakeholder requirements that are security-relevant. The stakeholder security requirements specify: the protection needed for the mission or business, the data, information, processes, functions, human, and system assets; the roles, responsibilities, and security-relevant actions of individuals that perform and support the mission or business processes; the interactions between the security-relevant solution elements; and the assurance that is to be obtained in the security solution. Systems security engineering activities provide the security perspective to ensure that the appropriate stakeholder security requirements are included in the stakeholder requirements, and that the stakeholder security requirements are consistent with all other stakeholder requirements.

G.2.2 *System Requirements and System Security Requirements*

System requirements specify the technical view of a system or solution that meets the stakeholder needs. The system requirements are a transformation of the validated stakeholder requirements. System requirements specify what the system or solution must do to satisfy the stakeholder requirements. Each system or solution is verified against its system requirements to determine that it was properly implemented. The system or solution is then validated against the stakeholder requirements to determine that it is effective in supporting the stated mission or business objectives.[61]

System requirements specify the capability and quality attributes of the delivered system. These requirements should be clear, concise, and capable of being verified. The system requirements are hierarchical and are decomposed relative to various levels of abstraction of the architecture of the system and the design of the system elements. The decomposition includes derivation of new system requirements as architecture, design, and implementation decisions are made throughout the engineering effort.

The hierarchical decomposition of system requirements provides details and refinements that transform the solution from an initial abstract statement of capabilities to the specific mechanisms and procedures to be implemented. The hierarchical decomposition of system requirements also reflects details of build versus buy versus lease/subscribe decisions, and reflects assurance details for verification at architecture, design, and implementation levels of abstraction. System requirements baselines are defined and configuration controlled at different levels of the system requirements hierarchy. These baselines are typically associated with key milestone or other reviews, and serve to manage the transition of the system as it matures through its concept, design, and as-built forms.

System security requirements are those system requirements that have security relevance. These requirements define the protection capabilities provided by the security solution; the performance and behavioral characteristics exhibited by the security solution; assurance processes, procedures, and techniques; and the evidence required to determine that the system security requirements have been satisfied. The decomposition of system security requirements is accomplished as part of the system requirements decomposition and is to be consistent with the different levels of hierarchical abstraction and forms of the system requirements.

---

[61] It is necessary to verify and validate the solution. It is possible for a successfully verified solution (i.e., a solution that properly implements its design requirements) to fail validation (i.e., it is ineffective or fails to satisfy stakeholder needs and expectations). Typically, a problem with either the stakeholder requirements or the transformation of those requirements into design requirements is the reason that a solution fails validation after being successfully verified.

Figure G-2 illustrates the two types of requirements and their relationship to the verification and validation of the system.

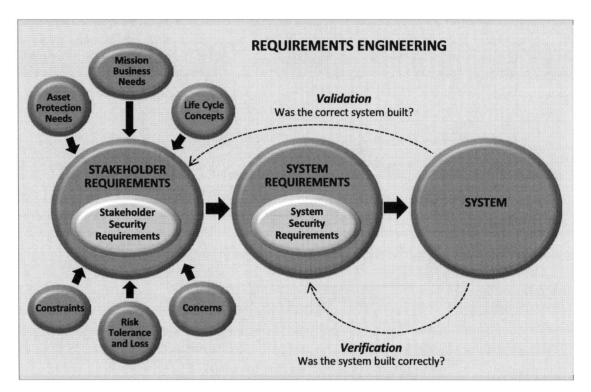

FIGURE G-2: STAKEHOLDER AND SYSTEM REQUIREMENTS

G.2.3 Types of Security Requirements

There are three types of security requirements that are important to consider in the systems security engineering effort including:

- **Security functional requirement:** Specifies the protection capability provided by the system, the capability for the system to protect itself, and the capability for secure management of the system;

- **Security nonfunctional requirement:** Specifies the security behavior, performance, strength-of-function, and quality characteristics and attributes of the system; and

- **Security assurance requirement:** Specifies the techniques and methods employed in the engineering effort to generate evidence that is used to verify that the system meets its security functional and nonfunctional requirements; to substantiate the trustworthiness of the system; and to identify the residual risk of the delivered system based on its intended use to support the mission or business.

G.2.4 Security Requirements in the Life Cycle Processes

The development of security requirements in all forms is the responsibility of the first five technical processes (i.e., **BA, SN, SR, AR,** and **DE**) described in Chapter Three. However, it is equally important to recognize that all of the remaining technical processes serve to *inform* the development of security requirements, with the *System Analysis* process providing data to support requirements analysis activities, and all of the remaining technical life cycle processes providing needs, considerations, and constraints that are specific to their process outcomes to inform the requirements analysis activities. Figure G-3 illustrates the requirements engineering process across key system life cycle processes.

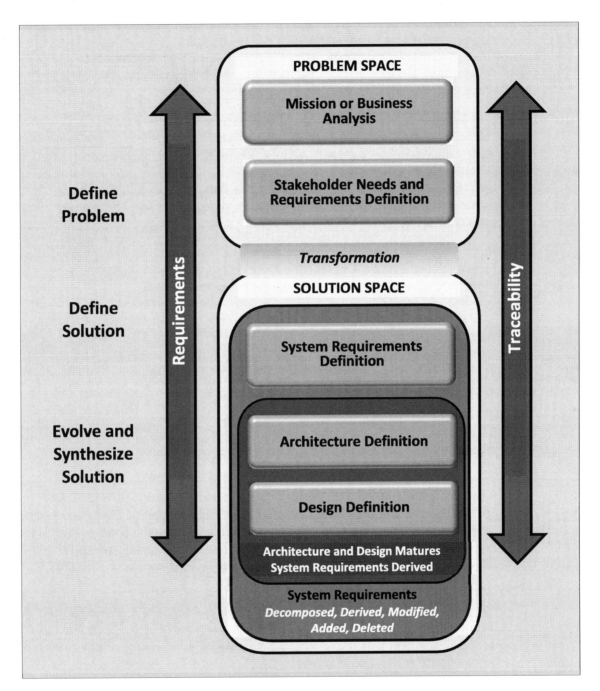

FIGURE G-3: REQUIREMENTS ENGINEERING ACROSS KEY LIFE CYCLE PROCESSES

Examples of information elicited and that informs security requirements analysis include, but are not limited to:

- *Business or Mission*
  - Environment of operation of the business or mission;
  - Processes, procedures, and interactions associated with the business or mission;

- Data and information;
- Proprietary/sensitive data and information;
- Roles, responsibilities, and interactions of personnel;
- Interactions with other organizations;
- Business or mission functions and function interaction;
- Criticality ranking and prioritization of business or mission functions; and
- Normal, abnormal, and transitional modes, states, and conditions of business or mission operations.

- *System Use*

  - Method of using the system to support the organization across all planned business or mission modes of operation and system modes of operation including operation in contested environments;
  - Interactions with other systems and services within the organization;
  - Interactions with other external organizations, systems, services, and infrastructures; and
  - Placement of the system within the organization (i.e., physical or logical placement).

- *Information*

  - Identification of information required to support the business or mission;
  - Method of using information to support the business or mission;
  - Sensitivity of information and concerns associated with its use and dissemination;
  - Identification of legal, regulatory, privacy, or other requirements that address information protection, use, and dissemination;
  - Information criticality and prioritization in supporting the business or mission; and
  - Impact to the business or mission, organization, or other organizations if the information is compromised, damaged, or becomes inaccessible.

- *Intellectual Property*

  - Identification of intellectual property assets that include data, information, technology, and methods associated with the system throughout its life cycle.

- *Enabling Systems and Other Systems of the System-of-Interest*

  - Identification of systems, services, or infrastructures used to support the business or mission;
  - Method of use for systems, services, or infrastructures supporting the business or mission;
  - Criticality of systems, services, or infrastructures supporting the business or mission; and
  - Impact to the business or mission, the organization, or other organizations if the systems, services, or infrastructures are compromised, damaged, or become inaccessible.

- *Disruptions, Threats, and Hazards*

  - Threat and hazard information associated with all system life cycle processes and concepts;
  - Identification of potential threat and hazard sources to include, but not limited to, natural disasters, structural failures, cyberspace and physical attacks, misuse, abuse, and errors of omission and commission; and
  - Plans, doctrine, strategy, and procedures to ensure continuity of capability, function, service, and operation in response to disruptions, threats, hazards, and inherent uncertainty.

- *Trustworthiness*

  - Policy, legal, and regulatory requirements and mandates;
  - Processes to be followed (e.g., acquisition, development, production, manufacturing, risk management, verification and validation, assurance, assessment, authorization); and
  - Agreements, arrangements, and contracts for services provided to or received from external organizations.

Figure G-4 illustrates the multitude of factors considered in security requirements analysis conducted as part of requirements engineering.

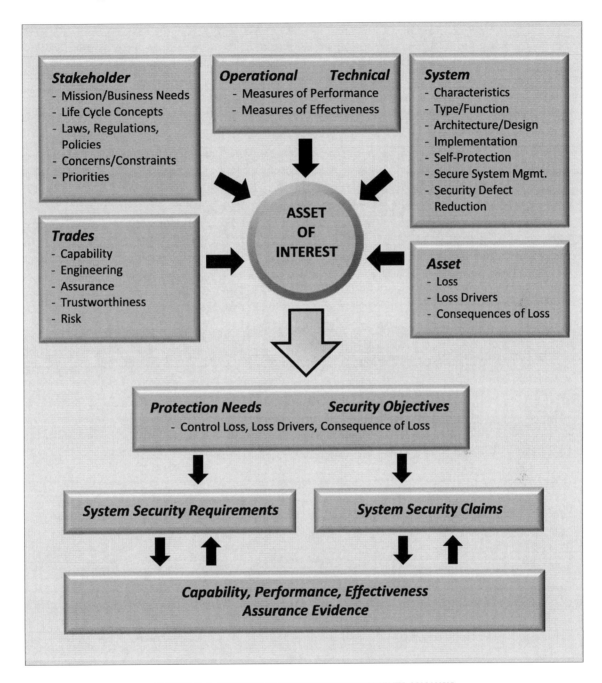

FIGURE G-4: FACTORS IN SECURITY REQUIREMENTS ANALYSIS

Security Requirements and Controls

The term *control* can be defined as the power to make decisions about how something is managed or how something is done; the ability to direct the actions of someone or something; an action, method, or law that limits; or a device or mechanism used to regulate or guide the operation of a machine, apparatus, or system. A *requirement* is a statement that translates or expresses a need and its associated constraints and conditions [ISO/IEC/IEEE 29148]. Requirements can express something that is needed or that must be done, or something that is necessary for something else to happen or be done.

The term control can be applied to a variety of contexts and can serve multiple purposes. For example, a safety control can be a mechanism designed to address needs that are specified by a set of safety requirements. Similarly, a quality control can be a mechanism designed to address needs that are specified by a set of quality requirements. When used in the security context, a security control can be a mechanism (i.e., a safeguard or countermeasure) designed to address protection needs that are specified by a set of security requirements.

From a systems engineering perspective, there is no single, prescribed, defined, or mandatory relationship between security requirements and security controls. The relationship is completely dependent on the systems engineering use of requirements which is formalized and grounded in a well-defined requirements engineering process. It is also dependent on the stakeholder's use of security controls, which may be dynamic and evolving.

G.3 SECURITY POLICY

Security policy is a fundamental security concept. Security policy provides a set of well-defined rules that determines aspects of the behavior, interactions, and outcomes of system elements that are deemed secure.[62] Security policy is enforced individually and in combination by human, physical, and automated system elements. In addition, security policy is enforced continuously (see Appendix F, security design principle on *continuous protection*) and is implicitly related to the concept of trustworthiness. One condition that must be satisfied for a system to be deemed trustworthy is that there must be sufficient confidence or assurance that the system is capable of enforcing security policy on a continuous basis. The implications associated with demonstrating the continuous enforcement of security policy at the system level is what distinguishes systems security engineering from its constituent security specialties and from the discipline of systems engineering and its related engineering specialties—particularly those concerned with accuracy, availability, fault tolerance, performance, reliability, sustainability, human safety, and general functional correctness.

G.3.1 System Security Policy Property Objectives

Security policy is typically expressed in terms of three security objectives: *confidentiality*, *integrity*, and *availability*:

- **Confidentiality:** Rules that govern access to, operations on, and disclosure of system elements (including, but not limited to, data and information). While confidentiality policy typically is considered in terms of information and data, it also applies to restrictions on the knowledge of and the use of system functions and processes;

- **Integrity:** Rules that govern the modification and destruction system elements (including, but not limited to, data and information) and that govern the manner in which system elements can be manipulated; and

- **Availability:** Rules that govern the presence, accessibility, readiness, and continuity of service of system elements (to include, but not limited to, data and information).

The responsibility for the *confidentiality* aspect of system security policy falls within the scope of the security discipline. The responsibility for system *integrity* and *availability*, however, spans numerous disciplines. For example, the ability of a software algorithm to perform calculations with sufficient accuracy and precision, and produce correct results in a delivered capability is not a security integrity responsibility issue. The ability of a device to continue to operate despite non-catastrophic faults is not a security availability responsibility issue. However, in each of the above situations, if the loss of integrity or availability results in a violation of security policy, then there are security-relevant concerns associated with those capabilities.

The integrity and availability scope and responsibility overlap leads to confusion when the basis for the protection need is not properly allocated or understood. The confusion is often the source of design conflicts and contradictions that are best resolved through informed trade space analysis among all impacted and contributing disciplines. Security policy distinguishes security-relevant aspects of integrity protections and availability protections from the integrity and availability

---

[62] Non-human system elements that exhibit behavior may do so on behalf of an individual. A protected binding between the system element and the individual associates the security-relevant attributes of the individual with the system element that executes on behalf of that individual. Such bindings make it possible to restrict the behavior of the process such that it can perform only those operations that the individual is authorized to perform. A computer process is an example a system element that executes on behalf of an individual.

protections that are addressed by other specialty disciplines. Figure G-5 illustrates the scope of security policy properties.

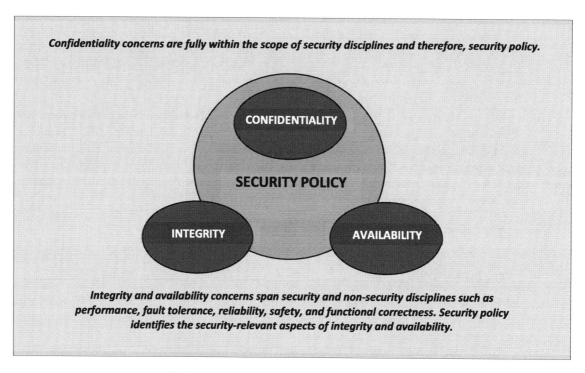

FIGURE G-5: SCOPE OF SECURITY POLICY PROPERTIES

G.3.2 Security Policy Hierarchy

The term *security policy* is used in several different ways including: *security policy objectives*; *organizational security policy*; and *system security policy*. There is a hierarchical relationship established among the uses of the term security policy (i.e., security policy objectives subsume organizational security policy which in turn, subsumes system security policy). Each use of the term *security policy* has a different context, authority, scope, and purpose as described below:

- **Security Policy (Protection) Objectives:** Security policy objectives include a statement of intent to protect identified assets within the specific scope of stakeholder responsibility and security loss and risk concerns. The objectives identify the assets to be protected and scope of protection (i.e., specifics of the protections to be provided). Security policy objectives are the basis for the derivation of all other security policy forms.

- **Organizational Security Policy:** Organizational security policy is the set of laws, rules, and practices that regulate how an organization manages, protects, and distributes its assets to achieve specified security policy (protection) objectives. These laws, rules, and practices identify criteria for according individual authority, and may specify conditions under which individuals are permitted to exercise or delegate their authority. To be meaningful, the laws, rules, and practices provide individuals with a reasonable ability to determine whether their actions either violate or comply with the security policy. The laws, rules, and practices that constitute an organizational security policy are highly dependent on the security policy objectives and the organization's analysis of life cycle threats. Organizational security policy defines the behavior of individuals in performing their missions and business functions and is used for development of processes and procedures.

- **System Security Policy:** System security policy specifies what a system with security policy enforcement responsibility is expected to do. It is the set of restrictions and properties that specifies how a system enforces or contributes to the enforcement of an organizational security policy. This includes, for example, defining how an operating system manages the use of system resources, including time (processes) and memory or how a firewall mediates the flow of incoming and outgoing data packets. System security policy may be reflected in semiformal or formal models and specifications. Mathematical methods and techniques (e.g., formal methods) may be used to demonstrate precisely and unambiguously the consistency and completeness of security policy models. The models and specifications are used as the basis for design and implementation of the mechanisms that must enforce the security policy. Verification activities demonstrate that the mechanism is a correct implementation of the security policy model. To minimize the semantic distance between security policy objectives and formal representations of security policy, problem domain expertise must be combined with versatility in the use of formal methods.

Security policy objectives and all subsequent security policy forms are derived from *protection needs*. Protection needs identified by requirements analysis activities are transformed into the security requirements that specify the security functions provided by the system. There is an intrinsic relationship between security requirements, security policy, security functions, and the security mechanisms that provide the specific security function (see Section G.4). Security policy objectives are allocated to all types of system elements during security architecture and security design activities. Such activities are carried out in a manner that is optimized across all technical and operational performance measures. Security policy goes through an iterative refinement process that decomposes an abstract statement of security policy into more specific statements of security policy. This occurs in parallel with security requirements allocation and the subsequent decomposition of requirements as the system design matures. Figure G-6 illustrates security policy allocation and the resultant enforcement responsibility.

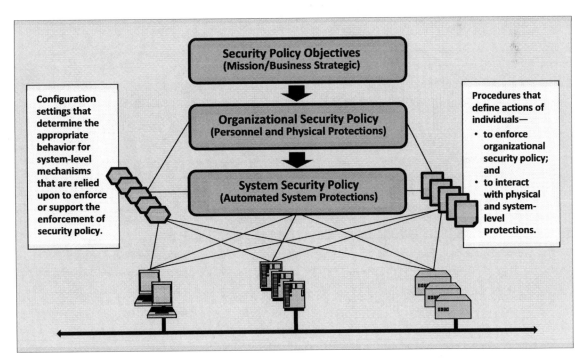

FIGURE G-6: ALLOCATION OF SECURITY POLICY ENFORCEMENT RESPONSIBILITIES

The scope of authority for system security policy enforcement is limited to the resources within the scope of control of the system. Thus, each instance of a system security policy enforcement is matched to the set of resources within the scope of control of the system and the capabilities of the security-relevant elements of that system to enforce the system security policy. Any resource operation not authorized by or specified by the system security policy violates the security policy objectives and organizational security policy. This has a direct linkage to the non-bypassability property of the *reference monitor concept* that is described in Appendix F. The transformation of an organizational security policy to a system security policy is supported by policy-driven verification and validation activities that are equivalent to those used to verify the system against its design requirements and to validate the system against stakeholder requirements.

G.3.3 System-Level Security Policy

Organizational security policy becomes relevant at the machine/technology system element level when these system elements are trusted to enforce organizational security policy objectives. The security architecture and design activities identify the aspects of an organizational security policy to be allocated to the machine/technology and the limitations, constraints, or restrictions that impact accurate translation of the organizational security policy into its system-level equivalent. The system-level security policy serves to *partition* the set of all possible system states into the set of secure states (i.e., what is allowed) and the set of nonsecure states (i.e., what is not allowed). A secure system is therefore a system that begins execution in a secure state and cannot transition to a nonsecure state. That is, every state transition results in the same secure state or some other secure state. The set of secure states includes the *secure halt state* and the *initial secure state*. Each state transition must also be secure. The set of secure state transitions include the transition from the secure halt state to the initial secure state, and the transition from a secure runtime state to the secure halt state.[63] Figure G-7 illustrates the set of secure state transitions.

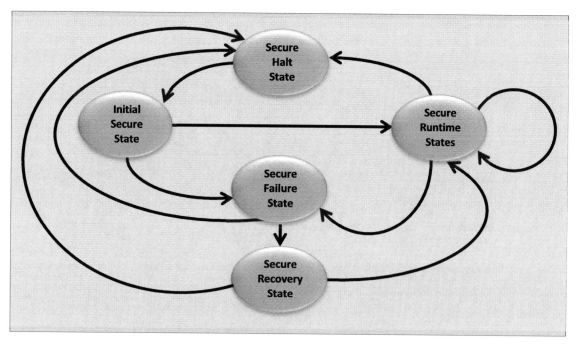

FIGURE G-7: IDEALIZED SECURE SYSTEM STATE TRANSITIONS

---

[63] This reflects the principle of *continuous protection*. That is, the protection required by security policy must be provided with a continuity that is consistent with the security policy and the security architecture assumptions.

While it is theoretically possible to engineer a system for which sufficient assurance can be provided to substantiate the claim that the "system is secure" (i.e., the system will only transition within the set of secure states), such a claim is impractical if not impossible. Therefore, security policies may include an additional partitioning that encompasses additional states and supporting state transitions that reflect concepts of *failure with preservation of secure state* and *trusted recovery*. Failure with preservation of secure state is the ability to detect that the system is in a nonsecure state or to detect a transition that will place the system into a nonsecure state. The ability to detect actual or impending failure relative to security policy enables two important capabilities. First, it enables responsive or corrective action that includes secure halt, and secure recovery to allow for continuation of operation in some reconstituted, reconfigured, or alternative secure operational mode.[64] Second, it enables a risk-informed basis to continue to operate in the current state despite it being not fully secure. This includes operating with the knowledge that an adversary has penetrated the system and may also have a sustained presence in the system.

Trusted recovery is the ability to effect reactive, responsive, or corrective action to securely transition from a nonsecure state to a secure state (or some less insecure state). The secure state achieved after completion of trusted recovery includes those that limit or prevent any further state transition, and those that constitute some type of degraded mode, operation, or capability. Trusted recovery may be accomplished via a combination of automated and manual processes.

G.4 DISTINGUISHING REQUIREMENTS, POLICY, AND MECHANISMS

The terms *requirements*, *policy*, and *mechanisms* are often used in abstract manners that allow them to be considered as synonyms. However, when used in the context of the engineering of trustworthy secure systems, these terms are distinctly different in their meaning and in their importance to specifying, realizing, utilizing, and sustaining systems in a trustworthy secure manner.

A requirement is a condition or capability that must be met or possessed by a system or system element to satisfy a contract, standard, specification, or other formally imposed document [IEEE 610.12]. A security policy is a set of statements with respect to what is and what is not allowed, whereas a security mechanism is an entity or procedure that enforces some part of the security policy [Bishop05]. The security policy states the behavior that is necessary to achieve a secure condition, whereas a security mechanism is the means by which the necessary behavior is achieved. The distinction between security policy and security mechanism extends to also differentiate security requirements (which specify the capability, behavior, and quality attributes exhibited and possessed by security mechanisms) from security policy (which specifies how the security mechanisms must behave in some operational context). Note that from the system standpoint, the human may serve as a security mechanism, is subject to secure behavior as stated by relevant security policy, and must have the capability to behave in a quality manner relative to relevant security requirements.

There is an important dependency relationship among requirement, policy, and mechanism. System security requirements specify the capability and behavior that a security mechanism is able to provide.[65] Security policy specifies the particular aspects of the security policy that a

---

[64] The *secure runtime states* in Figure G-6 includes normal modes, degraded modes, and variations thereof.

[65] An example would be the capability to mediate access to objects based upon individual user identity or groups of individual user identifies, and the operations that are authorized to be performed by those individuals or groups on a set of system-managed resources.

security mechanism must enforce to achieve organizational objectives.[66] This means that a secure system cannot be achieved if the security requirements do not fully specify the minimal capability necessary to enforce security policy. It also means that the satisfaction of security requirements alone does not result in a secure system, and that verification and validation activities must be accomplished separately and coordinated to ensure the individual and combined correctness and effectiveness of security requirements and security policy.

Figure G-8 illustrates the significance of the consistency relationship that must be maintained across interacting security requirements, security policy, and security mechanisms. Any security mechanism that fully satisfies its system security requirements may be deemed capable of enforcing the security policy that is defined for two different organizations. Each organization will utilize the same mechanism and will configure it to behave in a manner that enforces the rules of their organizational security policy. However, if the organizations were to switch mechanisms and keep the same configuration of the mechanism, they would achieve uncertain results (unless their security policy objectives required the exact same configuration of the mechanism). From this, the following conclusions may be drawn:

- Security requirements determine the capability for security mechanisms to behave in some manner;

- Security policy determines the behavior that is deemed "secure" behavior; and

- For a mechanism to be deemed secure, the requirements for the capability of the mechanism must be consistent with the security policy enforcement rules; the mechanism must satisfy the security requirements; and the mechanism must be configured to behave in a manner defined by the organizational security policy.

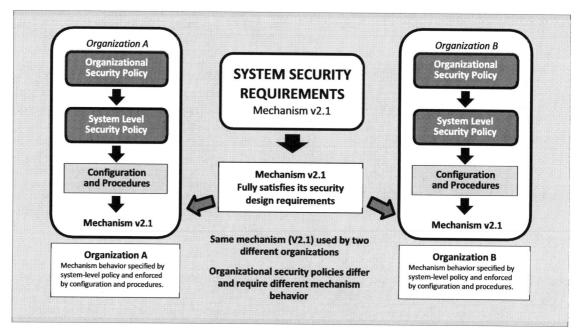

FIGURE G-8: RELATIONSHIP BETWEEN MECHANISMS AND SECURITY POLICY ENFORCEMENT

---

[66] An example would be authorizations for a specific set of individuals, groups of individuals, and the specific operations they are authorized to perform to accomplish mission/business functions.

G.5 SYSTEM SECURITY ARCHITECTURE, VIEWS AND VIEWPOINTS

System architecture, in general, is the fundamental concepts or properties of a system in its environment embodied in its elements, relationships, and in the principles of its design and evolution [ISO/IEC/IEEE 42010].[67] The system architecture conveys information about the system and its elements. It also conveys information about the element interconnections, relationships, and behavior at different levels of abstraction, different scopes, and encompassing multiple views of the system. An architecture *view* is a work product expressing the architecture of a system from the perspective of specific system concerns [ISO/IEC/IEEE 42010]. An architecture *viewpoint* is a work product that establishes the conventions for the construction, interpretation, and use of architecture views to frame specific system concerns [ISO/IEC/IEEE 42010].

The concerns that underlie architecture views and viewpoints include concerns of security and controlling the loss of assets and the associated consequences of asset loss. The *system security architecture* is the fundamental security concepts or properties of the system in its environment and is embodied in its elements, relationships, and in the principles of its design and evolution. The system security architecture parallels the notion of system security in that it embodies the security functions and the constraints levied on system functions to achieve the objectives of a trustworthy secure system. The system security architecture is reflected in a set of security views and viewpoints of the system architecture. The system security architecture conveys information, from a security perspective, about how the system is structured, decomposed, and partitioned into domains; the interactions among various system elements relative to structure, decomposition, and portioning constructs and abstractions; and the security-driven constraints.

The system security architecture demonstrates how security functions are allocated to system elements (making those elements trusted system elements); the nature of the trust relationships between the trusted system elements; the interconnections and information flows that realize the trust relationships; and how the trusted system elements combine and interact with each other and the other parts of the system to deliver the specified protection capability. Where applicable, the system security architecture also reflects the partitioning of the system into distinct security domains, which may reflect different levels of trust within the system, where those levels of trust exist, the information flows that occur within a specific trust level, and the information flows that cross trust level boundaries (i.e., cross-domain information flows).

The system security architecture leverages security design principles and concepts described in Appendix F including, for example: separation, isolation, non-bypassability, encapsulation, layering, and modularity. The system security architecture also composes with other system architecture properties to deliver capability in a form that enables stakeholders to achieve their mission or business assurance objectives.[68] These include, for example, objectives of reliability, resiliency, safety, sustainability, and usability. Finally, the system security architecture supports the security management of the system for all defined states and modes.

---

[67] The use of the term architecture should always be modified (e.g., system architecture, security architecture) to make its context and focus unambiguous.

[68] Architecture considerations for the achievement of defined stakeholder capability and assurance objectives are a multidisciplinary design problem. Security subject-matter expertise is required to help ensure that the appropriate protections and assurances are provided in all architecture and design views and viewpoints. This includes, but is not limited to: fault detection and recovery; exception handling; minimization or elimination of single-point-of-failure; load balancing; and defense-in-depth and *defense in breadth* techniques.

G.6 SECURITY RELEVANCE

In the broadest sense, *security relevance* simply means that there is some security-driven or security-informed aspect to a concern, issue, need, or outcome. Security relevance is an attribute of many engineering-related entities including, for example: requirements; architecture; design; functions; personnel, roles, and responsibilities; configuration; and policies, procedures, and documentation.

From the system design assurance and analysis perspective, the term *security relevance* is used to differentiate the role of security functions that singularly or in combination, exhibit behavior, produce an outcome, or provide a capability specified by the security requirements. Security relevance concerns inform architecture, functional allocation, design, and the associated trade decisions. Security relevance also informs verification and validation methods relative to security function criticality (see next section) to confirm and provide confidence that security functions operate correctly, exhibit no unspecified behavior, have appropriate strength of function, and are able to enforce relevant security policy.[69]

Security relevance is characterized and analyzed by using the following designations:[70]

- **Security-enforcing functions:** Security-enforcing functions are directly responsible for delivering security protection capability, to include doing so in accordance with making or enforcing security policy decisions. An example of a security-enforcing function is one that makes the decision to grant or deny access to a resource.

- **Security-supporting functions:** Security-supporting functions contribute to the ability of security-enforcing functions to deliver their specified capability. These functions provide data, services, or perform operations upon which security-enforcing functions depend. Generally, the dependence is at a functional level. Memory management is an example of a security-supporting function.

- **Security non-interfering functions:** Security non-interfering functions are neither security-enforcing or security-supporting but have the potential to adversely affect (i.e., interfere with or corrupt) the correct operation of security-enforcing and security-supporting functions. Security non-interfering should be interpreted as a *design assurance objective*, meaning that, by design, these functions have no ability to interfere with or alter the behavior of security-enforcing and security-supporting functions. The non-interfering objective is achieved through security-driven constraints on the requirements, architecture, design, and use of these functions.

All system functions can be identified as security-enforcing, security-supporting, or security non-interfering. The importance of the distinction is to design the functions to ensure that security non-interfering functions are in fact not able to interfere with the security-enforcing and security-supporting functions. The security relevance of functions is assessed within the context of the architecture and design to ascertain undesired behaviors, interactions, and outcomes. System security analyses determine options for the placement of a function in the system architecture in

---

[69] *Security policy* defines the rules that describe the allowed and disallowed behaviors, outcomes, and interactions.

[70] [ISO/IEC 15408-2] provides additional information on the types of security-relevant functions. While the notion of security relevance has roots in computer security, the implications have a very strong parallel to the notion of a load-bearing structure and associated members of a physical system—that is, members that fully support the load, members that enable the load bearing structure to exist but do not support the load (but if removed, the load bearing structure fails), and everything else. The purpose of the analyses is to understand where and in what capacity the load criticality (similar to protection criticality) resides and to design accordingly.

order to achieve its security non-interfering objective. System security analyses also determine the extent to which the functions may interfere with security-enforcing and security-supporting functions, and inform risk analysis and treatment to manage the associated risk. For example, to satisfy a size or form-factor constraint, a system function must occupy the same privilege domain as security-enforcing or security-supporting functions, thereby elevating the privilege of that security non-interfering function. If the size or form-factor constraint did not exist, it would be prudent to place that system function elsewhere to avoid giving the function elevated privilege—adding to the assurance that the security-enforcing and security-supporting functions are better isolated from the other parts of the system and will not be adversely impacted by their behavior or provide an avenue for attack.

The reason for distinguishing among the types of security relevance is to ensure that the system security analyses from different perspectives are properly scoped and performed to more accurately determine the potential for interference to the protection capability provided by the system. It also identifies the avenues for misuse and abuse that have the potential to produce undesirable behaviors, outcomes, or interactions, even in situations where the system is used as intended.

G.7 SECURITY FUNCTION PROTECTION CRITICALITY

Security function protection criticality reflects the degree to which failure of security-enforcing and security-supporting functions impact the ability of the system to deliver protection capability relative to the resulting consequences of such failure, and the level of assurance associated with delivery of the protection capability. Failure, in both intentional and unintentional forms, is determined relative to meeting security requirements and achieving only specified behaviors, interactions, and outcomes.[71] Failure is assessed, as required, across the spectrum from limited functional degradation to the complete inability to function.

Protection criticality analyses consider the assets that can be impacted by security function failure and the associated loss consequences; the security function allocation to system elements; and the manner in which the system function and element combination interacts with other system function and element combinations.[72] The protection criticality analysis focuses on the impact of failure, and does so independent of any specific events and conditions that might lead to the failure. The security design principles in Appendix F serve to guide and inform the protection criticality analyses. Security function protection criticality may also drive assurance levels and objectives, as well as the fidelity and rigor of architecture, design, and implementation methods employed to achieve those objectives.

G.8 TRUSTWORTHINESS AND ASSURANCE[73]

The concepts of security, system security, and adequate security establish an inherently context-sensitive and subjective nature to any assertion that system security objectives are achieved. No stakeholder speaks unilaterally for all system stakeholders regarding the valuation of system assets or for the need and sufficiency of security functions. Compounding this is the emergent nature of system security—that is, it is an outcome that is determined by how system elements and the constituent security functions compose. System security is not determined based solely on

---

[71] This may also be referred to as protection criticality.

[72] Protection criticality analysis is a type of system security analysis.

[73] Portions of this discussion are based on the principles and concepts described in [Neumann04].

a single system element or security function in isolation.[74] Therefore, requirements and associated verification and validation methods alone are necessary, but do not suffice as the basis to deem a system as being secure. Additional means are necessary to help address the emergent property of security across the subjective and often contradicting, competing, and conflicting concerns and needs of stakeholders. These means must also provide a level of confidence that is commensurate with the loss consequences associated with the valuation of assets.

The objective of such means is to be able to answer the questions "how good is good" and "how good is good enough" in a disciplined, structured, and evidence-based manner that is meaningful to stakeholders and that can be recorded, traced, and evolved as variances occur throughout the life cycle of the system. The means must take into account system capabilities, contributing system quantitative and qualitative factors, and how these capabilities and factors compose in the context of system security to produce an evidentiary base upon which analyses are conducted. These analyses, in turn, produce substantiated and reasoned conclusions that serve as the basis for consensus among stakeholders.

The notion of "good enough" is reflected in the term adequate security. Adequate security takes into account the complicating factor that system security is primarily focused on the uncertainty of "bad things that happen" to assets that result in unacceptable consequences.[75] It is through trustworthiness and assurance that adequate security is addressed in a disciplined manner. The concepts of trustworthiness and assurance are both based on a common, relevant, and credible evidence base. Together, these concepts constitute a trade space dimension that informs all engineering activities. Further, trustworthiness and assurance drive the level of fidelity and rigor in all engineering activities. This is increasingly important as asset loss consequences become increasingly unacceptable to accept.

G.8.1 Trustworthiness

Trustworthiness is defined as worthy of being trusted to fulfill whatever critical requirements have been specified and to produce or achieve intended behaviors, interactions, and outcomes [Neumann04]. Security trustworthiness does not just happen—it is a byproduct of purposeful architecture, design, and implementation supported by adherence to a fundamental set of security design principles, all grounded in verifiable security requirements and associated performance and effectiveness measures.[76] Trustworthiness also requires the rigorous application of system developmental processes that employ those security design principles. The trustworthiness of the individual system elements is determined by first obtaining evidence that provides assurance about how the individual security-relevant elements satisfy any *claims*[77] associated with the

---

[74] An individual security function can be verified for correctness and for the achievement of its specified quality and performance attributes. Those verification results inform the determination of system security but do not substitute for them.

[75] "Bad things that happen" means the system does something other than what it is supposed to do. This occurs as a result of system inherent misbehavior (i.e., faults, errors, failures) and the potential for forced system misbehavior (i.e., behavior resulting from an attack or abuse).

[76] Security design principles are discussed in Appendix F.

[77] A *claim* is a true-false statement that states the limitations on the values of an unambiguously defined property (called the claim's property), the limitations on the uncertainty of the property's value meeting the limitations on it, and the limitations on conditions under which the claim is applicable [ISO/IEC 15026]. Claims reflect the desired attributes of security functions and are best derived from risk concerns such as: how well the security functions are implemented; the degree to which the security functions are susceptible to vulnerabilities and contain latent errors; the ability of the security functions to exhibit predictable behavior while operating in secure states; and the ability of security functions to resist, respond to, or recover from specific threat events.

protections they provide, and how all system elements satisfy any claims regarding security-driven constraints.[78] Next, the security-relevant system elements that are composed to provide protection capability are considered in combination, and those system element combinations are considered in context of all other relevant system elements. This produces additional evidence about how the composed capability satisfies the claims associated with the protections they provide, taking into account specified and unspecified emergent behavior. The iterative building-block approach can be performed using abstractions such as architectural decomposition of the system, mission or business process flows and threads, and end-to-end data, information, or control flows. In each case, an assessment determines the degree of trustworthiness that can be placed on the protection capability and the acceptability of that degree of trustworthiness.[79] This assessment is conducted in a defined configuration that represents a system mode and its states and transitions, to determine that system security (i.e., the reasoned sum of all system protection capability) is adequate to support the specified mission or business operations while addressing all stakeholder concerns.

System security applies to all system modes, states, and transitions. Therefore, the trustworthiness of the system must also include recognition of insecure system states and the transition from insecure states to a secure state. This transition is accomplished through system functions such as recovery, reconstitution, adaptation, and reconfiguration. Note that the ability for a system to recover, constitute, adapt, or reconfigure does not imply it does so securely. The concept of *trusted recovery* is the ability of the system to reestablish a secure state and to do so in a secure manner (i.e., secure transition). Essentially, the system requirements must account for behaviors, interactions, and outcomes that comprise secure and insecure states, modes, and transitions. Once the foundation has been established that the system is able to function as specified in the absence of disruptions, the trustworthiness of the system can be established. This trustworthiness is based on anticipated disruptions, emergence, and uncertainty, and asset loss consequences that result.

G.8.2 Assurance

Assurance, in a general sense, is the *measure of confidence* associated with a set of claims. From a security perspective, assurance is the measure of confidence that the security functions for the system combine, in the context of the entire system, to provide freedom from the conditions that cause asset loss and the associated consequences. Security-oriented claims establish the basis for the assurance about system security. Security-oriented claims include, but are not limited to, the ability to satisfy stakeholder and system design requirements; to behave only as specified by those requirements; to achieve desired outcomes; to enforce security policy; to avoid, minimize, or mitigate vulnerabilities;[80] and to be effective despite defined disruptions. The initial security claims are based on assets and specific asset loss consequences. The security claims are refined

---

[78] Claims can be expressed in terms of functional correctness; strength of function; confidentiality, integrity, or availability concerns; and the protection capability derived from the adherence to standards or from the use of specific processes, procedures, or methods.

[79] The decision to trust the system for operational use includes the decision to accept residual risks.

[80] Not all vulnerabilities can be mitigated to an acceptable level. There are three classes of vulnerabilities in delivered systems: vulnerabilities whose existence is known and either eliminated or made to be inconsequential; vulnerabilities whose existence is known but that are not sufficiently mitigated; and unknown vulnerabilities that constitute an element of uncertainty—that is, the fact that the vulnerability has not been identified should not give increased confidence that the vulnerability does not exist. Identifying the residual vulnerabilities in the delivered system and the risk posed by those vulnerabilities, and having some sense of the uncertainty associated with the existence of the unknown residual vulnerabilities, is an important aspect of assurance.

and decomposed to address all aspects of the system that support the overarching claims of adequate security.

The level of assurance varies by adjusting the scope, depth, and rigor of the assurance methods and techniques employed to produce evidence.[81] Additionally, assurance is not a static level assigned unilaterally to the entire system. Levels of assurance may vary and may be allocated differently to different views and associated concerns related to the system. Ultimately, assurance is a key trade space parameter—with the objective of striving for optimal, cost-benefit trade-offs of assurance-driven effort expended and the confidence gained as a result of that expenditure. The assurance trade-off considerations can significantly influence the determination of the feasibility or the appropriateness of one security function over another. These considerations are an integral part of systems engineering and stakeholder trade decisions. They factor into the selection of security functions and the security constraints allocated to system elements.

The level of assurance obtained depends upon three interacting dimensions of *scope, depth*, and *rigor*.[82]

- **Scope:** Assurance increases (and becomes more complete) as a greater percentage of the system is considered in the analysis of system;

- **Depth:** Assurance increases as the analysis of the system reaches a finer level of introspection into the design and implementation of the system and into the finer aspects of supporting and enabling processes; and

- **Rigor:** Assurance increases as the methods, processes, and tools employed are more formal, structured, and consistently repeatable and provide increased fidelity and rigor in execution and results.

The level of effort required to achieve assurance therefore, increases as the scope increases, the depth increases, and the rigor of means and methods increase.

An important point about assurance is that the confidence obtained through analysis is not necessarily positive. Assurance evidence can support a compelling argument that counters a stated claim and supports a conclusion that there is insufficient confidence upon which to support a trustworthiness decision. That is, the system or some portion of the system is not sufficiently trustworthy and should not be trusted relative to its specified function without further action to establish a sufficiently credible and reasoned evidence base for its use.[83]

G.8.3 *Relationship to Verification and Validation*

Verification and *validation* activities generate evidence to substantiate claims made about the security capabilities, properties, vulnerabilities, and the effectiveness of security functions in satisfying protection needs. The evidence used to substantiate claims can be objective or subjective. For example, *objective* evidence could be pass-fail test results, whereas *subjective* evidence is analyzed, interpreted, and perhaps combined with other evidence to produce a result. There is no direct correlation between the type of evidence or the quantity of evidence and the amount of assurance derived from the evidence. Evidence may be obtained directly through

---

[81] The volume or amount of evidence does not necessarily translate to increased assurance.

[82] The three dimensions of assurance are defined in [ISO/IEC 15408-3].

[83] The alternative is to conduct a risk assessment as described in [SP 800-30] and make a risk-informed determination of the risk due to insufficient trustworthiness is acceptable.

measurement, testing, observation, and inspection, or indirectly through the analysis of the data obtained from measurement, testing, observation, or inspection. Due to the subjectivity associated with some forms of evidence, the interpretation of such evidence and the resultant findings may also be subjective. The credibility and relevance of evidence should be confirmed prior to its use. Some evidence can support arguments for strength of function, negative requirements (i.e., what will not happen), and qualitative properties. Subjective evidence is analyzed in the intended context and correlated to the claims it supports via rationale.

Security assurance-focused verification and validation activities are incorporated into each of the systems security engineering technical processes to build a security body of evidence. It is the accumulation of security evidence traced to outcomes of the engineering processes that builds assurance in the security functions and in the susceptibility of the system. Assurance evidence also serves as the foundation for substantiating the trustworthiness and risk associated with the security functions and system-level protection capability. The evidence required is therefore linked to security objectives, trustworthiness, and to loss and risk thresholds. An analysis of the security objectives and the loss and risk thresholds informs the trustworthiness and derivation of the security assurance claims for the system. Security assurance requirements then specify the evidence to be obtained and the verification and validation techniques and methods employed to acquire or generate the evidence.

Why Assurance Matters

The importance of assurance can be described by using the example of a light switch on a wall in the living room of your house. Individuals can observe that by simply turning the switch on and off, the switch appears to be performing according to its functional specification. This is analogous to conducting black box testing of security functionality in a system or system element. However, the more important questions might be—

- Does the light switch do anything else besides what it is supposed to do?
- What does the light switch look like from behind the wall?
- What types of components were used to construct the light switch?
- How was the switch assembled?
- Did the light switch manufacturer follow industry best practices in the development process?
- Is the light switch installed correctly? Installed without flaws?

This example is analogous to the many developmental activities that address the quality of the security functionality in a system or system element including, for example: the design principles; coding techniques; and code analysis, testing, and evaluation.

G.8.4 Security Assurance Claims

Security assurance claims reflect the desired attributes of a trustworthy secure system. These claims are derived from concerns such as how well the protections are implemented; the degree to which the protections are susceptible to vulnerabilities and contain latent errors; the ability of protections to exhibit predictable behavior while operating in secure states; and the ability of protections to resist, respond to, or recover from specific attacks. Claims can be expressed in terms of functional correctness; strength of function; specific confidentiality, integrity, or availability concerns; and the protection capability derived from the adherence to standards, and/or from the use of specific processes, procedures, and methods. Claims should not be expressed solely as a restatement of the security functional and performance requirements. Doing so only provides assurance that the security requirements are satisfied with the implicit assumption that the requirements are correct, provide adequate coverage, and accurately reflect stakeholder needs and all associated concerns. Claims restated as requirements are unable to address those aspects of security that cannot be adequately expressed by requirements, and therefore constitute an insufficient basis for reasoned decisions of trustworthiness.

G.9 SYSTEM SECURITY COST, PERFORMANCE, AND EFFECTIVENESS

The *costs* associated with security functions include, for example, the cost to acquire, develop, integrate, operate, and sustain the functions over the system life cycle; the cost of the security functions in terms of their system performance impact; the cost of developing and managing life cycle documentation and training; and the cost of obtaining and maintaining the target level of assurance. The cost of assurance includes the cost to obtain evidence; the cost to conduct the analyses with the fidelity and rigor defined by the assurance requirements; and the cost to provide the reasoning/rationale that substantiates claims that sufficient trustworthiness has been achieved.

The benefit derived from a security function is determined by the overall effectiveness of the function in providing the protection capability allocated to it; the trustworthiness that can be placed on the function; and the residual risk associated with the use of the function, given the value, criticality, exposure, and importance of the assets that the function protects. It may be the case that an optimal balance between cost and benefit is realized from the use of a combination of less costly security functions rather than use of a single cost-prohibitive security function. It may also be the case that the adverse performance impact on the system may preclude the use of a particular security function.

The cost of system security analysis to substantiate trustworthiness claims is also an important trade space factor. Given two equally effective design options, the more attractive of the two options may be the one that has a lower relative cost to obtain the assurance necessary to demonstrate satisfaction of trustworthiness claims. In all cases, the cost of system security must be assessed at the system level and must consider trustworthiness objectives and the cost that is driven by the assurance activities necessary to achieve the trustworthiness objectives.

54808205R10146

Made in the USA
San Bernardino, CA
25 October 2017